Adventurous Eating in Michigan

ADVENTUROUS
EATING IN MICHIGAN

101
Special
Restaurants
and
Recipes

Marjorie and Duke Winters

BEECH TREE PRESS
Holt, Michigan

Copies may be obtained from the publisher,
Beech Tree Press, 2673 Rampart Path,
Holt, Michigan 48842.

ABOUT THIS BOOK

Travel in Michigan and good food are two areas of interest that, when combined, may be greater than the sum of the parts. Long ago, sometimes out of frustration or disappointment, we wished for a perceptive and reliable guide to those elusive and special eating places: the best, the bargains, and the most beautiful. But, because such a book did not exist, we sought information wherever practical—from friends, from acquaintances, and then, since we're faculty members at Michigan State University, from *hundreds* of students on the East Lansing campus. After more than a decade, we compiled a lengthy list of restaurants that seemed particularly interesting and appealing, and this basis we decided to write this book.

But the greatest challenge was to sort out the very best of them. This required driving thousands of miles, visiting hundreds of restaurants, and talking with innumerable local citizens. Finally, after many months and much deliberation, we reduced the list (outside of Detroit) to 101 places that, in addition to good food, have something really special to offer.

We did not accept complimentary meals, and we neither requested nor received financial payment of any kind from any restaurant. The selection of establishments is entirely our own. We only asked that the restauranteurs provide us, if they wished, with recipes of their choice. Happily, most of them complied. In some cases the recipes specify a large number of servings. These we've either included verbatim, with our suggestions, or else have converted them to more manageable proportions. Except for three or four, because of the quantities involved, all the recipes have been tested in our kitchen. If a recipe is not credited to a restaurant, it's one of our own but, we hope, characteristic of the theme or cooking style concerned.

It wouldn't be unexpected for a restaurant listed here to decline in appeal and quality over a period of time. And we're also aware that some deserving places may have been omitted. In both instances we invite you to send your comments so that we can make changes accordingly in later editions.

Another problem concerns the uneven distribution of the restaurants, but, by the design of the project, this was out of our control—though we searched equally as hard for noteworthy places in the barren areas that appear on the maps inside the front and back covers.

Finally, we're pleased to report that there's a great deal of professionalism and creativity in Michigan's restaurant trade. The number of exceptionally talented young women and men in the business is impressive, and good opportunities exist for those well qualified. Our effort has left us with optimism and enthusiasm for a future of high-quality, adventurous dining in this wonderful state.

We wish to express our appreciation to Gary Manson and Richard Smith for administrative services; to Michael Lipsey, Bill Lardie, Kathleen Schoonmaker, and Ned Thomson for technical advice; to David Goldsmith for written comments on one of the restaurants; and to the many Michigan State University students who provided us with valuable information and opinions. Our very special thanks go to the restaurant owners and personnel who, with rare exceptions, were both cooperative and cordial. Bon appetit.

CONTENTS

1
TOSI'S
Stevensville

We've gone out of our way to visit Tosi's every chance we've had since 1966, when we saw it listed in *Time* magazine as one of the 22 best country restaurants in the United States. We still think that it is. Here in a comfortable, relaxed setting is fine northern Italian cooking at its best or, for steak lovers, a variety of substantial cuts grilled on an open charcoal hearth. The service by many experienced waitresses is friendly, helpful, and efficient. (And we do mean experienced—Elsa, a Tosi employee, two years ago claimed to be 81 years old.) The prices are moderate to high, but the value is very good to excellent. The full dinners are most generous, and for those not so hungry or not so solvent, Tosi's offers à la carte options (including salad and bread) and smaller portions of its entrees.

There are six rooms for dining: the VIP Room, very attractive for private parties and open to the public when not booked by larger groups; the New Walnut Room, added to the building in 1962; the Old Walnut Room; the Cypress Room, housing the charcoal grill (avoid the two tables by the kitchen here); the Venetian Room with white archways and murals; and the bar. Except for the VIP Room, the decor is not appreciably better in one room or another. Probably what you'll be most aware of is the red tablecloths and the crowds. The place has always been busy when we've visited. If you arrive early, we suggest that you have cocktails in the Sala Florentina, a very pleasant lounge with overhead arbor-like ceiling, slate floors, and a fountain. In warm weather you might prefer the patio or the garden adjoining it.

Eleven appetizers, about half of them Italian, are on the menu. Among the soups are *stracciatella* and a wonderful *minestrone*—not a vegetable soup with oregano but thick, sturdy, and peppery and almost a meal in itself. We usually order a salad with the house dressing: wine vinegar and Tosi's own custom-blended olive oil. Plain iceberg lettuce

1

and tomato wedges have never tasted more refreshing. The pastas include some of the commoner varieties plus an interesting *manicaretti à la Bolognese* (filled with tortellini, ham, and cheese and baked in a Mornay sauce) and *malfatti* (spinach rolls with a creamy meat sauce and mushrooms). We especially enjoy the veal entrées at Tosi's—that white, tender Provimi veal from Wisconsin—served Cordon Bleu (a spicier version than the usual), Parmigiana, Saltimbocca, Piccante, and Scallopini (with mushrooms and Marsala). Our own favorite dinner here is soup (one order serves two), an order of the smaller-sized veal Cordon Bleu, and an *à la carte* serving of *fettucine à la Romana*—these come with salad and bread—along with a bottle of Chianti Classico. All of this amply serves two people for under $25. In a way, it's a real bargain. For an accompaniment we urge you to order the spaghetti or vegetable in lieu of potatoes.

The breads, white and a light rye, are crusty and flavorful, and also available for purchase in Hans Kottman's adjacent pastry shop, the Bit of Swiss. For dessert, if you possibly have room for it, are some lovely alternatives: assorted pastries and a tasty Choccolino Valda, consisting of imported cocoa, a blend of liqueurs, espresso, and cream—all synthesized by steam.

Tosi's has quite a good wine list. The best of the collection are the red Bordeaux; about half were priced above $50 when we last visited, which is a measure of quality but also limits selection for those who want a more modest claret. The expensive reds include at least one of each of the five *premiers grands crus*, all vintage 1966 or 1967. The roster of red Burgundies isn't as impressive, but there are fewer expensive ones. Among the remaining offerings, which are numerous, you might search out the very palatable and lower-priced Spanish Torres wines, nearly lost among the Burgundies on the list. There's a fair selection of Italian red wines and an even larger number of California Cabernet Sauvignons (a reversal of these proportions seems more logical here). White wines are from France, Germany, and California, and, curiously, there are only three Italian biancos. Each waitress has her own leather-bound wine list, and the management is always willing to help customers in their selections. Customers are permitted, by the way, to visit the cellar, which contains about a third to a half of the restaurant's inventory. **Still one of the best country restaurants.**

TOSI'S, 4337 Ridge Road, Stevensville, MI 49127. Near Benton Harbor and St. Joseph; exit 23 off I-94, north on the Red Arrow Highway to Glenlord Road, then west on Ridge Road. Telephone (616) 429-3689. Hours: 5:30-11 p.m. (till midnight Saturdays, earlier off season). Closed Sundays, holidays, and during months of January, February, and March. Reopens on the Saturday closest to April 1. Bit of Swiss pastry shop open 8 a.m.-9 p.m. Full bar service. Children's menu. Background music, piano bar Wednesday and Saturday evenings. Free valet parking. Credit cards: MC, V. Call for information on reservations.

TOSI'S VEAL PICCANTE

For each serving, pound 4 veal slices to approximately ⅜ inches thickness (each should weigh about 1½ ounce). Dust veal in flour, and sauté in butter. When nearly done, add about ⅓ cup sauterne wine, place a lemon slice on each piece of meat, sprinkle with 1 tablespoon of capers (in all), and heat through. Place veal on serving dish, pour wine sauce over, and garnish with the lemon slices and capers.

Hints from the Winters: Plan on very fast cooking time. Have all ingredients prepared and measured ahead (we used about 2 tablespoons butter for each serving). The veal can be even pounded thinner; be sure to shake off the excess flour before sautéeing. If you've had veal Piccante (or Piccata or Piquante) before, we think you'll prefer this version: the sauterne, with its hint of sweetness, is an improvement on the very dry white wine often used in this lemon sauce.

2
THE BLACK SWAN INN
Kalamazoo

The Black Swan nicely combines popular American fare and creative cuisine. Chuck Houdeshell is an experienced and innovative chef, and our impression is that he and his wife Fran, who manage the restaurant, genuinely care about cooking and the pleasure of their guests. There is much here to commend, not the least of which is the Houdeshells' hospitality and that rare quality in restaurants, calm and restfulness. This is a lovely place, with a very attractive exterior of wood and cedar shakes and an interior featuring dark woods and a contemporary decor with Mediterrean touches. The dining room's floor-to-ceiling windows overlook scenic Willow Lake and its resident black swans and Canadian geese. A centrally located interior fieldstone fireplace has its own cozy seating area and provides contrast to the exterior view. The main dining area occupies a semicircle between these focal points. Some built-in seating and a slightly awkward traffic pattern in places may give some guests a feeling of being crowded on a busy night, but we believe this is a minor problem. You can also eat in the less dramatic lounge or ask for a sandwich menu here, but if you're looking for a little adventure, you'll opt for the main room.

The luncheon menu offers several classically prepared entrées, including a quarter of a roast duckling and veal Parmigiana with fettucine, as well as two daily specials. For dinner the most popular item is, as is often the case, prime rib or the always different evening special. There's something here to please most palates: steaks with mushrooms and Bordelaise sauce, four excellent veal dishes, beef tenderloin Cacciatore, breast of chicken Amandine, brandy-flambéed *tournedos*, steak Diane, flambéed shrimp Diana, and sautéed shrimp and scallops à *la Swiss*. Two experienced table cooks handle the theatrical numbers. Entrée prices are moderately expensive, but they do include a vegetable and your choice of tossed or spinach salad. The featured desserts are cherries Jubilee and strawberries Romanoff, but the fresh fruit crepes, chocolate fondue, and the various offerings on the dessert trolley are just as heart-warming. Or, if you prefer a dessert cocktail, try the Black Swan—Galliano, chocolate liqueur, Amaretto, and ice cream. A full line of dessert coffees are also available, among them, Spanish, Irish, Scotch, Jamaica, and Capetown.

The regular wine list has a pleasing selection and considerable variety. Connoisseurs should ask for the Captain's List—

which includes a few special, hard-to-come-by items such as four of the five *premiers grands crus* (no Mouton) and a fairly priced 1973 Beychevelle—as well as a shorter but good list of red Burgundies.

Graceful and gracious.

THE BLACK SWAN INN, 3501 Greenleaf Boulevard, Kalamazoo, MI 49008. Three miles northwest of I-94 Stadium Drive (E.) exit; off Parkview Drive in the Parkview Hills complex. Telephone (616) 375-2105 and 06. Hours: luncheon 11:30 a.m.-3 p.m., dinner 5:30-10 p.m. (Saturdays 5-11 p.m.), early bird special menu 4-7 p.m. Closed Sundays and most holidays. Full bar service. Children's menu (nice—with no hamburgers). Background music. Piano and singer Tuesday-Friday 7-11 p.m. in dining room. Casual dress, but no blue jeans. Free parking. Credit cards: DC, MC, V. Reservations recommended, especially for larger groups.

THE BLACK SWAN'S VEAL A LA SWISS

Trim 1 pound veal, slice thinly, and pound slices flat. Heat 4 ounces butter in skillet. Dredge veal slices in ¼ cup flour (with salt and pepper), and sauté in butter, turning carefully so as not to overcook. Upon turning the veal the first time, add ½ pound sliced fresh mushrooms, and roll the veal and mushrooms together. When the meat is done, add ¾ cup wine (half dry sherry and half sauterne). Burn off the alcohol, and add 2 tablespoons lemon juice. Roll again, and add 4 tablespoons diced tomatoes. Cook lightly. If the sauce is too thin, add a small amount of flour to thicken to desired consistency.

Put the contents of the skillet into a shallow casserole, and criss cross over the top 1 medium avocado (peeled and sliced) and 5 ounces Swiss cheese (sliced in strips). Bake in a hot oven long enough to melt the cheese. Serve with rice, noodles, or fettucine. The same recipe is good with seafoods. This dish is very rich and should serve 4 to 6.

Hints from the Winters: Aesthetically, this is a triumph. The combination of sherry and sauterne is slightly sweeter than one finds in many veal dishes cooked in wine; we found it a welcome and distinctive variation. Our only suggestion is, for convenience of serving and appearance (also to keep the dish hot) to serve it in individual casseroles or ramekins.

3
BACCHUS TASTEVIN
Kalamazoo

Tucked away unobtrusively in a shopping center, Bacchus Tastevin is decorated with vineyard motifs, including a rough plastered circular entryway suggesting passage into a Dionysian cave (for those of you who prefer Greek to Roman). The booths of sturdy timber are handmade, the table tops fashioned from the bulkheads of old cypress casks—most stains you see are from wine. Wine racks and 100-year-old barn beams form the walls, and the impressive salad bar rests on a solid old wine press. For seclusion, groups of six to eight may be seated in either of the two large replicas of wine vats, known as the "Barrels." An upper level, the Loft, offers another out-of-the-way dining area.

The luncheon menu includes the Sampler—bread, cheese, sausage, fruit—a few sandwiches, quiche Lorraine, red snapper baked in white wine, the salad bar, a changing special, and several other selections. For dinner Bacchus also offers a number of popular steaks and seafoods as well as two 8-ounce lamb chops (also popular and our favorite), chicken Supreme (served with rice and broccoli), duckling Grand Marnier, veal scallopine in a wine sauce with cheese, *coquilles St. Jacques* (scallops) in Mornay sauce, and seafood à la négociant (catch of the day). The "salad press," as at lunchtime, invests a well-worn theme with new life. Here is an assemblage of breads and cheeses to complement your wine choice and the fixings for a tossed salad of your preference. And we especially like the addition of assorted *crudités*. At both luncheon and dinner all prices include a taste of the featured "wine of the week," a pleasing touch. An after-hours menu is also available.

A special feature of Bacchus is an exceptional selection of the world's wines (at competitive retail prices) that may be consumed on the premises with no corkage fee. Wines may be had by the glass, with some 40 featured in a given week—though the greater chateaux are available only by the bottle. In all, more than 1,000 bottles of wine and 120 varieties are on hand. This is a fine place to learn more about wine: the list is comprehensive; you can try an appealing bottle with your meal; and, yes, if you like it, you may make additional purchases to take home with you—at the same prices (there's a discount on cases). The restaurant also includes cheese (30 varieties) and other delicacies for tasters, and some menu items are available for carryout. If there's a disadvantage, besides waiting in line on weekends, it's that prices are a little high for food, but this is balanced by the very good prices on wine.

Vintage quaint.

BACCHUS TASTEVIN RESTAURANT AND CHEESE SHOP, 6216 S. Westnedge, Kalamazoo, MI 49002. Located in Southland Mall; take the Westnedge exit off I-94 southbound, about 1 mile south. Telephone (616) 323-2411. Hours: luncheon 11 a.m.-2 p.m., dinner 5-10 p.m. (till midnight Fridays and Saturdays). Closed Sunday. Full bar service. Background music. Free parking. Credit cards: AE, MC, V. Reservations not taken Fridays and Saturdays.

BACCHUS TASTEVIN'S COQ AU VIN

We appreciate the appropriateness of this recipe—a dish cooked in wine from a Michigan restaurant that is geared to informing us about wine. The classic *coq au vin*, calling for red wine, is something we've never particularly cared for. We find this one more appealing. See what you think.

We've reduced the restaurant recipe so that it will serve 8. Disjoint 2 broiler chickers, and bake in a covered pan about 25 minutes at 250 degrees (possibly hotter in the home oven; try this at 300-325 degrees). Heat 3-4 tablespoons olive oil in a skillet or saucepan and brown 1½ cups chopped onions, 4 large sliced carrots, and 4 finely minced cloves of garlic. Blend in ½ cup flour, ½ cup minced fresh parsley, 2¼ tablespoons ground marjoram, 1½ bay leaves, 1½ tablespoons thyme, 1¼ teaspoon salt, and ½ teaspoon white pepper.

Add gradually, while stirring, the stock from the half-cooked chicken (see above). Remove from the heat and add 1⅔ cups dry white wine. Pour this mixture over the chickens and finish baking, about 25 minutes at 250-325 degrees. Serves 8.

4
THE GILKEY LAKE TAVERN
Delton

For those who haven't been to the tavern in some time, it's expanded and modernized, but that same marvelous country atmosphere is still here. (It's like being up North without driving so far.) There are a few structural problems, but the building is relatively well maintained. Some more festive nights have left traces—notice how many cars have driven into the front wall. But we sincerely hope that Dorothy Leinaar, the owner, isn't ever tempted to over-modernize. The Gilkey Lake Tavern, in business since the 1930s, ranks as a *bona fide*, off-the-beaten-track, rural gathering place, and for American home-style cooking it's as consistently rewarding as any place of the sort in Michigan.

In the bar area the worn wooden tables, moose horns on the backbar, bandstand, and pool table are probably the same ones we saw more than ten years ago. But there are now two new dining rooms with the same general utilitarian nondecor, and all three rooms open onto each other by sliding wooden doors. The extra space was needed; the tavern is as locally popular as ever. Saturday night tends to be busiest, but about 300 customers show up on a typical Sunday, and Mothers' Day might bring in more than 900! It's a fine place for all ages: the younger crowd can enjoy the band and dancing on weekends, and families will welcome the three all-you-can-eat specials. It's a bargain, it's good, and it's fun.

The menu includes more interesting selections than you might expect—for example, the breaded lobster, the fried rabbit, and an outstanding seafood platter of perch, shrimp, scallops, and frog legs. This is not a place for dieters; deep-fried food predominates. But the batters are excellent, and the food is hot out of the kitchen. For lunch, you might try the Wings (chicken) and Rings (onion—with an excellent beer batter), a very generous serving for less than $3. Two luncheon specials are also featured each day. There's a salad bar included with all entrees. Desserts and beverages are extra. Homemade soups include your choice of oyster stew, clam chowder, vegetable, or bean. But the specials are the real drawing card here. On Tuesdays an 18-ounce porter-house is the featured item (possibly the best steak bargain in Michigan); on Fridays it's perch, all you can eat; and our favorite is the Sunday specialty, family-style fried chicken with homemade noodles and biscuits—all of these at very low prices.

If you stop at the Gilkey Lake Tavern in the daytime, you might also plan a visit to the nearby Hickory Corners General Store and take some of the pleasant walks at the Kellogg Bird Sanctuary of Michigan State University Biological Station, just south of Hickory Corners. On a Friday, Saturday, or Sunday evening you might want to stick around and dance at the tavern; the band plays rock, country, polkas, and right now a lot of Elvis numbers. Dress down here.

Best country tavern in Michigan, a bargain.

THE GILKEY LAKE TAVERN, Route 2, Delton, MI 49046. About halfway between Kalamazoo and Battle Creek; 2½ miles north of Hickory Corners (just follow the sign). Telephone (616) 671-5870. Kitchen hours: 10 a.m.-9 p.m. (till 10 p.m. in the summer and on Saturdays). Full menu in effect all day. Full bar service. Children's plates. Jukebox; band starts 9 p.m. Fridays, 9:30 p.m. Saturdays, from 8-11 p.m. Sundays. No credit cards. Reservations taken only for holidays and on Saturdays if you want to be seated near the band (but plan to arrive by 6:30 p.m.).

THE GILKEY LAKE TAVERN'S
MARINATED CARROTS

This is a recipe we've reduced from some 60 or more servings to a more manageable 8 to 10. You can even cut it further if you wish; it'll still be good. And it's even better the longer you marinate it.

Mix the following ingredients together: ½ can cream of tomato soup, ⅓ cup vegetable oil, ⅔ cup sugar, ½ teaspoon each salt and pepper or to taste, ½ cup vinegar, ½ large onion (sliced), ½ large green pepper (sliced), and 4-5 cups canned, drained whole carrots (or cooked fresh carrots).

5
WIN SCHULER'S
Marshall

"It's not what it used to be." We've heard this said about Win Schuler's by many former customers who after several years have revisited the restaurant hoping to re-create a bygone experience. Yes, it *did* have an Olde English charm, and it *did* serve enormous relish trays, and the prices *were* better ten, twenty, fifty, and seventy years ago. But the changes appear to have been advisable or reasonable, and very few places or people are what they used to be. If we can stop being nostalgic about Schuler's (and we admit to being just that ourselves), what we find is a restaurant that is trying to combine the best of the past with modern innovations. Carole Parr, director of Schuler's public relations, was very helpful in enlightening us as to the developing ideas of the establishment.

We like the new decor. The main changes resulting from the $750,000 renovation completed in 1979 are the addition of the Courtyard and the restyling of the old Dickens Room, which has become the Inner Circle. The Centennial Room, the restaurant's main dining area since 1946 and the most traditional of the rooms, remains much the same. The familiar quotations on the ceiling beams, the lighted photomurals of historic Marshall, the rich dark woods, and the fireplace are still there, unchanged. The Courtyard, added to the east side of the building, has a light, airy indoor-outdoor effect, created by a window wall overlooking the patio, white brick walls, plants, and skylights. In the Inner Circle, a strikingly contemporary dining room, patrons are seated in comfortable banquettes or at tables in a semicircular sunken area in front of an attractively tiled fireplace. Smoked mirrors on the walls reflect the hanging lamps with pleated silk shades and the deep red and burgundy furnishings. As Hans Schuler, Win's son and president of the corporation (and an MSU graduate) notes, "With the decor variance, diners can surround themselves with three different looks. Depending on mood and preference, guests can select from the traditional, the Courtyard's open airy look, and the sophisticated, in-town surroundings of the Inner Circle."

Win Schuler has a network of eight restaurants throughout the state, but we believe the original establishment at Marshall is the most appealing—or perhaps we're just being sentimental. There is a greater sense of continuity here, too. Marge Hakes, for example, started as a waitress about 25 years ago and was personally trained by Win and Hans Schuler to take on her present position as kitchen supervisor. Carole Sanders, who for 25 years ran the gift shop, is now the assistant manager. The building is an official Michigan historic landmark, and restaurant has received the Holiday Fine Dining Award for more than 25 years.

Schuler's has long been famous for its meatballs by the crock, Bar-Scheeze, Swiss onion soup, roast prime rib of beef, fresh seafood offerings, London broil, corn and crabmeat chowder, and mouth-watering desserts. Aside from the regular menu items, each day for lunch and dinner there are "blackboard specials," including a "catch of the day." Other interesting possibilities include, for luncheon, barbequed beef ribs, Garden Quiche (with green vegetables, Swiss cheese, and mushrooms), and a creamy mushroom-cheese lasagne (the Vegetarian Delight); and for dinner, breast of chicken Stroganoff, seafood Rosellini, baked scallops de Jongh, and a delectable new appetizer, Crowned Mushrooms (caps filled with shrimp, crabmeat, and cheese). On football weekends there are special menus; call if you're planning a trip then.

There are two wine lists. The "Manager's Finest" surpasses the regular and less expensive list with an additional seven whites, nine reds, a rosé, several sparkling wines, and three Michigan offerings. The best on this list is an expectedly

12

expensive 1971 Lafite, but most wines cost less than $20. Wine is also available by the glass and carafe.

The cocktail lounge, Winston's, has been expanded and offers nightly entertainment as well as two special weekly affairs: Mug Night on Tuesdays (you can take home your ceramic beer mug) and Poco Loco Night on Wednesdays, featuring Mexican-American food and music by two authentic *mariachi* players. Prices for food and drink are typical for a better restaurant, and you should be prepared for waiting on busy night.

A Michigan tradition, with contemporary flair.

WIN SCHULER'S, 115 S. Eagle Street, Marshall, MI 49068.In city center. Telephone (616) 781-3961. Hours: luncheon 11 a.m.-2 p.m., dinner 4-10 p.m. (bar till midnight or later). Closed Christmas. Full bar service. Children's menu. Entertainment nightly. Casual attire, though you'll see lots of jackets. Parking in pay lot across the street. All major credit cards. Reservations accepted as long as there is space.

WIN SCHULER'S PEPPERMINT RIBBON PIE

For crust, combine 1¼ cup crushed chocolate wafers and 1/3 cup melted butter; pat into a 9-inch pie plate. Chill. For filling, after crust is chilled, fill with 1 pint softened peppermint stick ice cream. Cover with ½ cup cooled hot fudge. Freeze till firm. Add another layer of 1 pint peppermint stick ice cream; top with ½ cup cooled hot fudge. Top with peppermint meringue. Freeze till firm. Peppermint meringue: Beat 3 egg whites with ½ teaspoon vanilla and ¼ teaspoon cream of tartar until short peaks form. Gradually add 6 tablespoons sugar; continue beating till stiff. Fold in 3 tablespoons crushed peppermint candy.

Hints from the Winters: See our hot fudge recipe following the Blind Duck Inn (97). The recipe above doesn't say it, but you can, when ready to serve, quickly run the pie under the broiler as for a baked Alaska; serve immediately.

WIN SCHULER'S SWISS ONION SOUP

Cook 2 pounds thinly sliced onions in ½ cup butter until

soft. Stir in 1½ teaspoons paprika, then 6 cups beef stock, and bring to a boil. Make a *roux* by browning ½ cup vegetable oil and stirring in ¾ cup flour. Stir the *roux*, ¾ teaspoon celery salt, and salt and pepper (to taste) into the soup. Simmer at least 2 hours. Shortly before serving, sprinkle 12 slices of bread liberally with ½ cup Parmesan cheese and paprika, and toast them in the oven. Add 8 ounces dark beer to the soup, and allow it to return to serving temperature; then remove from heat. Pour soup into bowls; add a slice of toast to each, and sprinkle with additional Parmesan cheese. Serves 12. This recipe appeared in the *Holiday Magazine Award Cookbook*.

Hints from the Winters: Be sure to cook your *roux* on very low heat for at least 2 minutes to destroy the taste of flour.

6
CORNWELL'S TURKEY HOUSE
Marshall

City families with kids who think that a turkey is born and raised in a supermarket freezer can see the real thing on foot and enjoy an inexpensive meal at the same time. The 180-acre turkey farm dates to 1848 and was once the center of a thriving turkey business in the state. Years ago the Cornwells realized that the turkey sandwiches they sold at the Calhoun Country Fair by the thousands might be worth selling at the farm itself. So in 1968 they established a restaurant in a little one-room building behind the farmhouse. By noon of the first day they'd taken in only $26 and worried a bit. Now, over the past twelve years Turkeyville, U.S.A. is even considered a tourist attraction, a fact that surprises and amuses the Cornwells.

This is still a family-run business: the owners Wayne and Marjorie Cornwell live in the original farmhouse across from the restaurant, and their sons and grandson all contribute. Today only some of the turkeys served here are raised at the farm; the others are shipped in from an Orlando, Florida, turkey ranch. On an average summer's day the Cornwells will cook about forty large turkeys. All are milk-fed, and we think you'll agree that the turkey is exceptionally moist and tender.

The large complex of buildings includes the Turkey House, where assorted turkey dishes and excellent homemade pies are served cafeteria-style; the Turkeyville Ice Cream Parlor with white tile floors, striped awnings at the windows, and old-fashioned wire soda parlor chairs; an adjoining General Store, featuring candies and preserves; a gift store in the Granary; and an antique shop in the barn across the road—not to mention a field of some 2,000 white turkeys. The Turkey House dining room, decorated in early American style with ladder-back chairs and farm memorabilia, isn't air conditioned, but the large overhead fans are efficient. Or, if you prefer, you can eat at one of the very pleasant umbrella tables outside. Family dining is common here, and if the kids spill, it's not a crisis.

There are nine choices on the menu: five sandwiches (buttered turkey, turkey salad, Sloppy Tom, smoked turkey, and turkey dog) and four lunch or dinner plates (turkey hot plate—turkey, gravy, potatoes, stuffing, and cranberries; hot turkey and gravy on a bun; turkey chow mein; and the complete turkey dinner—the hot plate with the addition of cole slaw and roll). The plates include both light and dark meat; the sage dressing is quite tasty' servings are generous. And this should please families and the budget-minded: the most expensive menu item costs less than $3. Even though you must wait in line, the food is served hot and quickly, and it's simple to go back for more.

Who wants to eat with a bunch of turkeys? We do!

CORNWELL'S TURKEY HOUSE, 18935 15½ Mile Road (U Drive North), Marshall, MI 49068. Five miles north of Marshall; ½ mile west on I-69, N Drive North exit; 4 miles north of I-94 and I-69 interchange. Hours: 11 a.m.-8 p.m., Closed Sundays and for three months, the night before Thanksgiving to the end of April. No alcoholic beverages. Casual dress. Free parking. No credit cards or reservations accepted.

SAGE AND ONION POULTRY STUFFING

We were unable to persuade Wayne Cornwell to part with any secret turkey recipes. But we think you'll enjoy this dressing. It's an old family favorite of ours. Cube or tear into small pieces 1 large loaf of bread (1¼ pound loaf, or 12 cups bread cubes). Place in a large bowl with 1 cup chopped onions, 1 cup chopped celery, and 1½ teaspoons sage (or more, to taste). Mix together lightly, and let stand to dry overnight or several hours. Add 1-1½ teaspoon salt, ¼ teaspon pepper, and mix in. Add ¼ pound melted butter or margarine, and toss lightly. Add 3 beaten eggs, then ½ cup hot tap water, mixing in lightly after each addition. Moisten with ¼-½ cup milk or chicken broth. Dressing should hold together when squeezed lightly.

Stuff turkey loosely in both neck and body cavities, leaving a little air space for expansion of the dressing. This is enough for a 10-12 pound turkey. When working with smaller or larger birds, figure about 1 cup of bread cubes per pound of poultry and adjust the other ingredients proportionately. You can vary this recipe by adding ½ pound sliced, sautéed mushrooms and/or 12-16 ounces cooked, crumbled pork sausage.

7
TRUE GRIST, LTD.
Homer

There is no *one* thing special about True Grist—there are lots of things: a fascinating old restored building, a resident professional acting troupe, a profusion of authentic Americana, fine food and drink, and excellent prices. The theater restaurant is located in a white-painted mill by the bridge over the Kalamazoo River at the east end of the little town of Homer.

The mill, built in 1887, was operating until 1970, though True Grist has been in business for less than five years. We were first attracted to its culinary accomplishments after we read that it specialized in Middle Eastern and ethnic foods. Alas, the Middle Eastern gave way to Middle Western tastes, but there are still many options worth mentioning. The soups can't be faulted, especially the broccoli and the "cheesy chowder." The salad bar offers the makings for your own Italian or Greek salad as well as more familiar inclusions.

Sandwiches are designed for hearty appetites (try the hot beef and cheese or the barbeque). Among the daily specials are lasagne and Cornish pasties, the latter from Madelyne's in the Upper Peninsula. On Tuesdays the favorite item is the Mexican plate, including an enchilada, tostada, rice, and rolled taco.

The interior of True Grist is furnished with innumerable antiques: the desk in the lobby along with the two carved-back chairs are quite valuable, and the pressed-back chairs throughout the restaurant will enchant collectors. Overhead are hand-hewn oak and black walnut beams, hung with chandeliers fashioned from the old mill's drive wheels. The effect throughout is warm, cordial, and inviting. The main dining room is the dinner theater, but there is also a large lounge where one may eat even if eschewing the theater. It should be noted, though, that you cannot see the play without having dinner here. The dinner-theater package includes a lavish buffet, featuring an appetizer table, four entrées (round of beef, baked ham, fried chicken, and one revolving item), the salad bar, and several unusual vegetables (Lynn Westerman, the enthusiastic assistant manager, tells us that the buffet is especially popular with vegetarians). It's also available without theater tickets to customers in the lounge. For dessert you may order either baklava or the "Run of the Mill" (someone here likes puns), a fruit-filled nutty pastry with whipped cream cheese topping.

The wine list here is interesting. Six sparkling, nine whites, three rosés, thirteen reds, and six "Jim Miller Favorites" offer a good selection in type, variety, and price. The Grist could, however, add some French white Burgundies (or at least a claret), and a few more "distinguished" wines might serve them well.

We recommend the package for a pleasant evening's entertainment. Write for the theater schedule: True Grist Ltd., P.O. Box 127, Homer, MI 49245 or call. Groups of 25 or more receive special discounts on Thursday and Sunday. Generally dress is casual, but you might go a little more formal on weekends.

Old mill, new ideas.

TRUE GRIST LTD. DINNER THEATER, 109 N. Byron, Homer,

MI 49245. Off M-60, 24 miles southwest of Jackson. Telephone (517) 568-4151. Hours: luncheon 11 a.m.-4 p.m., dinner 5-9 p.m., buffet 6 p.m.-1 a.m. on Friday and Saturday, buffet 1-6 p.m. on Sunday. Closed Thanksgiving and Christmas (check on other holidays). Full bar service. Children, half-price on buffet. Background music. Credit cards: MC, V. Reservations required for dinner theater. Plays run Thursday through Sunday evenings and Wednesday matinées; curtain time Thursday-Saturday 8:30 p.m., Sunday 6:30 p.m., matinées 2 p.m. Dinner is available until ½ hour before curtain time on performance nights.

TRUE GRIST LIMA BEAN CASSEROLE

Soak 1 pound dry lima beans overnight. Drain. Cover beans with fresh water and 1 teaspoon salt. Cook till tender, 30-40 minutes (but do test). Drain; place in casserole. Dot with ¾ cup brown sugar and 1 tablespoon dry mustard. Sprinkle over beans. Mix 1 tablespoon molasses with 1 cup sour cream. Stir gently into beans. Bake 1 hour at 350 degrees. Serves 8.

Hints from the Winters: The sour cream may curdle—it did for us. We suggest a lower temperature (275 degrees) for 1¼ hours. Or mix in a tablespoon of flour (or for a foolproof sauce, mix ½ cup sour cream with ½ cup cream sauce, then add molasses). You can substitute frozen lima beans if you wish, 2 or 3 10-ounce packages (but the dried beans are better).

8
BILLINGSGATE
Horton

In a picturesque, erstwhile Methodist church built in 1906 and just recently designated a state historical site, Billingsgate is one of Michigan's most original and enjoyable restaurants. But perhaps that's the wrong word—it's really a dinner club, and dining here is possible only by appointment and for large groups (as this goes to press, 20 to 40 persons; but do call—it's possible that this year smaller groups may be able to make special arrangements for dinner).

The red brick building, overgrown with ivy and surrounded by a brown picket fence and graceful birches and evergreens, is an example of the Romanesque style of the noted American architect Henry Hobson Richardson. Except for the discreet sign on the front lawn, there's no indication of the culinary prowess regularly demonstrated inside. On the upper level antiques have been for sale for seven years in what was the nave of the church. In this room, with its resplendent stained-glass window, grand piano, and comfortable antique settees (on what was once the altar), diners can enjoy cocktails and appetizers before descending to the lower level for dinner. And what a dinner you can have here!

In a mellow English clublike setting with a subtle color scheme of earth tones, you'll dine by the light of nostalgic kerosene lamps or candles in burnished old brass candlesticks. Here you can arrange with the owner, James Beck, an entirely personalized feast for your family or friends. Do you want thematic table settings, entertainment, a particular table grouping, floral arrangements, or decorations for a special occasion? Ask, and it shall be done. And the entire church with its beautiful English garden is yours for the evening.

James Beck has a degree in architectural design from the University of Michigan. He lived in England for a few years, hence the name of the restaurant (ironic, of course—this is hardly a place that recalls Billingsgate, the venerable and lowly fish market of London). James and his wife Karen do most of the cooking, and his mother is the *chef du boulangerie* (her breads are exceptional). Dinners are price-fixed very fairly for the quality of the offerings and the individualized attention, but you will pay slightly more than the affordable going rate for certain more elaborate dishes. The procedure is to choose in advance from an extensive repertory of dishes that should appeal to the most discriminating diner.

Among the starters are filled mushroom caps, *pâté maison*, *vichyssoise*, gazpacho, and sausage quiche. Salad choices consist of spinach, Caesar, fruit, vegetable, avocado, or

mixed greens. The catalogue of entrées includes beef Wellington, beef Bourguinonne, Cornish hen à l'orange, wine-
poached fish fillets, stuffed herbed pork chops, seafood
crepes, and several first-rate chicken dishes (crepes, Cordon
Bleu, coq au vin, Kiev, and Neptune—see the recipe for it
below). Accompaniments can be selected from a list that
embraces such engaging items as curried fruit or vegetables,
spinach Parmesan, sherried braised celery, several potato
preparations, creamed eggplant with cheese, tomatoes Provençale, and glazed carrots Grand Marnier. The desserts
are dazzling: pies and cakes, Savarin Chantilly, meringues,
various crepes, cheese and fruit trays, or what is now becoming extremely popular, the dessert trolley with assorted
sweets, arranged on a 100-year-old serving cart.

The price of dinner includes starter, salad, bread, entrée
with vegetable accompaniment, dessert, coffee or tea. There
are no alcoholic beverages, but you can bring your own.
This is an opportunity to splurge on a better wine than usual,
at a retail price. For the cocktail hour, too, you can provide
your own liquor, and Billingsgate will dispense glasses, ice,
and napkins (for $1 per person). Mixes, drink garnishes, and
a few really appetizing appetizers are available at a small
surcharge by request. Almost anything can be arranged
with Billingsgate. For really special occasions, this is the
place to go.

For your own private culinary congregation.

BILLINGSGATE, 101 Main Street, Horton, MI 49246. Take
Spring Arbor Road (M-60) southwest from Jackson to Mos-
cow Road, which takes you to Horton. Telephone (517)
563-2943. Dinners served about 6:30 to 9 p.m., by prior
arrangement. Group dining only; $25 deposit required to hold
reservation. (The weekends are filled well ahead with lots
of regulars and whole families for special occasions.) Smaller
portions and reduced prices for children. Background music
(or bring your own records, if you want). Cocktails and wine—
bring your own. Free parking. No credit cards; personal
checks accepted. Reservations required.

BILLINGSGATE'S CHICKEN NEPTUNE

This is an unusual and creative combination of fish and fowl that works very well. The same sauce and stuffing would do nicely for various fish entrées. Measurements aren't exact—judge the amounts according to your taste; we include our suggestions in parentheses. First, skin and bone 12 chicken breasts, keeping each in one piece. Place in a large pan, and cover with chicken stock. Bring to a boil, and poach for 20 minutes.

For the stuffing, sauté 1 pound scallops in butter till tender; poach 1 pound monkfish in fish stock till tender; and poach 1 pound cod in fish stock till flaky. Place all these into a large mixing bowl. Mix in chopped sautéed onions (½-¾ cup) and chopped fresh parsley (¼ cup). Prepare Béchamel sauce by heating ¾ cup butter in skillet. Blend in ¾ cup flour, and cook slowly a few minutes. Gradually add 6 cups fish stock (use the poaching liquids), salt and pepper to taste, ½-¾ cup catsup, 2-3 teaspoons caraway seed. Mix half this sauce with the seafood (or enough to moisten).

Fill the chicken breasts with the seafood-Béchamel stuffing and place chicken breasts in a shallow baking dish. Thin the remaining Béchamel sauce with half and half (half milk, half cream), and pour over enough sauce to coat the chicken. Sprinkle with grated Parmesan cheese and sauteed fresh bread crumbs. Bake at 375 degrees for 45 minutes. Pour over the last of the sauce. Garnish with lemon slices, coarsely chopped green pepper, and parsley sprigs. Serves 12.

9
THE BRANDY WINE PUB
Jackson

Open only since June 1978, the Brandy Wine has attracted quite a following of loyal regulars in the Jackson area. It does no advertising at all, and yet on its opening night 125 people showed up—and left satiated and happy. The exterior is a modern version of American roadhouse style (meaning no windows and a location on a busy thoroughfare). But the interior has panache—barnwood siding on the walls, a gleaming brass church rail in the lobby, and a calculated, almost theatrical, use of stained glass throughout, including some ornamental ceiling treatments. The Brandy Wine boasts a large collection of stained glass—some Tiffany, some from English pubs. True, Tiffany lamps and stained glass are now almost ubiquitous in restaurant decor, but we doubt if you'll see them used more tastefully and effectively than at the Brandy Wine Pub. The Tiffany Room is especially fetching; we like the booths to the right as you enter—under lighted, colorful "windows"—and the four in the corners, particularly the one on your left beneath the 1915 poster advertising an MAC and U of M football game.

The Tiffany Room is also the most fashionable, but there are two other dining areas: the adjacent La Salle Room—more contemporary, no stained glass or booths but warm brick walls and illuminated paintings and prints—and the Upper Lounge, featuring a zebra skin and boar's head on its walls and overlooking the exceptionally inviting Lower Lounge with its expansive fireplace wall of cut fieldstone, hanging ferns, and a creative recycling of materials—for example, the old billiard table legs that flank the stairway.

As for cuisine, what impressed us first is something you're unlikely to see: the well-worn copy of *Joy of Cooking* on a kitchen counter. But you will see the menu. The Brandy Wine's cooking style might be described as *haute cuisine américaine*. Entrées—served with soup or salad, vegetable, and muffins—consist of Alaskan King crab legs, lamb chops, steaks, pork chops, chicken Cordon Bleu, spareribs, a vegetable plate, a few sandwiches, and some eloquent seafood. The latter are the most popular items of all and are flown in fresh from Boston: monkfish with *de Jongh* butter (a favorite here), fried haddock, a catch of the day, and others, if the catch is particularly good. The menu has changed about four times already, according to the inventiveness of the chefs and managers and by popular demand. Portions are large.

A special characteristic of the Brandy Wine Pub is that vegetables are treated with respect here. In fact, outside of the better vegetarian establishments, this may be the only place in Michigan where they are given their proper due.

The Variety Casserole, an entrée, is a most successful mélange of broccoli, cauliflower, and mushrooms with a cheese sauce. Receiving top billing with classic appetizers is a crunchy and colorful vegetable cocktail. And the salads are prepared with meticulous care. The greens—endive, romaine, cucumber—are tossed in the kitchen and served with tomatoes and varying garnishes. Yes, they're *tossed*, not drowned through a careless or exuberant pouring on of liquid. The house dressing is a perfectly balanced, well-seasoned oil and vinegar. Or you can toss your own: order oil and vinegar, and you'll get a tray with cruets as well as garlic, chives, lemon, and seasoned salt and pepper. Cooked vegetables, too, receive the same thoughtful attention. And the only potatoes are steamed redskins. We can't complain at all—there's nothing like a new, red-skinned potato steamed and swathed in butter.

But you might need to ask for the butter at the Brandy Wine. Though this is not exactly *nouvelle cuisine*, there is a tendency here to make us all a little healthier. The approach can't be faulted, as long as the food looks good and tastes good (and it cetainly does). All in all, vegetarians and calorie/cholesterol counters will revel in it. But the doctors-be-damned hedonists will enjoy it too.

One or two freshly made soups are available each day. And do ask about the specials; on our visit, mussels were offered as either an appetizer or entrée, and there was an additional vegetable (Italian-style zucchini) and entrée (lobster Creole). For dessert you can choose from eight acceptable and generally light possibilities, among them cheesecake, coconut snowballs, fresh fruit, and a dessert of the day. Three California house wines are available by the glass, and the list contains about twenty offerings. None are extra special, except possibly the Moet and Chandon Champagne, but all are reasonably priced—most between $6 and $8. We also understand that there's a "special" wine list but were unable to study it during our visit.

Superior seafood, voluptuous vegetables.

THE BRANDY WINE PUB, 2131 Horton Road, Jackson, MI 49201. Southwest of city center. Telephone (517) 783-2777. Hours: 5-10 p.m. (till 11 p.m. on Fridays and Saturdays). Closed Sundays and most major holidays. Full bar service.

Children's menu. Background music. Free parking. Credit cards: AE, MC, V. Reservations recommended Thursdays through Saturdays.

ZUCCHINI MARIO

This is very simple and satisfying, and it's a fine accompaniment to a meat course, especially lamb. Cut 1 pound small zucchini squash into ¼-inch-thick crosswise slices. Sauté in 1 tablespoon oil and 1 tablespoon butter on medium-high heat till crisp-tender, about 3-4 minutes. Salt and pepper to taste. Place in a shallow baking dish or 4 individual ramekins. Sprinkle with dry oregano leaves, crumbled (about 1 teaspoon). Add a layer of canned stewed tomatoes (1 pound can or larger, drained). Top with 1-1½ cup shredded mild Cheddar cheese. Bake at 400 degrees for 20 minutes or until cheese is melted and dish is hot. Serves 4-6.

10
CASA NOVA
Lansing

The usual (and often fatal) course a restaurant takes when it rebuilds or relocates is to expand its seating capacity, to attempt a more "elegant" decor, and to change drastically or increase unreasonably its menu selections. The Casa Nova, forced by a highway expansion program to move, didn't make that mistake, as its regular customers for many years will agree. The new building was erected about a mile away on the same street and is a near duplicate of the earlier premises in both exterior and interior. The Italian Mediterranean decor, the golden lights in the chandeliers, the curved bar with comfortable armchairs, and even the too-small entryway were all transplanted with little change. The reason, according to Bill Falsetta, one of the owners, was not so much traditionalism as feasibility. The result, we think, is that Casa Nova has lost none of its popularity and still offers some of the best bargains in the Lansing area.

There are three dining areas—the main room with the most comfortable seating at the booths along the wall, an elongated room parallel to it, and the lounge. Reservations aren't accepted (you take a number upon arrival), but we think it's worth the extra wait for a booth or a corner in the lounge. Some tables—those near the main entrance and off the kitchen door—should be avoided. During most of the year the Casa Nova is busy on Thursdays through Saturdays; it's a crush of people on Fridays in the summer. And don't be fooled if there are only ten or twelve people waiting near the door. The large overflow waiting room and bar downstairs might be filled with others already on the seating list.

Dishes that we particularly like, from the least to the most expensive (though all are moderately priced), are the six "giant" sandwich specials, the heavy cheesy pizza (you'll need a knife and fork), steak for two, barbequed ribs (highly recommended; probably the best for the money in all of Michigan), prime rib, and very nice Alaskan King crab legs. The French-fried onions are a good buy and much better than average. The Italian pasta entrées are somewhat pedestrian (the sauce a bit too sweet to our taste), but the veal scallopine is a standout (see the recipe following). Soups here are canned, we'd prefer a crustier Italian bread, and some of the seafood appears to come prebreaded and frozen. But if you stay with the items we mention above, you shouldn't be disappointed.

The wine list carries two house wines—Cribari and Villa Banfi white, red, and rosé—by the carafe and glass (we prefer the Banfi). It also features Bill Falsetta's favorite Lambrusco, several other Italian wines—Soave, Orvieto, Chianti, Valpolicella—Mondavi Zinfandel, champagnes, and a few others, most in both full-sized bottles and splits.

This is not a restaurant for intimate, quiet dining; and though once in a while you'll see even long, formal dresses here, more often it's bowling jackets and blue jeans. The Casa Nova is fine for families. There's no children's menu, but portions are large (ask for extra plates), and pizzas and sandwiches can be shared. The waitresses are cheerful and efficient for such a busy place, and some have been here for years. For example, Hazel Oliver, a favorite of ours, came here

from England as a World War II war bride and has been
keeping things running smoothly for as long as we remember.
Tops for pizza, ribs, steaks, crab—and a bargain.
CASA NOVA LOUNGE AND PIZZERIA, 3015 S. Logan Street,
Lansing, MI. Three miles southeast of the city center; 1 mile
south of I-496, Logan St. exit. Telephone (517) 882-6697.
Hours: 11 a.m.-2 a.m. Closed Sundays, holidays, the week of
July 4th. Full bar service. Background music. Free parking.
Credit cards: AE, CB, MC, V. Personal checks accepted.
Reservations not taken.

CASA NOVA'S VEAL SCALLOPINE

This is a creamy veal dish quite different from the usual
scallopines in both cut of meat and method of preparation.
The rich-tasting final product belies its orgins in some "convenience" ingredients. We received the restaurant's own
recipe, calling for 10 pounds of veal and have rewritten it
for 6 servings.

Cut 2 pounds of veal (from the rump or round) into 1-inch
strips. Roll in a mixture of ½ cup flour, 1 teaspoon salt, and ½
teaspoon pepper plus a dash of garlic powder. Heat 2 tablespoons oil and 2 tablespoons butter in a roasting pan. Add
the meat, and brown in a hot over (about 400 degrees) for
1-1½ hours, stirring occasionally. When nicely browned,
remove from the oven and add 5 tablespoons chopped fresh
green pepper, 2 tablespoons dry minced onion, an 8-ounce
can of mushrooms (drained), and 3 tablespoons cooking
sherry. If the mixture appears dry, add up to ½ cup water.
Cover with foil and return to a 250-degree oven. Bake slowly
about 2½-3 hours till very tender. This much can be done
ahead. For the final cooking, put meat into 6 individual
casseroles or ramekins. Top with Campbell's canned cream
of mushroom soup (2 cans mixed with 2-3 tablespoons cream
or milk). Sprinkle with shredded Mozzarella cheese (about 2
cups in all). Bake about 20 minutes in a 400-degree oven.
Serves 6.

Hints from the Winters: We think the recipe is excellent as
is, but you can improve it slightly by substituting fresh
chopped onion (about ¼ cup or more to taste) and fresh

sautéed sliced mushrooms (add these to the meat just before reheating). But don't substitute another sauce; use the soup. It's easy, it's lower in calories than its flavor and consistency in this dish suggest, and we assure you it won't taste like mushroom soup.

11
THE CITY FISH CO.
Lansing

Five or six years ago, a regular customer of the City Fish Co. decided that it wasn't enough merely to buy a fresh fish fillet and insisted on eating it on the premises. So three beer cases were pushed together to form a makeshift picnic table, and the ever-obliging proprietors cooked him his fillet. Today the City Fish Co. still cooks anything to order for its patrons, but it has expanded from a thriving fish market to a small seafood restaurant as well.

On entering, for a fleeting moment coastal natives might think they're back in Boothbay or Tillamook. The pervasive odor of fish could be considered an advantage or disadvantage, depending on one's view. We like it and hope they never find a way to deodorize the place. And we especially like the City Fish for a light, reasonably priced lunch after shopping nearby. It's also within walking distance of the Capitol, so tourists might wish to consider it as an alternative to one of the more expensive restaurants in this part of town.

Don't "dress" for the City Fish, and don't expect "atmosphere" in the usual, awe-inspiring sense. The decor, if you can call it that, is minimal: overhead fluorescent lights, rough cement floor, six tiny high wooden tables with stools (avoid the wobbly one in the corner), three lower tables, and a few cedar shakes and fishnets to make it all credible. The three owners—Jim Hauff, Hunt Sweitzer, and Jerry Zimmerman—and their help did the decorating, and they're the first to admit that they're better cooks than masons and carpenters.

Customers line up at the serving bar and order from the signs and blackboards; there's a serve-yourself side counter for beverages. The place overflows at lunchtime, but the turnover is fast. And it's a showcase for people-watching: the wide variety in clientele is likely to include state senators, local basketball stars, well-dressed society matrons, and young people sporting some of the oldest, most profusely patched jeans in town.

The fish and seafood served here are either broiled or deep fried. On the menu are shrimp cocktails in two sizes, fish and chips, shrimp Creole, broiled seafood kebab, and a combination platter. There is always a daily special; side orders of rice, French fries, cole slaw, and rolls are also available. Or, if you see something in the market you'd prefer, the restaurant will cook it for you with 30 minutes or more advance notice (including boiled lobster). All the fish is fresh, with some rare exceptions, such as the popular white bass. In the fall and winter the City Fish makes a tasty clam chowder as well. Anything you order can be packaged for takeout, and cold beer and wine may be purchased to go (but not for consumption on the premises).

If your lunch here leaves you still savoring seafood (and it probably will), you might wish to stop at the market in the adjacent room and buy something for dinner. The fish store has been operating since 1916. Fish, flown or trucked in fresh, is purchased from throughout the country—San Francisco, Seattle, Virginia, New Orleans, Florida—and from the Canadian government. Even though the cost of fish has been going up as much as that of beef, there are some bargains at City Fish. Check out the "fish of the day" and the "fillet of the day," for example. And Hunt Sweitzer has been encouraging his customers to try shark steak in lieu of swordfish—at a third of the price. Julia Child's touted monkfish can be had here, too, at a low cost. In addition, the City Fish has a lobster tank; freezer items such as bulk packages of shrimp, frog legs, crab; and a small stock of seafood necessaries (lemons, breading mixes, seasonings). A welcome touch that will appeal to novice or experimental cooks is the wall file of complimentary recipe cards near the rear entry.

Close your eyes, and you're on the New England coast. THE CITY FISH CO., 124 E. Washtenaw Street, Lansing, MI 48933. In city center, 1 block east of Washington Street. Telephone (517) 482-4815. Hours: 11 a.m.-7 p.m. (till 8 p.m. on Fridays). Closed Sundays. No alcoholic beverages. Children's plates. Free parking in rear. No credit cards or reservations accepted.

CITY FISH OYSTERS ROCKEFELLER

In a large bowl mix ¼ cup minced onion, 2 crushed bay leaves, 1 teaspoon salt, 1 pinch cayenne pepper, 1 cup minced raw spinach, 1 tablespoon minced parsley, and 1 teaspoon Worcestershire sauce. Melt ½ pound butter in a saucepan; add 3 tablespoons sherry and ½ cup bread crumbs (1 cup in all). Stir, and combine with seasonings in bowl, mixing well. Arrange 3 dozen raw oysters (opened, on half-shell) on a cookie sheet. Spoon mixture onto oysters; then sprinkle with remaining ½ cup bread crumbs and ½ cup grated Parmesan cheese. Bake in a preheated 400-degree oven for 10 minutes or until golden brown. Serves 6. Variation: substitute clams, mussels, or diced escargots in mushroom caps for the oysters.

Hints from the Winters: For attractive serving, you might prefer to arrange the shells on individual ramekins filled with rock salt (both to steady the shells and keep the dish hot). The original recipe for oysters Rockefeller is attributed to Antoines in New Orleans, which maintains secrecy as to its ingredients. But one additional flavoring was used—first, absinthe and, later, Pernod. You might try it in the recipe above, but go easy. It's powerful, and just a drop will do.

CITY FISH SHRIMP CREOLE

In a medium skillet, saute ¾ cup minced onion, 1 clove minced garlic, 1 minced green pepper, and ½ cup finely chopped celery in 2 tablespoons butter until tender. Remove from heat. Stir in an 8-ounce can tomato sauce, ½ cup water, 1 crushed bay leaf, 1 teaspoon minced parsley, ½ teaspoon salt, and 1 pinch cayenne pepper. Simmer 10 minutes. Add additional water if needed. Add ½ pound of peeled raw shrimp. Bring mixture to a boil. Cook, covered, over medium heat for 5 minutes. Serve over boiled rice. Makes 2 generous servings.

Hints from the Winters: The prime hint here is *not* to overcook the shrimp, a mistake that both restaurant and home chefs frequently make. Think of shrimp as you think of soufflés. When you're spending that much money on them, don't let them turn into hard, tasteless little nuggets. Cook shrimp till just pink, curled, and opaque—the 5 minutes is probably a *maximum*. We like this dish with a good big pinch of cayenne (almost ¼ teaspoon). We also find that ⅓ cup water is sufficient; add water only if necessary. Two "generous" servings is right—½ pound shrimp in this dish will satisfy 3 (or maybe even 4), especially if you're serving other courses.

12
JIM'S TIFFANY PLACE
Lansing

The Vlahakis family has owned and operated Jim's since 1914, though its present location dates to 1937. The building qualifies as a historical site, but the Belle Epoque interior and the food are what contribute to the restaurant's special appeal. The new sidewalk solarium, the Greenhouse, has an outdoor cafe atmosphere and is particularly pleasant for cocktails or lunch. For dinner here, however, we much prefer the booths in the lounge to the main dining room, though an attempt has been made here to provide quiet, intimate dining by partitioning tables. The decor throughout the restaurant has, as its name implies, a turn-of-the-century flavor and is a showcase for one of the three largest and finest collections of authentic Tiffany lamps in the world—more than 100, with no two alike. About 60 of the lamps are on display at any one time, in addition to many rare prints with antique frames and other late nineteenth-century memorabilia.

The luncheon menu includes a changing Greek specialty of the day served with an Athenian salad and rolls. Favorite dinner entrees are prime rib (in three sizes and prices); *pikilia*, a Greek sampler platter of *moussaka* (eggplant and beef casserole); *dolmades* (stuffed grape leaves); *spanakopita* (spinach in *filo* pastry); and lamb (braised shank) with rice pilaf. Our own favorite is shrimps Skorpios, lightly battered, deep-fried shrimp served in a ramekin over rice and topped with a delicious tomato sauce and Feta cheese, then broiled. Dinners include cheese and crackers, tossed or Greek salad, rice pilaf or potato or vegetable, and a loaf of bread. We have heard that sometimes the vegetables are overdone—but we can't recall ever having a crisp vegetable in Athens either.

For an appetizer, we adore the *saganaki*, a succulent fried Greek cheese flamed in Metaxa and lemon juice (our own recipe follows). One order is more than enough for two and can serve four. We also recommend the splendid *avgolemono* soup. Try at least one or the other. (We generally order both.) Popular desserts include *baklava*, *crème caramel*, and rice pudding (*rezogdo*)—prepared at Jim's by Uncle Peter since 1914! In addition, the evening menu offers several chef's specials and a seafood of the day. The small but versatile wine list features Greek wines, all sold by the half-liter as well as by the bottle. There's also a variety of unusual nonalcoholic drinks and several house cocktails, notably the Metaxa Sour.

Jim's attracts downtown Lansing businessmen and government employees, especially at lunchtime. You'll see lots of jackets and ties here, but clean jeans are completely acceptable. The kitchen is open for inspection at all times. The service is friendly, efficient, and professional. In fact, professionalism and dedication to good restauranteurship seems to be a theme of this restaurant and certainly characterizes Angie Vlahakis, its present owner, and his staff. This attitude and effort provide Jim's with a consistency that we think you'll appreciate.

Greek professionalism.

JIM'S TIFFANY PLACE, 116 E. Michigan Avenue, Lansing, MI 48933. In city center, two blocks east of the Capitol. Telephone (517) 372-4300. Hours: luncheon 10:45 a.m.-4 p.m., dinner 4-10 p.m. Closed Sundays and holidays. Full bar service. Children's menu. Free parking after 5 p.m.in adjacent lot. All major credit cards. Dinner reservations recommended.

JIM'S CHEF HUNTLEY BURROUGHS'
KOTA KAPAMA

Arrange 2½ pounds frying or roasting chicken (cut up) in a glass or earthenware bowl (you can substitute lamb). Rub thoroughly with lemon juice. Allow to stand while heating 4-5 tablespoons sweet butter and vegetable oil (mixed) in heavy braising pot. Slip chicken into fat; cook over medium heat, turning with tongs to avoid pricking the flesh. Sauté till light chestnut in color. Heat ½ cup dry white wine in a small pan (optional). Pour over the chicken. Shake the pan, and continue cooking over low heat. Stir in 1½ pounds fresh or canned tomatoes (peeled, chopped, and drained) and 1 tablespoon tomato paste diluted with ¼ cup water. Slip 1 large cinnamon stick among the pieces of chicken. Cover, and simmer over lowest possible heat for 1½ hours or till the chicken is tender and the sauce thickens. Or transfer to a 325-degree oven to complete the cooking. Season with salt and pepper. Serve warm with cooked rice.

Hints from the Winters: We especially like this recipe with boned and skinned chicken breasts instead. If the sauce doesn't thicken enough, add a mixture of 2 tablespoons chicken broth and 1 tablespoon cornstarch. We prefer a light red wine with this dish.

SAGANAKI

A curious phenomenon attaches to this dish. Almost every Greek restaurant we've visited over the years claims to be its originator. But whatever the truth of the matter, *saganaki* is a winsome appetizer.

Slice Kefolotiri or Kasseri cheese into 2-inch squares about ¼-inch thick. (Mozzarella can also be used successfully, and it's easier to find.) Dip the cheese first into a mixture of beaten eggs with a little milk added, and then into dry bread crumbs or flour. Fry the cheese squares in hot olive oil (about ¼ inch oil in a skillet) till brown on the bottom. Turn, and cook the second side half as long. Pour Metaxa or brandy over, and ignite. (Now's the time to shout "Opa!") Sprinkle the cheese with fresh lemon juice. Serve with a crusty bread.

Exact quantities will depend on personal tastes. Two or three squares of cheese seems reasonable. Use about 1 jigger brandy and the juice of ½ lemon for every 6 slices of cheese. After trying this once, you might want to use more or less brandy and juice. Be careful when igniting the brandy; remove the pan from the stove before flaming, or you might also ignite the stove hood. Also be sure the brandy is hot (watch for rising fumes), or it won't flame.

13
ROBERT'S
East Lansing

Robert's may be the most handsome and stylish restaurant in the Lansing area. Upon entry to this below-street-level establishment, you'll be immediately impressed by the Mediterranean archways, the warm browns and rich textures of wood and upholstery, of brick and burnished copper. Widely spaced tables provide intimacy and comfort, and there are a number of private and semiprivate dining areas—for example, the Governor's Room, a secluded setting for groups of six to ten. But our favorite of the four dining rooms is the Middle Room, with its ingenious wood and mirrored ceiling and high-backed upholstered armchairs. We especially like the charming booth here that adjoins the wine cellar. Also most appealing is the Director's Room, with the same sort of seating. We might even say that rarely have we been more comfortable in a restaurant. Adding to the ambience is the background music (tapes made by the staff): a tasteful mix of soft jazz, classical, and female vocals. Other small touches, too, are thoughtful—the matchbooks printed with your name if you reserve ahead, the fresh white rose on each table, the promptly emptied ashtrays, the constant but unobtrusive attention of the staff to your needs.

The cooking at Robert's (by the way, the "t" is pronounced) is Continental with an accent on French. Prices are high, but the quality is high, too. Among several more customary appetizers are two less common ones: the *gravlax* (salmon in dill) and an insinuating *galantine* with Cumberland sauce. Popular entrées are veal Oscar, roast rack of lamb, and fresh seafood. The seafood platter Bouquetiere for two persons is a delectable combination of lobster tails, jumbo shrimp, crab legs, and perch, garnished with fresh vegetables—

broccoli and asparagus with Hollandaise, cauliflower, carrots, tomato, and potatoes Delphine. On menu options are *tournedos Rossini*, Chateaubriand for two, chicken Kiev, duckling *à l'orange*, scallopine of veal Marsala, and shrimp *à la* Robert (sautéed in Cognac, sherry, garlic, and butter, on a bed of rice). Daily specialties from the chef are also offered, on the order of whole Maine lobster or medallions of pork Calvados. Dinners include salad, rolls, a vegetable of the day—well prepared and tender-crisp (sometimes a shade too crisp)—or Robert's featured potatoes Delphine (whipped and blended with seasonings, then deep fried; these are excellent). The baked goods and pastries are prepared on the premises. Or, to finish, you might instead prefer one of Robert's creamy dessert cocktails. For four or more persons, the chef and *maître d'hôtel* will be happy to help in arranging a special dinner for any occasion upon 48 hours' notice.

You may visit the kitchen, and when we did, we found it to be very clean and, even more impressive, redolent of shrimp and garlic. You can also observe the small, refrigerated wine cellar. The wine list on an earlier visit wasn't large (in fact, was a bit disappointing); but recently when we dined at Robert's, we found it much improved, with more than fifty selections. And there's also a Captain's List on request, including, in small quantities and at high prices, some exceptional offerings. A house wine may also be had by the glass or carafe.

Leo Farhat, the young, knowledgable, and gracious manager, learned some of his trade from Topinka's in Detroit. Robert's is a relative bewcomer to East Lansing, and if the cuisine and service continue to match the attractive decor, it should earn in a short period of time a reputation as one of Michigan's finest restaurants.

Tasteful, subtle, and sophisticated.

ROBERT'S, 101 E. Grand River Avenue, East Lansing, MI 48823. In the city center. Telephone (517) 351-8505. Hours: 5-10 p.m. (til 11 p.m. Fridays and Saturdays). Closed Sundays and holidays. Full bar service. Background music. Jackets for men suggested. Parking is a bother; Robert's has no lot. Try a nearby city lot. Credit cards: AE, MC, V. Reservations recommended.

ROBERT'S COLD FRUIT SOUP

Dissolve ¾ cup sugar in 2 cups water. Add 1 cup dark sweet pitted canned cherries (drained), 1 cup fresh strawberries, 1 cup canned, drained peach slices, 1½ cups canned Mandarin oranges with juice, the juice of 1½ lemons, and ¼ cup raisins (optional). Cook no more than 10 minutes. Dissolve 2 tablespoons cornstarch in ¼ cup cold water, and add to 3 cups warmed orange juice. Add this mixture to the fruits. Chill well. Add ½ cup heavy cream and 2-3 tablespoons brandy. Garnish with mint leaves. Makes 12 servings, 5 ounces each.

14
BEGGAR'S BANQUET
East Lansing

Liver *pâté*, baked clams Leone, casserole of shrimp Bordelaise, eggs Florentine, veal scallopine Marsala—these don't sound like menu selections from a restaurant popular with college students. The Richard M. Nixon Memorial Bologna at $1, hard-boiled eggs, chili, BLTs—now, these do. Yet all of them are among the many offerings at the Beggar's Banquet, a restaurant near Michigan State University that is fast becoming an institution itself. The flexible menu meets all tastes. The clientele comes in all varieties. The prices are for every pocketbook.

You enter through the often noisy and crowded bar that doubles as a waiting room during busy periods. The restaurant consists of three high-ceiling, elongated, ground-floor rooms that were once part of a row of stores on a side street in the East Lansing business district. Some first-time customers are most interested in the setting: old barn siding and beams, wooden tables and floors, numerous antiques including a variety of farm implements, a cigar-store Indian, a moose horn from Ontario, leaded stained-glass, assorted plants, and an array of generally tasteful paintings by local artists (for sale). Other initiates to the Beggar's Banquet are fascinated by the clientele, tending toward a university-flavored avant-garde. Most patrons, however, forget all first impressions on later visits and concentrate on whetting their appetites for the consistently well-handled American/French food.

Brunch is served on Sundays from 11 to 2 and consists of some fine omelettes and egg dishes (including Benedict, Florentine, our favorite Princesse, and Mundane—"topped with absolutely nothing"), quiche, French toast, and several salads and side dishes. What we most like about this brunch is the table service rather than the increasingly ubiquitous buffet style.

Luncheon Mondays through Saturdays offers much of the Sunday brunch menu plus a variety of sandwiches (the roast pork is good), a daily special or two, very good to excellent soups, and what may be the hottest chili served regularly anywhere in the world. Servings are generally adequate, though a few sandwiches could be more generous.

But dinners at Beggar's Banquet are by far the best meals here. The list of entrées, ranging from four standard steaks to eight or ten more interesting items offered on a regular basis, as well as two or three daily specials, provides a happy variety of choice. Dishes are prepared and served with concern for both quality and appearance. Our favorite regular entrée is the near-incomparable chicken Kiev (too often we've been disappointed in prepackaged, frozen versions); the scallops à la Lyonnaise are most commendable; in fact, there is nothing here we couldn't recommend. Vegetables (and they're seldom overcooked) are included with the entrée along with salad, bread, and coffee or tea. One welcome feature of the menu is that the cost of some dinners varies according to portion size—a thoughtful touch, indicating that the Beggar's is interested in accommodating its customers.

The wine list is large but unusual because only California wines are available. The climate-controlled cellar contains about 4,000 bottles and was described in the New York Times in 1976 by Frank Prial. You should be able to find something of interest, though this list will particularly appeal to those who prefer domestic wines. An adequate house carafe (California, of course) is also available.

The best seating is in the north room, or "dining room" (but away from the entrance). And if tables here aren't free, try for one of the more intimate wooden booths in the "middle room." Above all, avoid tables in traffic areas and especially those in the bar if you want a relaxing dinner. This food deserves your attention, and the bustling bar is, we think, too distracting. Also, you might enjoy the background music here, some of it classical (ask for the Vivaldi tape) and all of it taped by the staff.

We think you'll like the Beggar's Banquet's sense of originality in cooking and generally comfortable and informal atmosphere. Reservations are honored quite promptly (but football Saturdays present problems); and once seated, you won't be rushed. Prices are fair, about average for a better restaurant. and if you really want to splurge, you can arrange with the Beggar's for a $125 special dinner for four, including appropriate wines. One disadvantage, especially for those unfamiliar with the area, is the lack of a parking lot, although city lots are located across the street and behind the building.

Doing its own thing nicely.

THE BEGGAR'S BANQUET, 218 Abbott Road, East Lansing, MI 48823. In city center (across from the State Theater). Telephone (517) 351-4573. Hours: 11 a.m.-2 a.m. for luncheon and dinner, Sunday brunch 11 a.m.-2 p.m. Closed Christmas. Full bar service. Background music. No dress code (anything goes), but you might see some jackets at night in the dining room. Credit cards: MC, V. Reservations recommended.

TOMATOES JERESA

This is attractive and flavorful as an accompaniment or garnish with almost any entrée. Mix in a shallow bowl 1 egg with 1 tablespoon cream. In a second shallow bowl place ½ cup purchased Italian-style dry bread crumbs (or a mixture of ½ cup dry crumbs, ½ teaspon mixed Italian seasonings— or ¼ teaspoon each dry oregano and basil—and 1 tablesspoon grated Parmesan cheese). Slice tomatoes crosswise about ½-inch thick (or more). Dip first into egg mixture, then into crumbs. Heat about ¼ inch vegetable oil in a skillet over high heat. Fry tomato slices, turning once, till golden brown on each side. Measurements are for 2 medium-large tomatoes, about 8-10 slices.

15
THE STATE ROOM
East Lansing

We admit a bias in this entry, but we do believe that most visitors will agree with our assessment of the MSU campus as one of the most attractive in the country, especially in the spring and fall. One way to enjoy it more fully is to eat at the State Room and then take a short walk through the beautifully landscaped grounds of the university. The State Room is housed in the Kellogg Center for Continuing Education, one of the foremost adult education centers in the United States. As headquarters for nearly all conferences held at Michigan State, it hosts over 400 meetings and short courses and serves about 150,000 people each year. It also serves as the campus inn, and among many other facilities is its public dining room, the State Room.

Redecorated in the mid-1970s in a traditional walnut and brick scheme, the room is comfortable and semiformal and features on its walls a collection of photographs giving glimpses into the historical development of the university. It can be very busy during a large convention, and there's a slight institutional flavor here—but we think you'll enjoy your meal and a visit to a major university campus. The best tables (for nonsmokers) are near the windows, and the alcove is a pleasant, more private area for larger groups. But do try to avoid a table near the entryway or the swinging door to the kitchen.

Both luncheon and dinner menus change daily and offer interesting variations on basic American cooking at moderate prices. Over the years for lunch we've enjoyed the chicken salad plate, open-faced sandwiches (especially the mushroom and cheese), the French dip and beef patty, braised lamb shanks, soufflés, and numerous delicious muffins. Breakfast, too, is particularly agreeable in the State Room— the food is well prepared and the atmosphere relaxed. At dinnertime the most popular entrée is roast lamb, accompanied by a choice of vegetable and potato and a sauce that varies. The menu also includes a "Gourmet's Corner"that on one evening might feature chicken Kiev and on another, baked stuffed salmon. Desserts are a specialty here, and aside from the ever popular sundaes, the State Room offers some excellent, freshly baked cakes and pies.

After your meal (it's likely that you'll pay Betty Ennis, who has been cashier for the last fourteen years), we suggest that you take a leisurely walk out the rear entrance, cross the Red Cedar footbridge, pass Jenison Fieldhouse (who can forget Earvin "Magic" Johnson?) and Football Stadium, all the way to Farm Lane bridge. Return on the opposite side of the river past the canoe livery; the Administration Bulding, named in honor of John Hannah, probably the university's most distinguished past president; and the library. Then stroll through Beal Botanical Gardens, and cross the river again at the bridge near "Sparty" to return to Kellogg Center. This will take about an hour, but it'll give you an especially charming view of a splendid campus. By the way, there are several footbridges that can shorten your journey if you tire or don't have enough time.

Number one in the Big Ten.

THE STATE ROOM, Kellogg Center, S. Harrison Road, East Lansing, MI 48823. On the campus of Michigan State University. Telephone (517) 332-6571. Hours: breakfast 7-10 a.m., luncheon 11:30 a.m.-2 p.m., dinner 5:30-8 p.m., Sunday breakfast 8-11 a.m. and dinner noon-4 p.m. Closed holidays and holiday weekends. No alcoholic beverages. Background music. Parking in adjacent pay lot. Credit cards: AE, MC, V. Reservations not taken.

THE STATE ROOM FRUIT TORTE

This delectable cake can be made with pineapple, blueberries, or strawberries, either fresh or frozen; but if you use frozen strawberries, be sure to drain them, thicken the juices, and fold the berries back into the juice so that the mixture can be spread as a heavy sauce on the whipped cream. For the cake batter, cream together ½ cup butter or margarine and ½ cup sugar. Slowly add 4 egg yolks. Sift together ⅔ cup cake flour, 2 teaspoons baking powder, and a pinch of salt. Add the flour and ¼ cup milk alternately to the creamed butter mixture. Mix 3 minutes at slow speed of an electric mixer. Pour into two greased and paper-lined 9-inch round cake tins.

For the meringue, beat 4 egg whites till foamy. Slowly add ½ cup plus 2 tablespoons sugar and ¼ teaspoon vanilla. Beat till soft peaks form. Divide meringue into 2 equal parts, and spread over cake batter. Sprinkle with ¼ cup chopped nuts, and bake for 20-25 minutes in a preheated 325-degree oven. Mix the filling: whip 1½ cups heavy cream and sweeten to taste. Add ¼ teaspoon vanilla. When the cake is done, remove one layer from pan and place on a plate with the meringue side down. Cover with half the whipped cream. Put the fruit on the cream evenly, and cover with remaining cream. Place the second layer on the cream with meringue side up. (This will probably take longer to bake in the home oven.)

16
THE BLACK SHEEP TAVERN
Manchester

There's an untouched quality about Main Street in Manchester. The storefronts, the old feed mill, and its adjoining millpond recall the quieter pace of the nineteenth century. But today Manchester is probably best known for the Black Sheep Repertory Theater and the Black Sheep Tavern. Since 1873 there's been a tavern on this site, and we'd guess that the present one is the best of them all. It's a designated historic site, and care has been taken to retain and re-create the atmosphere of its early days. The decor throughout is rustic and nostalgic—solid oak tables, lots of worn wood, antique signs, chopping blocks, agricultural paraphernalia. And you really must look at the beautiful stand-up bar with copper foot rail and mirrored backbar—it dates to the first Black Sheep Tavern of more than 100 years ago. To one side of it is a collection of the beers that have been served over the years in the tavern. In the basement is a second appealing dining area, the Williamsburg Room, occupying what was once a bakery. Here the walls are stone and the floors brick, all original and now restored.

Luncheon seems to be almost an afterthought at the Black Sheep, understandable enough in a small village. If you plan to travel especially to visit the tavern, it's wiser to go in the evening or on a Sunday. The midday menu is dominated by some very predictable sandwiches, and the only thing possibly worth going out of your way for is the daily special. But dinner is another thing entirely. The soups are freshly made and hearty—onion, seafood bisque, and a soup of the day, possibly lentil, beef barley, split pea or bean in ham broth. Appetizers include oysters on the half shell, fried clams and smelt, and steamed mussels. The Fisherman's Catch varies daily and is the customers' favorite (if possible, try the swordfish). But there's an entrée to please everyone: steaks, chops, and seafood as well as duckling, lamb shanks and rice, knackwurst and sauerkraut, poached finnan haddie, and braised rabbit, plus some combinations (steak and crab, lobster, or shrimp; rabbit and pork chop). More comprehensive combinations are listed under the heading "dedicated to those who can't make up their mind": Fisherman's Feast (fish, shrimp, clams, crab) and Land Lover's Lust (lamb shank, pork chop, and rabbit). Dinners include a salad bar, freshly baked bread, and a choice of German potato salad, stewed tomatoes, baked potato, fresh corn on the cob, or cottage fries (these are tops, and not what you'd expect). To finish, you have a choice of cheesecake, fresh pie, Irish coffee, or "hot apple mountain"—a luscious concoction of ice cream and spiced fresh apples on a shortbread biscuit, topped with whipped cream and dusted with cinnamon. Wines are modest; the beer list exceeds that of wines—and perhaps this is as it should be in this old tavern.

Spring, summer, and autumn are the theater season in Manchester. In conjunction with the Black Sheep Repertory Theater across the street, the tavern arranges dinner packages with a discount for groups of ten or more on Wednesdays, Thursdays, and Sundays. Another arrangement, mainly limited to theater packages, is the series of Williamsburg Dinners, served in season on weekends in the lower-level Williamsburg Room. These are price fixed at about $8 and include a choice of four entrées (braised rabbit, chicken Creole, steamed rainbow trout, and roast leg of lamb), accompanied by wild rice, bran muffins, and salad bar. When the summer theater is on, a guitarist plays in this room. On weekends in the main dining room there's a pianist.

A timeless tavern.

THE BLACK SHEEP TAVERN, 117 E. Main Street, Manchester, MI 48158. South of I-94 between Jackson and Ann Arbor, in village center. Telephone (313) 428-7000 or (517) 788-2670. Hours: luncheon 11:30 a.m.-2 p.m. (till 4 p.m. on Saturdays), dinner 5 p.m.-closing (about 12-I a.m. on weekends), Sunday dinner 2-11 p.m. Closed Thanksgiving, Christmas, New Years Day. Full bar service. Children's portions. Entertainment weekends and in summer. Packages available with theater. Free parking in rear. Credit cards: MC, V. Reservations recommended.

THE BLACK SHEEP'S TOMATO RELISH

This was a popular item featured on the tavern's buffet in the past. It's a good recipe for a group, it's very simple to put together, and you can prepare it in advance. Needless to say, it's at its best with tomatoes fresh from the garden in summer. Mix together the following ingredients: 1½ gallons (24 cups) diced fresh tomatoes, 6 stalks celery cut into 1-inch julienne strips, 3 green peppers cut into 1-inch julienne strips, 1 minced onion, 4 tablespoons horseradish, 8 teaspoons salt, 3 cups red wine vinegar, 2 cups sugar, 4 teaspoons mustard seed, ½ teaspoon ground cloves, and 1 dash pepper. Refrigerate overnight; keeps about 1 week. Serves 25-30.

Hints from the Winters: For 8-10 servings, use these measurements—8 cups tomatoes, 3 stalks celery, 1 green pepper, about ¼ cup minced onion, 1 tablespoon plus 1 teaspoon horseradish, 2½ teaspoons salt, 1 cup red wine vinegar (Dell'Alpe brand is excellent), ⅔ cup sugar, 1½ teaspoons mustard seed, ⅛ teaspoon or more cloves, dash pepper.

If you like our recommendations, tell the proprietor. If you don't, tell us. Write Beech Tree Press, 2673 Rampart Path, Holt, Michigan 48842.

17
HATHAWAY HOUSE
Blissfield

Though there are a few Continental and Oriental dishes on the menu, Hathaway House is 100 percent American—from the 1851 building to the furnishings, from the table settings to the service. Originally a private residence, the stately Greek-revival home hasn't changed much since its construction. Though converted to a restaurant in 1961, the feeling here is still that of a warm, friendly, and relaxing home, albeit a magnificent one. The Weeber family—Art, Mary, and Mike, the chef—took over the management in 1963 and are dedicated to making their guests feel welcome and very special.

The building is worth studying. The monumental facade is representative of the architectural movement that swept over the South and Midwest prior to the Civil War, a revival of the Doric Order of Greece that dates to four centuries before Christ. Some typical features incorporated in Hathaway House are the fluted columns and the triangular tympanum they support. It's an imposing exterior—those large white pillars, the crisp green canopy over the entrance, the low wrought-iron fence surrounding the grounds, and the well-manicured lawns and shrubbery. Imposing, but inviting, too. There are six dining rooms in all—three on the first floor and three on the second level that can open into one large room for banquets and during the weekend's entertainment. Each gracious room is decorated in a different color scheme, and the decor is essentially early American, though the fireplaces and woodwork retain the classical lines of the building's architectural style.

The menu is dominated by good American cooking and goes far beyond limited steakhouse fare. Yes, the steaks, chops, lobster, and shrimp are here (and are very well prepared), but there is much, much more. For preliminaries you can go to the appetizer table, included with your entrée (salads, relishes, steaming homemade soup, and spicy meatballs Romano) or order one of the classic starters from the menu—*coquilles St. Jacques* in a Mornay sauce, "natural-stuffed crab" (stuffed with crab), *escargots*, and others. At least thirty entrees make an appearance: Hawaiian shrimp, beef Stroganoff, planked lake trout, shrimp Newburgh, baked ham with brandied raisin sauce, colonial chicken pie (the chef is justifiably proud of this one), Tempura-style prawns, tiny and tender frog legs, delicately crisped scallops, and chicken served family style.

At luncheon some of the same items are available as well as an assortment of favorite sandwiches and five refreshing salads (shrimp, chicken, chef's, vegetarian, and the "Exotic" turkey and water chestnut). The daily buffet at lunch is popular, consisting of four hot dishes, assorted salads, and rolls. And on Sunday there's a smorgasbord featuring roast beef and ham at a good price; the meat is carved to order and is complemented by six other hot dishes and at least 25 salad varieties.

The breads are mouth-watering (be sure to try the cinnamon rolls). And though we're not enamored of salad bars or buffet tables, this one works well. The tables are in a separate room so that seating is not disrupted by traffic to and fro. The desserts should be forbidden, but we're glad they're not: ice cream drinks (the Amaretto Alexander is a knockout), lots of good coffees (Jamaican, Irish, Spanish, Mexican, Scotch, etc.), warm cherry and apple pie, a number of delectable cakes, and flambéed *babas au rhum*, cherry Alaska, and cherries Jubilee. Splurge on dessert here.

At the rear of the restaurant, next to the cloakroom, is a Spice Shop that sells spices, extracts, candies, and teas. It opens onto the rear lawn, where umbrella tables are set up on the patio in the summer and where the annual Hathaway House picnic takes place on the first or second Sunday in July—complete with clowns, pony cart rides, entertainers, a flea market, artists, and a barbeque. On Friday and Saturday in the Ballroom Eddie and Diana, country/folk recording stars, sing and play instrumentals. (Book well ahead for this; there's a $2 cover.)

There are lots of nice little touches at Hathaway House. On the tables are pressed glass stemware, fresh flowers, and petal-folded cloth napkins. The children's menu is a prize winner—literally. We've seen lots of placemats and coloring books, but for the Little Guests here are magic slates; on

the back the dishes (good selections, too) are named after famous Americans of the Revolutionary War period. The menu won a silver medal from the National Restaurant Association. **Deserves a gold medal for all-American cuisine.**
HATHAWAY HOUSE, 424 W. Adrian Street (U.S. 223), Blissfield, MI 49228. About halfway between Ann Arbor and Toledo, Ohio. Telephone (517) 486-2141. Hours: luncheon 11:30 a.m.-4 p.m., dinner 4-9 p.m. (till 10 p.m. Fridays and Saturdays); luncheon buffet 11:30 a.m.-2 p.m.; Sunday brunch 11:30 a.m.-4 p.m. Closed Mondays, December 24 and 25, and New Years Day. Full bar service. Children's menu. Background music, entertainment on weekends. Free parking. All major credit cards but CB. Reservations highly recommended, especially on Saturdays.

HATHAWAY HOUSE
DEEP-FRIED ARTICHOKE HEARTS

This is a stunning appetizer for one of your special parties. Sift together ½ cup flour, ¼ teaspoon baking powder, and 1 teaspoon salt. Combine ½ cup milk and 1 beaten egg. Blend into flour mixture. Using 1 small can of artichoke hearts (well drained) and 1 cup bread crumbs, first dip the hearts into the batter and then into the crumbs. Deep fry in 360-degree oil until crisp, approximately 2 to 3 minutes. Drain and serve with sour cream, mixed with chives and seasoned with garlic salt to taste.

HATHAWAY HOUSE VEGETABLE DIP

Chef Mike Weeber thinks this is great for all fresh vegetables. We think so, too, and it has an advantage of being prepared with ingredients that are probably already in your refrigerator and on your shelves. This is a good last-minute appetizer when you need one.
Combine 2 cups sour cream, 2 cups salad dressing (preferably Kraft's Miracle Whip), 1 teaspoon dill weed, 1 medium minced onion, 2 teaspoons Worcestershire sauce, 1 teaspoon celery salt, ½ teaspoon Tabasco sauce, and 1 teaspoon minced garlic.

18
THE SPAGHETTI BENDER
Ypsilanti

Here is one of the happier meeting places of town and gown. Located near Eastern Michigan University, the Spaghetti Bender, under the able direction of Tom Ciccarelli, has nicely bridged the gap between young and old. It started up modestly in 1973 with one dining room, the present Old World Room, and then started growing. There are now several rooms: the Mona Lisa Room (and, yes, she's there smiling enigmatically on the salad bar); the Mirror Room, our own preference, with walls reflecting the Tiffany lamp collection and massive old pieces of furniture; and the Garden Room, one of the darkest gardens we've seen anywhere, apparently named for the profusion of hanging preserved ferns. This last might also be called the Room Where the Action Is—the bandstand's here, and it swings on weekends. Red-checkered bistro clothes on the tables, bottles and plants suspended from the ceiling, brick walls with old pictures—there's a lot to look at, including the varied clientele.

As you might guess, spaghetti is the number-one vote getter here, followed by lasagne, pizza, and the veal offerings. These are particularly tempting: the Veal alla Ypsilanti, on a bed of fettucine, is topped with a rich tomato sauce, mushrooms, and Mozzarella; another possibility is Piedmontese veal, tips of veal combined with a Marsala wine-beef gravy and served with rice or fettucine. Other entrées are chicken Florentino, baked Italian pork chops, and a few non-Italian items—baked chicken, steak, roast beef, ham steak, Boston scrod, and liver and onions.

There are twenty pasta dishes on the menu, many of them imaginative renditions of the traditional and many of them original with the Spaghetti Bender. The spaghetti Vesuvio, for example, has a barbeque-flavored sauce and is topped with chicken, mushrooms, onions, and green pepper. The Donaldo Verde is a blend of fettucine noodles, buttery cheese sauce, and basil. And there are two vegetarian pastas based on eggplant. The pizzas here also offer plenty of variety:

assorted cheeses, different crusts than the customary, and some unusual combinations such as the Inferno, a "Mexican" pizza; the Mother Nature, with a whole-wheat crust and vegetables; the Polynesian (better than it sounds); and the especially recommended pizza Lorraine, billed by the restaurant as "better than quiche." One pizza we haven't seen often in restaurants is an individual six-incher called the Little Rascal. The Spaghetti Bender suggests Chianti with pizza—we suggest beer.

If you want something lighter, there's a good selection of soups and salads (plus a salad bar) and sandwiches—with oldtime Hollywood labels (the Laurel and Hardy, the Mae West Burger, et al.). We like the W. C. Hoagie—a mixture of steak, onions, mushrooms, green pepper, Mozzarella, and sauce on a sub roll. A good one for vegetarians is the Swiss and Colby sandwich with sprouts, tomatoes, and onions. Incidentally, there's reason beyond just humor behind the unusual and amusing names given some of the dishes at the Spaghetti Bender. Tom Ciccarelli is proud of his products— all the restaurant's own creations—and to give them more commonplace names might set up the wrong expectations. After all, how can you be disapponted in anything called Pasta di Popeye (with spinach, of course)? Each item on the menu is well described so you won't make many mistakes. And if you're bored with the company, read the menu—it's amusing and chatty.

We like the choice of rice dishes, prepared in several ways: with Oriental vegetables and chicken, Calabria style (Italian vegetables, chicken, mushrooms); alla Marsala (veal, mushrooms, and Italian vegetables); Siciliano (Italian sausage, vegetables); and Genovese, billed as a "terrific dish for rice connoisseurs" (steak, peppers, onions, mushrooms on a bed of seasoned rice with a barbeque sauce on the side). Portions are huge; you might think about sharing here. The salad bar has 60 to 70 items on it—one of the state's most bounteous. And somehow we don't mind it in this place. In the Spaghetti Bender, one expects customers to be milling around, and a walk to the salad bar gives you an excuse to peer in at the other rooms.

The prices are very good. In addition, there are all kinds of specials and "deals" with the management. The tab on lasagne is reduced on Mondays, and spaghetti costs less on Sundays. Wednesday is Rebate Night—you get a raincheck of 10 percent of your bill to use on a return visit. Specials on wine are offered Tuesdays; Thursday is Ladies' Night; and on Friday and Saturday till 9:30 in the evening is an Italian Wedding Buffet—all you can eat of lasagne, rice, spaghetti, chicken, meats, cheeses, salad, pizza, and dessert (for less than $7), a superbargain for voracious eaters.

Speaking of bargains, Dad, take a look at the kiddies' menu; it beats a drive-in any day. The list includes ravioli, baked chicken, pastas with butter and cheese or meatballs— these are only 99 cents ($1.19 for the meatball dish). Here also are teeny pizzas and several other choices. It's certainly one of the best children's menus we've seen, both in number and variety of selections and in prices.

The wines are suitable and well chosen for a restaurant of this kind—mostly Italian, mostly modest. The house wines are from California's Sebastiani. But as the menu points out, "beer is good for what ales you." (Ouch.)

You might want to make an evening of it here. After the Wedding Buffet is over, about 9:30 p.m., an uncanny metamorphosis takes place in the Spaghetti Bender. Without any effort on the part of the management but through some sense of group hypnosis, the place suddenly transforms itself into a nightclub. Recently the Cafe Rouge, a five-piece swing band with female vocalist, has appeared regularly; but the entertainment varies. Over the years there have been mime shows, big bands, and Italian opera. And music and dancing aren't the only entertainment; you can play pool or ping pong, too. Reservations aren't taken, except for large parties, so be aware of this if you arrive on a weekend. On a Friday or Saturday night, the Spaghetti Bender might seat 380 people. Football weekends are exceptionally busy.

As you leave, you may notice the sign in front: "This Restaurant Will Be Here Forever." We certainly hope so and hope you'll agree with us.

Mind-bending, pocketbook-stretching.

THE SPAGHETTI BENDER, 23 N. Washington, Ypsilanti, MI 48197. Exit 183 off I-94, downtown Ypsilanti. Telephone (313) 485-2750. Hours: Monday through Thursday luncheon 11:30 a.m.-3 p.m., dinner 5-10 p.m., Friday and Saturday dinner 5 p.m.-midnight, Sunday 4-10 p.m. Closed major holidays. Full bar service. Children's menu. Background music, entertainment and dancing Wednesday through Saturday evenings. Carryout pizzas. Credit cards: MC, V. Reservations not accepted except for special parties and large groups with advance notice.

19
COMPLETE CUISINE, LTD.
Ann Arbor

A cooking school, a store, a food shop, a bakery, a *patisserie*, a restaurant, a spectacle, an event—in business only three years, Complete Cuisine is the brainchild of Sandi Cooper, who studied at La Varenne in Paris and the Cordon Bleu in London, and her husband Steve, who teaches microbiology at the University of Michigan in the daytime and cooking classes once or twice a month in the evenings. As Sandi describes the establishment, it probably has "the least decor and the most atmosphere" of any restaurant in the state. We won't go into all the wondrous cookware and gourmet foods sold in the store proper—though you might like to know, to get idea of the completeness of Complete Cuisine, that this is the place to buy your *crème fraîche*, your dipping chocolates (seven types in all), and the preserved lemons for your Moroccan cooking.

The school is a mecca for the home cook, the chef, the would-be chef, the cooking teacher, and the just-plain-fascinated epicurean who wants to see how it's all done. In the "beautiful" category are classes in cake decorating, Chinese cuisine, and spectacular desserts. In the "bargain" category there are workshops in *pâté* and bread making and two-hour classes in such creative activities as chocolate cookery, crepe making, and the production of a Mexican French, or Italian dinner from starters to sweets. But the greatest bargain of all is the free classes on Wednesdays. A few recent ones focused on one-pot meals, desserts made with nuts, and a series of "know your food" tastings (cheese, chocolate, coffee, oil, vinegar, mustard). In the "best" category are full-fledged courses in any number of procedures and any number of cuisines, culminating in occasional visits by foremost teacher-chefs. Guest *professeurs de cuisine* have included Paula Wolfert, Marcella Hazan, Bernard Clayton, Jacques Pepin, and Simone Beck—who thrilled her class by merely cutting up a chicken. (If you don't remember Ms Beck, affectionately known as Simca, she was Julia Child's collaborator for the famous two volumes of *Mastering the Art of French Cooking*, books that introduced French cooking to millions of Americans.)

On Tuesdays Creative Cuisine offers luncheon classes; these might be based on a particular cuisine of the world or possibly on menus of great restaurants. Each is different, and at each you both learn how to prepare the dishes and then enjoy them for your lunch. The charge is slightly higher than for the regular menu offerings. Private and group classes are also available. And, men, don't be shy; usually about a third of Creative Cuisine's students are male. (From all the evidence, if this isn't a good meeting place for singles, it should be.) And if you love to cook and love to eat, Complete Cuisine will put you on the mailing list for *Soupçon*, a monthly newsletter with a calendar of classes and events, a recipe of the month, and some informative cooking articles; send $1 for a year's subscription.

But, yes, we did mention that Creative Cuisine is also a restaurant. The tables, set up at the rear of the store, seat only up to 22. Nancy Kozak is the talented and accomplished *chef de cuisine*, who with help of her small but enthusiastic staff offers some of the most delightful luncheons in Michigan. Nancy has her roots in Polish cuisine and retains a healthy respect for sound, basic food and the use of the best fresh ingredients (which is, after all, the essence of that much abused phrase "gourmet cooking"). The recipes used are all original, and the menu is printed daily. Surprisingly, the prices are quite reasonable, comparable with those of places serving much less interesting and innovative food.

Entrees might include fettucine Belgique—freshly made (!) egg pasta tossed with Belgian endive, *crème fraîche*, and Dijon mustard—*pâté de campagne*, mushroom and Cheddar quiche, golden lemon fish mousse, Bretonne crepes filled with Nova Scotia salmon in a sour cream and dill sauce,

Senegalese carrot soup, *poulet Dijonnaise* in *filo* pastry, a cold summer soup synthesizing peaches and brandy, an exceptional *ratatouille* (distinguished by the fresh herbs Nancy uses and a crisper texture than the usual), or a fine Belgian endive salad with walnuts and black olives. If it's on the menu, don't fail to order the pasta—Nancy even makes her own spaghetti. And don't miss the desserts: her pear *sorbet* with ginger brandy is a refreshing, icy treat; her chocolate mousse is remarkable (with rasberries, it's doubly delicious); and her strawberry tarts are as beautiful to look at as to eat. No wine with lunch—a pity.

We mentioned a bakery and *patisserie*, too, didn't we? Next door to Complete Cuisine and under its auspices is a charming spot, Ian's Patisserie. Baked goods, pastries, and coffee can be had here from 7:30 a.m. to 1 in the morning, offering a fitting finish to an evening out. The decor is light and airy with crisp blue and white table linens, and the light walls also serve as a local art gallery with changing displays of paintings, textiles, and *objets d'art*. In warm weather there are tables outside, too. Ian Titterton developed his skills in Great Britain and personally attends to the creation of dozens of rich European delicacies: *croissants*, Dundee cakes, scones, *brioches*, cheesecakes, and tortes. Mousses, French pastries, and Nancy Kozak's fruit tarts are also on the menu. The bakery, an adjunct to the pastry shop and café, offers carryout purchases of some exceptional breads. The peasant varieties are noteworthy—whole wheat with hazelnut, sourdough rye with sunflower or flax seeds, Lithuanian pumpernickel, and Irish soda bread. And the French bread is as close to the genuine article as you can get a continent away. The oven is a marvel—fitted with an internal steam jet to insure the proper crispness and texture. Look closely at some of the prize-winning cake decorations in the glass display case at the entry. What looks like Alençon lace is really icing, hard as it is to believe. And what looks like a cookware store in Ann Arbor is just that—and much, much more.

Completely delightful.

COMPLETE CUISINE, LTD., 322 S. Main Street, Ann Arbor, MI 48104. In city center. Telephone (313) 662-0046. Hours: luncheon only 11:30 a.m.-1:30 p.m. in three seatings—patrons seated on the half hour, last seating at 1:30, Tuesday through Saturday. Call ahead, though; when famous guest chefs are here or when a cooking workshop is scheduled, lunch is not available. Hours of Ian's Patisserie are 7:30 a.m.-1 a.m. Closed Sundays and Mondays. No alcoholic beverages. Background music (WUOM radio) and a few clanking pots and pans. Daytime metered parking in rear. Credit cards: MC, V. Reservations recommended.

20
THE CRACKED CRAB
Ann Arbor

If you've spent any time in New England, you'll sense a familiar seaboard aura as you set foot in the Cracked Crab. Those black-and-white tiled floors, marble tabletops, and dark bentwood chairs will call up an unmistakable, nearly clairvoyant vision of steaming, fragrant crustaceans. There are two rooms, one with a long bar, and an adjacent, more recent addition, both decorated in the same style and seating some 150 people. We prefer the barroom for its breezy, casual atmosphere and the nautical touches here and there (including a fishing boat with lobster trap hanging above the front windows). If this area has a problem, it's that a few seats are too close to the traffic from the kitchen. But in this sort of place, maybe that's not a problem at all, but an advantage—the odors are particularly appetizing here. True, the scents aren't quite as heady as in a Boston seafood bar, but Don Merke, the affable and accommodating owner, is working to get the aroma of crab back into the restaurant. (We hear that years ago it was much more insistent and has now been all but destroyed by modern filter systems.) The seafood, after all, is what the people have been coming for during the last ten years. And they flock here from all over, students in blue Michigan sweatshirts and the "mink girls" from Barton Hills. This is a prime place for people watching.

As for the seafood, the Cracked Crab is a good (whoops—we almost said "viable") alternative to the Gandy Dancer, Chuck Muer's well-known restaurant in a fascinating old depot nearby. We like both places, but here the prices border on bargains for high-quality, completely fresh fish and seafood. (And, thankfully, there's no salad bar.) Moreover, since Captain Jack, the new chef, has arrived, the possibilities are much more exciting than oldtime patrons might realize. This may even turn out to be one of the great mergers in the Michigan restaurant scene: Captain Jack, who came in 1979 from the Sherman House in Chicago, and the imaginative Don Merke, owner and manager of the Crab. With this combination and their enthusiastic, hard-working young staff it's difficult to see how they can miss.

The luncheon menu includes four starters: steamed clams, oysters or clams on ice—with a fine, snappy red sauce, well laced with horseradish—and steamed mussels—sixteen black-shelled beauties served with broth, melted butter, and lemon. Soups comprise chowders (better than ever under Captain Jack's watchful eye), a notable Cajun-style gumbo, and one or two daily specials. The sandwiches at the Cracked Crab rise far above the commonplace: beer-battered fish or shrimp on a toasted bun, an open-faced steamed fish, soft-shell crab, smoked Baltic herring on rye, and finnan haddie.

Some of the same items are dispensed in the evening, but the offerings are more numerous. Both the shrimp and Dungeness crab are treated inventively, first seasoned with a hot, spicy mixture (don't ask; it's a well-kept secret), then steamed. The lobster tails, also steamed, are the most expensive thing on the menu here (as elsewhere), but these are mammoth tails; ask about the going price. There are daily specials at both lunch and dinner—and they're really special. Don Merke, a seafood convert who admits to hating fish before he was married, is meticulous about his catch and goes out of his way to provide new and appealing dishes, depending on what's available—such as Danish smoked eel, fresh scrod, and monkfish (which Captain Jack either broils or sauteed in sherry sauce and served over rice). Some of the best items on the bill of fare are the dinners for two, varying daily; these are bargains at less than $20. The entree might be on the order of northern jack from Ontario, stuffed with rice and cucumber, or Icelandic cod with a filling of oysters and pistachios. If you see them on the menu, you'd be well advised to consider the South Australian fish cakes, Fisherman's Stew, or (in the summer) Fisherman's Salad—

a medley of cold steamed monkfish, shrimp, and King crab.

Only two desserts are listed: liqueur parfaits and a topnotch Jewish cheesecake from Detroit. There's a chalked Drink of the Day above the bar. The wines are minimal, and we wish some better Chablis were available. But the Crab doesn't want to up the prices with very expensive wines; we applaud the sentiment. House wines only. While you're lingering over your coffee, you might notice that the background music doesn't just fill a void but is actually worth listening to— light classical, big bands, and jazz from 1910 to 1920.

Special seafood, special prices.

THE CRACKED CRAB, 112 W. Washington, Ann Arbor, MI 48104. Downtown, just west of Main Street. Telephone (313) 769-8591. Hours: 11 a.m.-11 p.m. (till midnight on Fridays and Saturdays), Sundays and holidays 5-11 p.m. Closed Thanksgiving, Christmas, New Years. Full bar service. Background music, Parking a problem in the daytime; after 6 p.m., parking in large bank lot at rear. Credit cards: AE, MC, V. Reservations not accepted.

THE CRACKED CRAB'S
FISH FILLETS A LA BONNE FEMME

Place 4 fillets of fish in a buttered, flameproof shallow casserole, and cover with ¾ cup finely sliced mushrooms, 1 small bunch minced green onions, and 1 teaspoon chopped parsley. Gently pour ⅔ cup dry white wine into dish. Cover and simmer 10 to 15 minutes. Remove the fish onto a hot shallow ovenproof serving dish. Boil the pan liquids until reduced by one-half. Stir in ⅔ cup Veloute sauce (or cream sauce made with fish stock) gradually into the wine until blended. Pour the sauce over the fillets, and broil until the sauce is lightly browned. Serve with boiled new potatoes. Serves 2.

CAPTAIN JACK'S FISHERMAN'S STEW

In a 6-quart pan mix 3 cups diced canned tomatoes, 1 can condensed cream of tomato soup, 1½ soup cans water, ½ teaspoon salt, ¼ teaspoon pepper, ¼ teaspoon Accent,

1 teaspoon oregano, a good pinch of saffron, 1 teaspoon Worcestershire sauce, 1 teaspoon concentrated fish stock. Bring to a boil; then simmer, and add ½ cup each of your choice of diced vegetables, such as potatoes, carrots, celery, onions, turnips, and parsnips. When vegetables are halfway cooked, add 2 cups fresh fish in large chunks (any good inexpensive variety like cod, monk, flounder, or haddock). Stir gently to avoid breaking up the fish. Serve over wide buttered noodles. Serves 4-6.

Hints from the Winters: If you can't find concentrated fish stock and don't keep stocks in your freezer, you might try (as we have with other fish recipes) 2 or 3 teaspoons of dried Chinese shrimp (available in specialty food stores).

21
RAJA RANI
Ann Arbor

If you never believed those fairy tales about genies coming out of bottles, Raja Rani may change your mind. Here a prodigious array of culinary successes comes out of an amazingly tiny kitchen—we think there's some magic at work. Nowhere, not even at the celebrated Veeraswamy's in London, have we tasted any better east Indian food than at this little place in Ann Arbor. The restaurant takes its name from the Indian words for "king" and "queen," and we'll let you guess why that name is appropriate. According to the obliging and attractive Loveleen Bajwa, one of the owners and originally from the Punjab state in northern India, the restaurant has never advertised and does mainly a word-of-mouth business. The word seems to be getting around more and more; we've even heard Raja Rani described as the best restaurant in Ann Arbor.

The dining room seats only about 36 people. It's simply and cleanly decorated—tables with gold and white linens and plates banded with blue are set under a near-matching blue ceiling, and the Indian prints on the walls are softly lighted by shining pierced-brass hanging lamps. Indian background music contributes to the understated ambience.

East Indian cuisine is one of the greatest in the world and is developed most highly in northern India, where dishes are more subtle and less aggressively seasoned than in the south. But north or south, the use of spices and herbs is perhaps the most distinctive characteristic of the cuisine. Unfortunately too many people have grouped all Indian dishes into a homogeneous "curry" and have no idea of the wide variety of flavors—pungent and mild, hot and warm—that results from the centuries-old craft of blending spices in India.

First-time customers here usually—and probably should—order the Raja Rani special dinner for two (or three): *mulgatani* soup, *tandoori* chicken, egg and vegetable curries, *pullao* (rice), *dal*, *chapathi*, *papadams*, and chutney. The soup is delicate and flavorful. Each of the two curries has its own assertive character. The *dal* consists of lentils cooked with cream, butter, and seasonings; and the *pullao* with green peas is moderately and compellingly spicy. *Chapathi*, like all the breads served here, is based on an unleavened whole wheat dough and differs from the others mainly through the cooking process. It's almost impossible not to become enamored of the chicken *tandoori*, breast of chicken which has been marinated in an amalgam of spices, citrus, and yogurt and then is broiled or charcoal-grilled to golden perfection. The color alone, from the saffron and turmeric, is aesthetically satisfying. As for the *papadam*, Americans—who spend millions a year on potato chips—should be delighted with this paper-thin, crisp delicacy made of lentil flour, one of the more distracting appetizers in the restaurant world, complemented by Raja Rani's exceptionally cool and refreshing pale green chutney (or you can order a sweeter chutney, if you prefer).

Most likely, once you've tried all these, you'll want to return and sample some other dishes at the restaurant. Habitués at Raja Rani are particularly fond of the fiery hot Madras-style lamb Vendaloo and the *tandoori* chicken Masala (served with a creamy tomato sauce—*masala*, by the way, means "sauce"). The Vendaloo, we think, is one of the best of its genre. Only lamb, chicken, prawns, and shrimp as well as numerous vegetables are served here. But the flavors vary considerably, and each dish is well described on the menu. We can vouche for the *tandoor* mixed grill, consisting of *tandoori* chicken, chicken *tikka* (juicy boneless chunks of white meat), shrimp *tandoori*, and *boti kebab* (broiled lamb), garnished with *tandoor*-cooked mushrooms and peppers. A number of entrees will appeal to vegetarians, too. All meat and seafood entrees are accompanied by peas *pullao*; and any dish may be spiced according to your taste—mild, medium, hot, and "Indian hot" (go easy on the last). We suggest that you order some *raita* with the more incendiary dishes; this is a creamy yogurt and mint sauce that acts as both a palate refresher between tastes of different dishes and as an almost essential tongue cooler after an injudicious mouthful of the Vendaloo.

Several other *pullaos* are on the menu, prepared with shrimp, lamb, vegetables, and—the house specialty—chicken. Desserts include *kheer* (a golden rice pudding), fresh fruit, *jaman* (milk cake balls in syrup), and the very sweet *burfee* (fudge cake flavored with either almond/cheese or coconut and pistachio). If you're unfamiliar with Indian food and interested in learning, ask for an assortment of any dishes of your choice—Raja Rani is very willing to please, you'll find. And we further suggest that you plan on sharing your dishes as the Indians do. Simply let your waitress know, and she'll serve you family style.

Beverages, unfortunately for those who like cocktails before dinner, are all nonalcoholic. There's a choice of a fruit and rose-petal drink, fresh lemonade, *lassi* (a cool, sweet yogurt drink), and two captivating teas: Darjeeling and Masala—the latter with a persuasive hint of cinnamon and cardamom, served hot or cold. Perhaps the only concession to American tastes is the availability of soft drinks. (It was gratifying not to see a New York strip steak or hamburger on the menu.) Don't let the lack of bar service deter you; stop first for a cocktail at one of Ann Arbor's little bistros. We like the Blind Pig at 208 S. First Street, a restored historic site and agreeably funky bar, and Leopold Bloom's Gallery, 118 W. Liberty, another historic site with a 1920s atmosphere.

Food fit for a maharajah.

RAJA RANI, 1133 E. Huron Street, Ann Arbor, MI 48108. At the intersection where Washtenaw merges into Huron, about 1 mile east of Main Street. Telephone (313) 995-1545. Hours: 5:30-9:30 p.m. Closed Mondays, some holidays. No alcoholic beverages. Background music. Carryouts. Free parking on the west side of the building. No credit cards, but personal checks are accepted. Reservations taken only for 5:30 p.m.

TANDOORI CHICKEN

For the marinade, combine in a mixing bowl 2 cups plain yogurt, ⅓ cup lime juice, 2 tablespoons lemon juice, 1 clove garlic put through a press, ½ teaspoon ground cumin seed, ½ teaspoon ground coriander seed, 2 teaspoons ginger, 1 teaspoon turmeric, 2 teaspoons salt, ¼ teaspoon cayenne pepper, ½ teaspoon red food coloring. Cut 4 whole chicken breasts in half, and skin them. Place in a shallow pan. Pour over the marinade, and turn the chicken so each piece is coated. Cover and refrigerate 24-48 hours, turning occasionally.

Cook chicken over a hot charcoal grill, basting with melted butter (⅓-¼ cup). Start with the bone side up and cook until slightly charred; then turn, meat side up, and cook until done (prick with a fork; juices should run clear). Serves 4. The same recipe may be used for chicken Tikka; bone the chicken, and cut into small pieces, about 1 x 2 inches. Grill, turning, till done.

22
THE GANDY DANCER
Ann Arbor

For railroad buffs and admirers of Victoriana, the Gandy Dancer is a must. The building is a designated Michigan and national historic site, and while that sounds a trifle flat, it does convey a very special aspect of the restaurant. The green plaque out in front reads "Michigan Central Railroad Depot: Built in 1886 and conceived by Frederick Spier, the design of this granite block building was influenced by the Romanesque style of the great American architect Henry Hobson Richardson. The massive arch and two-foot thick walls are balanced by the simple, precise detailing. Carefully preserved, this depot is a symbol of the elegance and vitality of 19th century rail transportation." Conversion of old railway stations into restaurants is becoming nearly ubiquitous, but in this case both the station itself and the restaurant, a Chuck Muer seafood house, are worth going out of your way for.

The depot was known in railroading days as "the finest station between Buffalo and Chicago." And today, we conjecture, it's one of the finest stations in the country. Lending authenticity and even greater appeal to the Gandy Dancer is the auxiliary stone building on the west that now serves as the Amtrak station on the main line between Chicago and Detroit. Yes, the trains are still rumbling by. When the restaurant opened in 1969, customers applauded somewhat self-consciously at the sight of a passing engine and its entourage. Now they cheer in vociferous appreciation, and the bells start ringing.

The interior has been handsomely restored by the Muer Corporation, and the patina of age and character remains untouched. The main—and what for years was the only— dining room occupies the site of the original waiting room, with one long bench still there, dividing the room into two smaller areas. Take a few moments to look at the chandeliers; the ornate wooden ceiling; the red brick fireplace, attesting to the skillful masonry of almost a century ago; and the marvelous old Seth Thomas pendulum wall clock from the Reading Railroad system. Adjoining this room is a newer addition to the restaurant, and now the most popular with customers: the Garden Room, with floor-to-ceiling windows, trailing foliage, and effective track lighting on the expansively high ceiling. The tables for two along the windows, just fifteen feet from the railroad tracks outside, are favorites of ours. We like the furnishings here, too—parquet wooden tables and comfortable bentwood and cane armchairs.

At the far east of the building beyond the granite arch in the Garden Room is still another engaging area, the Baggage Room, accented by Oriental rugs, varicolored granite walls, and high arched windows. Here there are three tables for six and at one end a large, varnished library table that seats ten—it's a good room for groups.

Opposite the main entrance from the original dining room

is the Roundhouse Saloon, featuring cozy mirrored booths (with baggage racks above them) and a stainless steel and wooden bar. (Around the corner, by the way, is an oyster bar.) Off this area is a staircase to the upstairs lounge, with a piano bar and several low, comfortable sofas and lounge chairs, warmly lit by hanging chandeliers with gold satin, tasseled shades. The room seats about fifty, and its wrought-iron balcony overlooks the entryway and main dining room. Each room in the restaurant is so interesting and well designed that we hope you'll stroll all the way from the upstairs lounge in the west to the small, intimate Baggage Room on the east. And if you're in Ann Arbor and have other plans for dinner, we strongly recommend that you at least stop in at the Gandy Dancer for drinks or a snack.

Seafood and New England dinners predominate here, as at the other colonies of the Muer empire. Chuck Muer's restaurants are noted for their seafood, and it is indeed very good. The quality is centrally controlled, and all menus and recipes are chosen by Executive Chef Larry. Prices border on the expensive, but the high quality justifies it. At luncheon you might start with a cheering Bucket of Charley's Chowder (see the recipe below) or any of several choice shellfish appetizers. Entrées include various fried and broiled fish and shellfish as well as Boston scrod with crabmeat stuffing, scallops Provençale with rice pilaf, poached smoked schrod, and the Boston Blue Plate assortment. The side dishes included in the price consist of hot cracked wheat bread, slaw, and "steak fries" or stewed tomatoes. Luncheon specials vary daily; Monday's quiche and Tuesday's lamb chops Riviera are the most interesting. In such an impressive setting as this, all the pluses on the menu are slightly tarnished by the somewhat awkward instructions to get "your salad fresh from the baggage cart" and to "take all you want—eat all you take."

In the evening the menu is more extensive. Dinners for two are the specialties: the Chesapeake Bay Bucket, a downeast clambake (Maine lobsters, Dungeness crabs, steamers, mussels, corn on the cob, and redskins); a steak and crustacean platter (steak, lobster, crab, corn); and Bouillabaise Chef Larry. Many of the other offerings are the same as those served at lunch, with the addition of sautéed rainbow trout, baked crabmeat Larry, baked stuffed lobster Larry, steamed or chilled Dungeness crab, rack of lamb, and a few more. The menu has a section of "Helpful Hints" with diagrams on how to eat a whole lobster and suggestions on handling the protean clambake. On both luncheon and dinner menus, the Daily Fisherman's Catch is the most popular item. At least three fish—always fresh—are featured.

There's a smaller "Johnny Come Early" menu for those who arrive before 6:30 in the evening. And if you're with the family, the children's menu is a double treat: the little ones have a choice of catch of the day, scallops, fried chicken, a daily special, and a share in the grownups' clambake, and then the menu itself folds into a fire chief's helmet. The wines here are the same as at the corporation's other restaurants. Some of you are familiar with the "Passport"-like list with more than forty entries in the medium to medium-low price range, organized by countries with accompanying maps. It provides a decent selection that is fun to review the first time through. The house wine at our last visit was from Paul Masson.

To put a bit more adventure into your experience with the Gandy Dancer, there's an easy round-trip train ride on the Amtrak from Detroit to Ann Arbor. It'll drop you off for about four hours, long enough for a leisurely meal and a relaxing time listening to the resident pianist in the lounge before the return train arrives.

Depot dining at its best.

THE GANDY DANCER, 401 Depot Street, Ann Arbor, MI 48104. Six blocks north of the business district. Telephone (313) 769-0592. Hours: Monday-Thursday 11:30 a.m.-11 p.m., Friday 11:30 a.m.-midnight, Saturday 5-11 p.m., Sunday 3-10 p.m. Closed Thanksgiving, Christmas, New Years Day. Full bar service. Children's menu. Background music. Pianist in balcony lounge nightly at 7 p.m. Free parking. All major credit cards. Reservations recommended, especially on weekends.

CHARLEY'S CHOWDER
FROM THE GANDY DANCER

Heat 2 ounces (¼ cup) olive oil in a large pot until very hot. Add 3 medium cloves of garlic (smashed). Cook until golden in color. It's important that you don't burn the garlic. Remove the cloves from the oil. Add 2 ounces finely chopped onions (about ½ medium onion) and cook a minute or two. Add a pinch each of basil, oregano, and thyme and cook 1 minute. Add 3 ounces finely chopped celery (about 1 stalk), and cook until translucent. Add 6 ounces stewed tomatoes, chopped very finely (can use canned stewed tomatoes, either a 6-ounce can or half a 16-ounce can). Cook about 20-25 minutes, stirring to prevent sticking. Add 12 cups water, 1 pound boneless fish (pollack or turbot), 2 ounces clam base, and cook for an additional 15 minutes. (If clam base is not available, substitute 12 cups clam juice for the water.) This last 15 minutes of cooking should be on high heat with the pan uncovered, to remove excess moisture and extract oils for flavoring the chowder. Add salt to taste, cover the pot, and cook 20 minutes on low heat. Stir often by whipping to break up the fish and blend the flavors. Just before serving, add 1 ounce chopped parsley (2-3 tablespoons). Serves 6.

23
THE GOLDEN HUNTER
Howell

If we were writing a full-fledged article on the Golden Hunter, we might entitled it "The Evolution of a Gourmet Restaurant" (possibly subtitled "The Supreme Holiday Inn Dining Room"). And it's still evolving (and it's still supreme). It hasn't yet divorced itself from the banality of the salad bar or emerged from the cocoon of popular taste to become a gastronomic butterfly. But the cycle has begun—in fact, is well on its way. Only a few years ago, the innovative manager and Innkeeper, Dale Smeltzer, introduced just three "gourmet" dishes. Today diners at this most unstereotypical of Holiday Inns have such options as sweetbreads and oyster stew, tarragon-baked pheasant, country-style quail, and rock lobster tails broiled with sherry butter.

The decor is unobtrusive, the seating comfortable at well-spaced tables with armchairs (but avoid those near the salad bar), the menu highly impressive, the wine selection at our last visit mediocre (but we hear that soon a special list may be available for connoisseurs), the music emanating from the nearby lounge soft and pleasant, the service cheerful and accommodating. And the Golden Hunter is convenient for dining at almost any hour—three wonderful meals are served here daily.

The breakfast omelettes can be filled with your choice of—not just ham, bacon, cheese, but—shrimp, crabmeat, and lobster. Malted pancakes and waffles, too, provide a nice change of pace. And you'll see other things on the menu that are hardly the usual Holiday Inn fare: English farmers' mixed grill (eggs with bacon, sausage, kidneys); Toad in the Hole (pork sausages baked in pancake batter); Scotch eggs (first boiled, then wrapped in sausage, breaded, and fried); and Innkeeper Dale's Special—a grilled English muffin topped with poached eggs and served with veal sweetbreads.

The midday menu offers a number of salads, some classic and some inventive: shrimp-stuffed cucumber, the Golden Hunter's version of *niçoise* (with smoked salmon), and the Salade Palace Court (with chicken, lobster, and Russian dressing). Soups include a delicate cream of watercress, a succulent oyster and scallop stew, and a refreshing cold split pea with mint. The sandwiches are pretty standard, but we applaud the appearance of the breaded pork tenderloin—more restaurants should serve it. Several fine crepes can be ordered; two memorable ones are the Terrie Jane (lobster and veal in Mornay sauce) and the Suedois (with smoked salmon and chopped eggs in a dill sauce). The seafood selections number, among others, sautéed lobster, oysters Rockefeller, poached salmon, brook trout, and shrimp in garlic butter. Other choices include London broil, lamb or pork chops, liver, kidneys, brochette of beef as well as baked avocado with shrimp filling and chicken Cordon Bleu and Tetrazzini. For the self-servers, there's also a daily buffet served from 11 to 2, including soup and salad bar.

If all this for breakfast and lunch is unexpected, you can imagine what awaits you at a Golden Hunter dinner. Your favorite prime rib, steaks, and chicken are here, as well as numerous other possibilities for the more adventurous: veal kidneys sautéed with ham, onions, and tomatoes; broiled trout on a bed of fennel, flamed with Cognac; parslied rack of lamb *bouquetiere*; broiled or poached Dover sole with toasted almonds; and the list goes on and on. The entrées, as you'll notice, tend to be creative variations on classic cuisine—such as lime vichyssoise and flounder stuffed with lobster. Presentation and garniture, too, receive the devoted attention of Chef Jim Neubacher. For example, the brace of quail, filled with cornbread stuffing, is nested in potato shells to hold their juices and piped with *pommes Duchesse*. The entire creation rests on a wooden plank and is served with a rich brown sauce. There's a decent range of prices, and you can eat here moderately, depending on what you order. The Sevruga caviar as an appetizer, though, might send you into bankruptcy (it goes for about $280 a pound—$22 a portion at the Golden Hunter).

The vegetables are fresh and flavorful; don't pass up the crisply gilded deep-fried zucchini slices. Served at each table is a loaf of banana-nut bread, which we found very tasty but not particularly compatible with most of the entrées. Take home what's left in a doggie bag—of foil (golden, of course)—and it will be as good the next day as it was the night before. You'll see lots of little golden bags leaving this restaurant. The wine list needs some refurbishing (and that's coming, as we mentioned). On our visit there were only two chateaux, both lesser (Lafon Rochet and Ponet Canet), one Burgundy (Beaujolais)—in fact, the total of the French connection is only four red still wines, three Champagnes, and one white (Muscadet). Little touches elsewhere might also be improved. The butter is unwrapped, for example, but the cream comes in little plastic cups.

For years the Golden Hunter has been locally noted for its buffets. There's a brunch on Sunday, and on Wednesday evening crepes are featured. But the Friday seafood buffet is what you'll hear most about. It's no longer the bargain it once was, but it's certainly a good value and seafood has gone up more than beef in the past year. Reservations are not accepted, so if you don't want to wait, arrive before 6:30. On the buffet table are assorted salads, smoked oysters, clams, cold shrimp in the shell, a whole baked salmon, four or five other baked fish, fried shrimp, crab legs, frog legs, a round of roast beef (!), vegetables, redskins, and fresh fruit—all you can eat, of course. During the time of the buffet, however, one can also get full menu service. A sandwich menu, too, is always available during the dinner hour for lighter appetites. **Pure gold.**

THE GOLDEN HUNTER, 125 Holiday Lane (in the Holiday Inn), Howell, MI 48843. Exit 137 (Howell exit) off I-96; about 1 mile south of the city center. Telephone (517) 546-6880. Hours: breakfast 6-11 a.m., luncheon 11 a.m.-5 p.m., dinner 5-11 p.m., Sunday brunch 9 a.m.-1 p.m., Sunday dinner (no lunch) 1-10 p.m. Closed Christmas. Full bar service. Children's menu. Background music, live entertainment in lounge nightly. Free parking. All major credit cards. Reservations recommended, not taken on Friday evenings.

THE GOLDEN HUNTER'S
SWEETBREADS MONTEBELLO

Soak 1 pound sweetbreads in cold water for 1 hour. Place in a saucepan, and cover with water and 1 tablespoon lemon juice. Bring to a boil; then simmer 5 minutes. Drain and cool, Remove skin and sinew. Dust sweetbreads in seasoned flour (with salt and cayenne to taste). Saute in 2 ounces butter, 5 minutes a side. To serve, place sweetbreads on 2 Dutch Rusks. Cover half with tomato sauce (¼ cup, thinned with Champagne) and half with Hollandaise sauce (¼ cup, thinned with Champagne). Garnish each serving with a truffle slice. Serves 2.

24
AH WOK
Novi

It's gradually changing, but we in the United States too often gain our first impressions of Chinese food from chop suey, chow mein, fried rice, and egg foo yong without appreciating the centuries-old tradition of Chinese cuisine, one of the greatest in the world. But somewhere between our first taste of chop suey and our first taste of Peking duck or moo shu pork, we begin to recognize the signals to all our senses that this cuisine, almost beyond any other, offers. Texture—crisp young vegetables, smooth and sophisticated sauces. Aroma—elusive, sometimes subtle, sometimes pungent, as important to the Chinese as flavor. Color—the golden clarity of chicken consommé, the brilliant greens of a young Bok Choy. And flavor—from the almost endless condiments and spices of the Orient: ginger, coriander, sesame oil, hoisin and soy, red chili peppers, mustard, star anise, and garlic, perhaps the most versatile cross-cultural herb in existence. Though the style varies from one province to another, Chinese food at its best is an artistic study in sensual contrasts.

And Ah Wok is a place of which even our demanding Chinese friend Jimmy Wang would approve (well, maybe not—he's a perfectionist; but his wife Vera would love it). The shopping-center location might at first put you off, but once inside you'll find a modern, trim decor with red tablecloths, globe lighting, well-spaced tables and booths (best for two persons) along the walls, partitioned by Chinese import crate tops—the only obviously Oriental accessories in the room. The service is courteous and helpful, and the food, exceptional.

The restaurant, in business for six years, specializes in Mandarin and Cantonese dishes. The Mandarin is hotter, spicier, and the ingredients more finely cut than in south China's more familiar Cantonese. The menu here is quite comprehensive and features many such seldom-seen Chinese treats as the always wonderful shark's fin soup (the Chinese equivalent of caviar, truffles, and *foie gras* wrapped up in one), sizzling soups (chicken and shrimp), steamed whole fish redolent of ginger and soy sauce, velvet chicken (and it's just that), sweet-sour chicken with lichee fruit, rice paper shrimp, and Mandarin pancakes with Mik Yee shredded meat. The Szechwan hot and sour soup is outstanding. On three days' notice, Ah Wok will provide you with a whole sea bass with ginger and scallions or with Peking duck. For those unfamiliar with the latter, this is a classic dish, one of China's most prestigious and served at feasts all over the country. It must be prepared well ahead to assure a skin free from fat and perfectly crisp and yet a flesh that is moist and flavorful. The luncheon menu offers many of the same dishes

66

and several combination platters as well.

On Tuesdays and Thursdays Ah Wok offers an all-you-can-eat Cantonese-Mandarin buffet at a reasonable price. And at any time the chef promises to prepare a Chinese favorite of yours that's not on the menu. Furthermore, if you can get together ten people, the restaurant will arrange a lavish banquet of eleven courses or more—call ahead on this one. It's a way to savor Chinese cooking and service at its most enchantingly characteristic.

Ah, the winning wok.

AH WOK, 41653 W. Ten Mile Road, Novi, MI 48050. About 1 mile east of Novi Road, off I-96, northwest of Detroit. Telephone (313) 349-9260. Hours: 11 a.m.-10 p.m. (Fridays and Saturdays till midnight), Sundays noon-10 p.m. Closed Mondays, Thanksgiving. Full bar service. Background music. Takeouts. Free parking. All major credit cards. Reservations highly recommended on weekends.

AH WOK'S PEANUT CHICKEN

Cut 2 to 3 chicken breasts into 1-inch slices. Marinate for 1 hour in a mixture of ¼ cup cornstarch, 6 egg whites, and 1 tablespoon vegetable oil. Heat 2 cups oil in a wok or large saucepan. Cook chicken for 3 minutes in the hot oil, drain, and set aside.

In another pan add 3 tablespoons oil, and heat over a hot flame. Add ¼ cup diced bamboo shoots, ¼ cup sliced water chestnuts, ¼ cup green peas (fresh or frozen and unthawed), ½ cup fresh roasted peanuts. Stir-fry for 2 minutes. Add the chicken and ¼ cup chicken broth. Bring to a quick full boil. Add ½ teaspoon sugar, ½ teaspoon sesame oil, ½ teaspoon Accent (monosodium glutamate), and salt, Tabasco sauce, and hot ground pepper to taste. Mix 4 tablespoons cornstarch with ½ cup water. Add gradually, stirring, to thicken as desired. Serve over boiled rice. Serves 2-3.

If you like our recommendations, tell the proprietor. If you don't, tell us. Write Beech Tree Press, 2673 Rampart Path, Holt, Michigan 48842.

25
MITCH'S
Pontiac

For MSU students this is THE most popular restaurant in either peninsula of Michigan. The portions are stupendous, the quality high, the atmosphere casual and comfortable, the food straightforward and mouth-watering, and—if you order wisely— it's a bargain. Mitch's opened its doors in 1952 as a tavern serving only beer and wine, and within three years, not by the choice of the Mitchells but by the demand of the customers, pizzas went on the menu. Today Mitch's is practically an institution in the southern end of the state and serves, in addition to its famous pizzas, some of Michigan's best barbequed ribs, Italian pasta, and salads.

But as this goes to press, some big changes are being made. Oldtime Mitch's patrons recall the scaling paint and the sagging structure—the building has been described as looking like it's slowly sliding into the lake. As sentimentalists we're sad to see the old place doomed to destruction. But the new building on the same property has enough similarities that we're sure you'll still feel at home, whether a regular or first-time visitor. The exterior is a lot different—dark red brick, roughsawn siding, and a Western-style veranda. But, inside, the bar is in the same position; there are still two levels and the same knotty pine walls and wooden floor so the shock won't be too great when you realize that the old Mitch's is gone. The new building seats a few more people, but the menu is the same, thankfully, and Nancy, the hostess for the last fourteen years, is still there to greet you. One nice addition is the eight-foot barbeque pit—we think those ribs are as worth watching as eating.

So, then, what's so special about Mitch's? You'll like the wine liter full of ice water on each table. And while you're waiting, you'll be served a basketful of salt bread—chewy and buttery hot bread sticks: fables in flour. These are positively addictive and, unless you're careful, guaranteed to ruin your appetite for what's to come. (Please be careful; there's more to Mitch's than the salt bread, hard as it is to believe.) The Greek salad is refreshing perfection, served on ice-cold plates and faultlessly dressed. It accompanies certain dinners, or you can order it instead of the tossed salad at a slight additional charge. And you really should plan on sharing it; one salad is enough for two and could suffice for four. Or, when you're in a group, think about ordering the large size, serving eight to ten—a real bargain. If you don't care for a Greek-style starter, try the chef's salad or the antipasto, two more winners.

The barbequed ribs are the best we've had in Michigan (though ribs tend to encourage controversy among their devotees). The rigatoni in a rich, creamy, garlicky sauce with mushrooms and green pepper is indescribably palatable and will easily serve four people. Again, share. There's a lot of sharing at Mitch's, so much so that the restaurant even has a "sharing charge" of $2 per table—it's still worth doing. Or, if you simply do not want to share, the pasta dishes are available in half portions (*huge* half portions). Our own preferences at Mitch's are the ribs, pizza, and rigatoni. But also on the menu are fried and barbequed chicken, steaks, stuffed crab, fried shrimp and fish, and broiled whitefish. Pastas include spaghetti with several sauces, rigatoni with meat sauce, linguine with clam sauce, lasagne, and that heavenly "special rigatoni."

The service is attentive and fast. We suggest beer with ribs or pizza and Chianti or Lambrusco (sweeter) by the glass with the pastas. "Come as you are" seems to be the dress code. On our last visit a well-coifed lady swathed in Tourmaline mink was nearly rubbing shoulders with a young sport in Adidas at the next table who had obviously just finished work at a nearby factory or machine shop.

Pure pleasure.

MITCH'S, 400 Cass Elizabeth Road, Pontiac, MI 48054. In Waterford Township, just west of Cass Lake Road. Telephone (313) 682-1616. Hours: 11 a.m.-11 p.m. daily. Closed Christmas and Thanksgiving. Full bar service. Free parking. Carry-outs, across the road; call 681-3400. No credit cards or reservations accepted.

RIGATONI WITH CREAMY GARLIC SAUCE

The recipe for Mitch's special rigatoni is a well-guarded secret, but we started experimenting and came up with a reasonable facsimile. It's not as good as at Mitch's, but it's darned good. We hope you'll agree. It's also a very economical main dish. Serve it with a salad and some crusty bread.

Heat 1-2 tablespoons butter (or half butter, half oil) in a skillet. Add ½-¾ pound sliced fresh mushrooms, and saute for about 4 minutes on medium-high heat. Remove and set aside. Add more butter or oil to the pan if necessary, and saute 2 sliced green peppers (with stem and seeds removed) for another 3 or 4 minutes until tender-crisp. Remove and set aside. In a large saucepan, heat 2 tablespoons butter and 2 tablespoons olive oil. Add 4 large cloves garlic, put through a press (about 4-5 teaspoons pressed or finely chopped garlic). Cook on medium to medium-low heat for 2 minutes, watching carefully and stirring so that it doesn't burn. Stir in ¼ cup flour, and cook slowly 2 minutes, without browning. Gradually add 2 cups half-and-half (half milk, half cream). Salt and pepper to taste. Blend in ¼ cup grated Parmesan cheese and the sauteed mushrooms and peppers. Cook ¾ to 1 pound rigatoni (a large round hollow pasta; about 20 for each portion) according to package directions—about 15 minutes in boiling water until *al dente* (tender but slightly chewy). Drain, and combine with the sauce. Makes 4 generous servings.

26
LA FAMILIA
TRINI AND CARMEN'S
Pontiac

To judge Mexican food on the basis of a taco is like judging Italian cuisine from a pizza. Both are popular snacks (and full meals can be made of them), but Mexican cuisine, like that of other countries, has a long history and comprises a wealth of varied dishes, many of them going back to Montezuma, the famous emperor of the Aztecs. The finished products are rooted in native bounty: chiles (more than 140 varieties grown in Mexico alone), tomatoes, corn, avocados, cocoa, pineapples. Of all the Mexican restaurants in Michigan, three were consistently mentioned by MSU students:

the Beltline Bar in Grand Rapids and the more authentic La Familia Martinez and Trini and Carmen's, both in Pontiac.

The two Pontiac restaurants are under the management of the Martinez family, Trini and Carmen and their twelve children: seven boys and five girls, who bus, wait tables, and eventually play every role in the business. (All except little Trini, a teenager who has yet to be beckoned by the culinary arts.) La Familia has been open since 1966 and is beginning to show the wear and tear, but the effect is comfortable and relaxed all the same. The main dining room is adjacent to a long bar that seats about twenty, and there's an overflow room in back. But the action is up front in the American tavern-like setting with a few Mexican touches (including Latin music on the jukebox).

Trini and Carmen's opened its doors in 1978 and seats about the same number of customers (up to 150) but is roomier and modern and has more personal touches, mementos from Mexico brought back by the family. Though neither place is quite the equal of Mexico City's El Refugio, either one is worth visiting if you like or want to try some good, authentic Mexican food. And unlike in Mexico itself, it's easier here to get *hielo* and *mantequilla*.

Desayuno isn't served, and we're sure that the Martinez women make some great *huevos rancheros*. Maybe these will come in the future. But you can have a fine *comida* (dinner), *cena* (late supper), or *merienda* (light snack). And as Linda Martinez, the charming young manager at La Familia, points out, all Mexican food is not peppery hot. Theirs is subtly spiced, and if you like it hotter, add the tables sauce. Among the appetizers are *guacamole* salad, corn chips *con queso* (with cheese), *crispa con queso* (flour tortilla—*delicioso*), *quesadilla* (flour tortilla with meat, cheese, and *guacamole* filling), and the Micro Mini (a small portion of *nachos*). All the familiar items are here: tostadas, burritos, tamales, and enchiladas. We suggest the combination dinner if you'd like to sample more than one. The *nachos* are a particularly agreeable blend of tortilla chips, peppers, tomatoes, beef, and two cheeses (available in two portion sizes). For the *postres*, try the Mexican cookies or *munelos* (deep-fried flour tortillas with cheese and honey, similar to *sopapilla*). There's a limited number of American sandwiches for the nonadventurous. Specialty drinks include imported Mexican beer and Margaritas.

Por una comida excelente.

LA FAMILA MARTINEZ, 848 S. Woodward Avenue (Business Route 10), Pontiac, MI 48053. About 3 miles south of the city center. Telephone (313) 338-8477. TRINI AND CARMEN'S, 1715 N. Telegraph Road, Pontiac, MI 48055. Telephone (313) 332-6851. Hours: 11 a.m.-midnight, Saturdays noon-midnight, Sundays 4-11 p.m. Closed most holidays. Full bar service. Background music. Free parking. All major credit cards. Reservations not accepted (on weekends, a 45-minute wait is common unless you arrive early).

GUACAMOLE

Use this as a salad dressing or for Nachos (see recipe index) or tostadas. You can buy guacamole canned or frozen, but your own homemade version will be better—if you can get the right avocado. Sometimes it requires a search. If you plan ahead, start watching for those small avocados that when ripe are dark green to nearly black in color and soft to the touch, though with the skin fully intact and not broken. Sometimes these are sold on sale in large supermarkets.

Peel and pit 2 ripe avocados and scoop out the interior (the meat near the skin should be bright green and that near the pit light green or yellow; if it's all brown, it's too ripe). Mash the avocados in a small mixing bowl. Add 1 medium clove garlic put through a press or finely minced, 2 tablespoons finely minced onion, 1 teaspoon chili powder (or to taste), 2-4 drops Tabasco sauce, salt and pepper to taste. Mix in 2-4 tablespoons mayonnaise (homemade or Hellman's brand). Use immediately; or if you must make it ahead, cover the entire surface with plastic film so it won't discolor. (Don't just cover the bowl; the film must touch the surface of the guacamole.) Makes 1-1½ cups.

27
MEADOW BROOK HALL
Rochester

This is the stuff of which dreams are made. You'll love it, your children will love it, Anglophiles will adore it, Francophiles will grudgingly acknowledge (and secretly rejoice in) the tasteful Gallic touches throughout, art buffs and antique buffs will marvel at it. And gastronomes will enjoy an exceptional meal in one of Michigan's grandest settings. "Grandeur" is not an exaggeration. We hope that everyone in Michigan at some time is able to tour Meadow Brook Hall, certainly the state's most "stately home."

Once the residence of Matilda Dodge Wilson and now part of Oakland University and a state and national historic site, Meadow Brook Hall, set within rolling, glacially contructed hills, was built in 1926-1929 for 3½ million dollars (imagine what it would cost today, if it could be built at all). Matilda Dodge, widow of the auto pioneer John Dodge, married Alfred G. Wilson in 1925, and soon after their marriage the couple left with architect William Knapp for a trip to Europe, where they toured the many English palaces and manor houses that inspired plans for Meadow Brook Hall. In 1957 the Wilsons donated their estate and surrounding farm land to Michigan State University for the establishment of another campus, which in 1970 became an independent institution, the present Oakland University. The Hall today is a residential conference and cultural center for continuing education.

A blend of Tudor and Elizabethan architecture, the 100-room mansion is one of the most impressive buildings in the state. The exterior of brick and sandstone, with windows inset with decorative stained glass, is enhanced by 42 brick chimneys extending from the gabled tiled roof to serve 24 fireplaces, all of individual design, as suggested by those at Hampton Court in England. The formal garden, rose garden, fountains, gazebo, carriage house, and circular entry drive at least equal those we've seen at stately homes in England. For the children, there's even a secret staircase—but no dungeon.

It's like stepping into another century as you enter the Great

Hall, with its majestic table, needlepoint draperies, wood paneling, carved woods, stone arches, and oak ceiling beams. Leading from the Great Hall is our favorite room, the Main Gallery, patterned after that of Knole House, with the inside wall consisting mostly of windows that open onto the magnificent Grand Ballroom on the floor below. The Christopher Wren Dining Room, accented by walnut paneling, ornate light fixtures, and an elaborately carved ceiling, seats 36 at the gleaming inlaid dining table and with the smaller tables in the room will serve up to 84 persons. The ceiling is worth study—it required six artisans six months to complete. Suggested by Grinling Gibbons carvings at a Lincolnshire manor house, it was first modeled to scale in clay and then through many laborious stages was completed in sections under the direction of Detroit architectural sculptor C. J. Parducci.

Throughout the mansion are priceless antique furnishings and decorations in a variety of periods and styles—English and French chairs, African and Russian onyx tables, Persian rugs, Chinese porcelains, Jerusalem brass trays, Spanish urns, Meissen tiles—as well as paintings by Rembrandt, Rousseau, Gainsborough, Reynolds, Murillo, Constable, Turner, Hobbema, Bonheur, Van Marcke, Van Dyck, Baptiste, and many more, all personal choices of the Wilsons for what was, after all, their home. And this fact is what lends Meadow Brook Hall the fascination, but not the coldness, of a museum.

And, yes, visitors may dine in this splendor. In July and August the Summer Tearoom is open, and on pleasant days there's outdoor dining nearby. Exceptional buffets are served on Sundays throughout most of the year in the impressive Christopher Wren Dining Room, but in July and August it offers the same *à la carte* menu as the tearoom. At least four entrées and a profusion of assorted other dishes appear on the buffets, and the price is fair. However, dining at Meadow Brook is only possible in conjunction with tours and conferences, but this shouldn't deter you—the tours are a pleasure. The Hall welcomes some 75,000 visitors a year. You might even consider arranging your own group tour—available year round by appointment and including lunch or dinner.

A special annual event is Christmas at Meadow Brook Hall in early December. The mansion is stunningly decorated by florists for the occasion, the fireplaces are glowing, and light lunches are served in the Carriage House. Is it worthwhile and popular? Just ask the 16,000 visitors who showed up for this event in 1979.

Our own magnificent obsession.

MEADOW BROOK HALL, Oakland university, Rochester, MI 48063. Telephone (313) 377-3140. Tour hours: 10 a.m.-5 p.m. (last tour at 4 p.m.); tours last at least 1 hour. Dining hours: Summer Tearoom open July and August 11 a.m.-3:30 p.m., Sunday buffets 1-5 p.m. year round except in July and August (in July and August, Wren Dining Room has same menu as in tearoom). Group tours, including luncheon or dinner, available year round by appointment. No alcoholic beverages. Free parking. No credit cards or reservations.

MEADOW BROOK HALL'S BEURRECKS

The best beurrecks we've had lately have been those of Belma Baskett, a gracious lady recently arrived from Turkey and an authority on, interestingly, the writer Kurt Vonnegut. This recipe from Meadow Brook Hall is the Greek version. These are wonderful appetizers, and the finished product looks much more involved than the actual work that goes into producing them. For the cheese filling, add 2 egg yolks and 1 pound of Feta cheese to ½ cup very thick Bechamel sauce. If the cheese is very salty, cut in chunks, set in a bowl of cold water, and then squeeze dry in cheesecloth. Purchase 1 box of prepared *filo* pastry for this amount of filling. Brush 1 sheet *filo* with melted butter. Place second sheet on top, and brush with butter. Cut this double layer in strips (5 across). Place 1 tablespoon cheese filling at the end of each strip so there is room to fold a triangle of dough over it. Continue to fold triangularly until each strip is a closed triangle. Brush front and back with butter, and place on a baking sheet. Repeat this process till all the *filo* and cheese filling have been used. Bake the beurrecks for 5 minutes at 425 degrees until lightly browned.

Chef's note: Heat expands cheese. If the filling begins to

ooze out, remove triangles from oven immediately before they burst. If they haven't yet browned evenly, allow the internal temperature to cool before replacing in oven to finish baking. Beurrecks must be watched carefully while baking. Place them on a doily or cloth-covered tray and serve hot. Makes 6 dozen appetizers.

Hints from the Winters: For the Bechamel sauce, see our recipe index; this one is thicker, and we suggest using 3-4 tablespoons flour to 1 cup liquid.

28
THE COOPER'S ARMS
Rochester

This is another of those places in Michigan that doesn't have an especially imaginative cooking style or elaborate menu but that is becoming very well known for its well-prepared, fresh seafood. The restaurant, on the main street of Rochester, has been in business only eight years, but it looks like it's been there forever. The Cooper's Arms is named after what is believed to be the oldest public house in Kent, England. Accordingly, its facade has a British accent, and the decor is Tudor, with soft lighting, lustrous dark beams on walls and ceilings, latticework, and leaded glass. The main dining room is at the front of the restaurant, and adjoining it is a more intimate room with a fireplace. But for seclusion and an even more pub-like atmosphere, our choice would be one of the partitioned booths in the rear dining area.

The offerings here are typically American and of high quality: prime rib (as always, the most ordered item), steaks, lobster tails, King crab legs, steak kebabs with Greek rice pilaf—augmented by a small salad bar and *à la carte* baked potatoes, onion rings, and sauteed mushrooms. The appetizer list is small but acceptable (French onion soup, *escargots*, and a couple of others), and the soup of the day is choice (if available, try the cream of broccoli). Interestingly, in light of the fine beef dishes offered, the favorite at luncheon is the broiled whitefish; and at dinner tying for first place with the prime rib are, even more interestingly, the broiled monk-fish and sauteed *mahi-mahi* (dolphin).

The daily specials, too, are well worth considering, and prices are reasonable. At lunchtime there might be tenderloin tips, omelettes, barbequed ribs, calves liver, or quiche as well as the regular sandwich offerings, fish, and steaks. Frequently featured at dinner are roast duckling and rack of lamb. English-style fish and chips are on both menus.

The wine list, limited to about twenty selections, is the type that places more emphasis on how to pronounce the name than on its vintage. But this is commonplace in Michigan, and you'll need to be satisfied with undistinguished offerings here. You may even prefer the slightly lower-priced red, white, and rosé carafe wines.

A cheerful American pub.

THE COOPER'S ARMS, 306 Main Street, Rochester, MI 48063. In city center. Telephone (313) 651-2266. Hours: luncheon 11:30 a.m.-4 p.m., dinner 5-10:30 p.m. (till 11:30 p.m. Fridays and Saturdays). Closed Sundays and holidays. Full bar service. Children's plates. Background music. Occasional entertainment in Uncle Bela's Pub adjacent. Free parking in rear. Credit cards: AE, DC, MC, V. Reservations not accepted Friday and Saturday evenings.

29
JOHNSON'S
Mount Clemens

If you'd like to recapture the experience and atmosphere of the wooden framed roadhouses so common four or five decades ago, try Johnson's, outside of Mount Clemens. Yes, there's a new screen door out front, and someone jammed a room air conditioner into one of the windows as well as improving the parking lot with a couple of loads of crushed rock, but thankfully the old Johnson's remains. On the outside of the one-story building is waterfront-weathered wood, painted blue with a large red neon sign spelling out the owner's name. The place started out as a gas station-*cum*-grocery store and after several additions evolved into an eatery. A long, old, well-stocked bar extends along the west wall, and eight or ten tables occupy the remaining area (avoid the table for two nearest the kitchen). Some of the furnishings are new, but most first-time visitors over age 40 will probably be impressed by the nostalgic aura of a place that opened in 1937 and has stayed much the same.

For lunch Johnson's offers about twenty sandwiches, including a low-cost homemade grilled frankfurter and a liverwurst on dark bread (ask for an onion slice). Soup and chili are always available and a creamy New England clam chowder (the real article) is served on Fridays, Saturdays, and Sundays.

About twenty dinner entrées are on the menu, two-thirds of them "seafood." By far the most popular—and deservingly so—is the broiled Boston scrod with lemon butter. Some 400 pounds of it is consumed each week at Johnson's, and we highly recommend it. The deep-fried lake perch and pickerel (walleyed pike) are also outstanding, and the beef is prime. Servings are generous; dinners include a relish tray, salad, potatoes, and bread sticks.

We wish we could tell you that the prices are low, but they aren't. "Moderate" is a better description, but the value increases as you come to appreciate the authenticity of the place. This is one of those half-hidden marvels that you're glad to know about. Even getting there is a small adventure as you drive east from I-94 along North River Road and pass Selfridge Air Base with its variety of planes and an occasional takeoff or landing and as you notice the increasing clutter of all kinds of boats in various stages of repair both in and out of the water along the nearly continuous row of marinas and docking facilities on the shores of the Clinton River and Lake St. Clair.

Finally, if you get a glimpse of a tall but a bit slouchy white-haired gentleman over 60 with a long, handsome face, it's probably Fred Johnson himself. Born in Massachusetts and later a runaway with the Ringling Bros. circus, he's now a friendly member of the local "Old Crowd." He's run a good restaurant for years, and if you enjoy your meal, we're sure he'd like it if you tell him. If you're a circus buff, ask Mr. Johnson about Emmett Kelly; if you're a seafood buff, he can tell you the difference between scrod and schrod.

A remarkable roadhouse.

JOHNSON'S, 32003 N. River Road, Mount Clemens, MI 48045. North River Road exit from I-94, eastbound past Selfridge base about 3 miles. Telephone (313) 469-9656. Hours: luncheon 10 a.m.-3 p.m., dinner 5-10 p.m., Sunday dinner 2-10 p.m. Closed Christmas, New Years Eve, New Years Day. Free parking. No credit cards. Reservations not accepted.

JOHNSON'S BROILED BOSTON SCROD

Ideally, you should use freshly caught fillets of scrod weighing under 2½ pounds. Johnson's uses only the thickest part of the fillet and trims away the small part of the tail and the belly part. Cut the fillet in half, brush the skin side with lemon butter, and place skin side down in a pan of flour. Shake off loose flour, and lay fish in a broiler pan with the floured side down. Brush the top of the fillet with lemon butter and dust lightly with paprika. Place under broiler flame. It should be cooked in about 5 minutes (test center with fork; if translucent, it's done). Serve with melted butter and sliced boiled potato. Garnish with chopped parsley.

Hints from the Winters: We found it necessary to brush the pan with butter before broiling so the fish wouldn't stick. As we've said before, a restaurant oven is hotter than the home range. The fillet will probably take closer to 10 minutes. You can go by appearance, too. We like the surface of the fish a golden brown with the beginnings of burnt edges. Don't worry about the thinner portions getting overdone—they'll be delicious. We've all heard scrod described as a sort of poor man's lobster. But we think it deserves recognition on its own merits. This recipe, though, is good for any other fleshy fish, too. On the side you might want to substitute, in season, steamed new potatoes mixed with parsley butter.

JOHNSON'S POACHED FINNAN HADDIE

This is a dish that appears on very few restaurant menus. Here are two ways that Johnson's prepares finnan haddie,

both delicious. (1) Use only the thickest part of the fillet.
Poach it in milk with a bay leaf until it flakes easily. Sprinkle
with chopped parsley. Serve with melted butter and sliced
boiled potatoes. (2) The tail pieces and thin cuts from the
above fillet can be poached as above and flaked, discard-
ing the skin. Add the haddie to cream sauce, and serve on
toasted English muffins. Garnish with sliced boiled eggs and
chopped parsley.

Hints from the Winters: To poach the fish, place the fillet in
a skillet, add milk to come halfway up the fish, bring to a boil,
cover and turn heat down to a simmer. This will take about 20
minutes. In the second recipe, which we like best—especially
for brunch—make about 1 cup of cream sauce for 1 pound of
fish. Leftover finnan haddie is good cold, too.

30
THE VOYAGEUR
St. Clair

Established about a decade ago and named for the rugged
French-Canadian canoe men of the late eighteenth century,
the Voyageur affords a singular view of the St. Clair River
traffic for just about all visitors, including those sitting at the
bar. The well-designed building is immediately adjacent to
the river, and large windows combined with different floor
elevations make most seating arrangements highly satisfactory, although the best tables, as always with a vista, are by
the windows. The chef, Frank Krzywiecki, makes a superb
clam chowder (but for some reason we don't understand,
only lets his customers enjoy it on Friday—and sometimes
Saturday), is willing to try an occasional gourmet night, but
concentrates mainly on providing sound, basic food. The
result is fifteen seafood and eleven other (beef, fowl, ham,
veal) entrées that may be ordered either as part of a complete
dinner (including soup, salad, and coffee) or à la carte for
$1 less. We suggest that you consider the chef's own favorite,
stuffed flounder—fresh, not frozen, and prepared on the
premises. Daily specials are offered as well as the familiar

variety of appetizers, salads, and sandwiches. A salad bar is available during the evening meal.

The large, elongated dining room has an open floor plan and a decor that is modern and practical, but not especially distinctive. The ceiling is beamed, the main colors greens and blues, but these are much less apparent than the compelling riparian view of Canada. It is the scenery outside that sets the tone of the Voyageur, particularly in the daytime. Background music is soothing, and the interior is pleasant; but when one of the big lake vessels churns by, all attention goes out the window.

The restaurant is well suited for groups of varying sizes; and if you're in a party of five or six, you might appreciate the somewhat special table in a circular niche on the upper level. The Voyageur is also a place that attracts a variety of age groups, and if you have children with you, you'll be comfortable in its relaxed atmosphere. We suggest that, while in the area, you also take a stroll along St. Clair's attractive river walk to an appealing shopping plaza not five minutes from the Voyageur.

Of the three restaurants on the St. Clair River, we list this as the least expensive and the most informal. The meals are not cheap; but they're competitively priced, they're well prepared, and the servings are generous. The à la carte options and availability of children's portions will gratify the the budget-minded. If you prefer the elegant or are feeling extravagant, go upstream to the River Crab or St. Clair Inn. If you don't need or want that sort of thing, we're sure you'll enjoy the Voyageur.

For the best view of the St. Clair River.

THE VOYAGEUR, 525 S. Riverside, St. Clair, MI 48079. Telephone (313) 329-3331. Hours: 11 a.m.-11 p.m. Full bar service. Background music. Children's portions. No credit cards. Reservations not accepted, except for parties of 15 or larger.

31
THE ST. CLAIR INN
St. Clair

Here is a place with a grand old tradition, which is now undergoing renovation and the addition of a pool, sauna, and 34 more sleeping rooms to take the place of the old companion houses north of the main building. The Tudor-style inn was bult in 1922 on the site of the old St. Clair sawmill on the riverfront and is charmingly decorated in Old English style, with many furnishings to interest the collector. The grounds are attractively landscaped, and in the rear are a very pleasant boardwalk and patio near the water for outdoor relaxation and cocktails.

Both the River Lounge and the Coach Room serve cocktails and light dinners and are warm and comfortable. There are four other, more formal dining rooms, but our favorite is clearly the South Porch with windows on two walls that offer, aside from the patio, the best view of the St. Clair River and its water traffic.

Michael LaPorte, the manager, is young but experienced, personable, and helpful. We think you'll be well satisfied with the friendly and efficient service. But one person you won't meet but will admire is busily at work in the kitchen—Evelyn Mary Cowan, who has been making the inn's famous strawberry pies for nearly 37 years.

The St. Clair Inn is open for three meals a day and tends towards American cooking. The dinner menu includes daily specials as well as such interesting entrées as Boston scrod with crabmeat (topped with cheese sauce), broiled fillet of young shark Amandine, baked chicken Kiev, and Swedish beefsteak. The most frequently ordered items are the steamed Alaskan King crab legs, the sautéed frog legs, and, of course, Evelyn Cowan's fresh strawberry pie. And the scallops may be the best in the area. On Friday and Saturday evenings in the summer, steaks are grilled outdoors on the patio and served with corn on the cob and a salad bar.

The inn maintains a very large wine cellar, and connoisseurs may wish to ask for the special wine list. The dinner menu includes a less extensive selection of mainly French,

82

American, and German wines. Carafes are also available.
Sophisticated, scenic, serene.
THE ST. CLAIR INN, 500 N. Riverside, St. Clair, MI 48079.
Ten miles east of I-94 near the city center; 1½ block north of
St. Clair on M-29. Telephone (313) 329-2222. Hours: 7 a.m.-
10 p.m. (till midnight Fridays and Saturdays). Closed December 24, 25. Full bar service. Background music. Sing-along at
the piano bar in the Coach Room Wednesday-Friday; dancing
to a trio in the River Lounge Tuesday-Saturday. Free parking.
Credit cards: AE, MC, V. Reservations recommended.

KATH HUNTER'S STEAK AND KIDNEY PUDDING

There is much that's authentic about the Old English decor
at the St. Clair Inn. But the menu lacks one essential English
specialty, so we'd like to include it here (since we were
unable to get Ms Cowan's strawberry pie recipe)—the marvelous English steak and kidney pudding of Ms Kath Hunter
of East Lansing, a good friend, a native Londoner, and an
excellent cook. Have this on a cold winter day, ideally with
the typical British "two veg's" on the side.
Mix suet pastry. Place 2 cups flour, 2 teaspoons baking
powder, and 1 teaspoon salt into a mixing bowl. Stir to blend.
Add 3-4 ounces grated or finely diced beef suet, and mix in.
Add about 1 cup water, and stir to make a sticky dough that
will leave the sides of the bowl clean after being well mixed.
Divide the dough into ⅔ and ⅓ portions.
Prepare ingredients for the filling. Cut 1 pound stewing
beef into 1-inch cubes. Mix together 3 tablespoons flour, 1
teaspoon salt, and ¼ teaspoon pepper in a smaller bowl. Roll
meat in this mixture. Cut ¼-½ pound lamb or veal kidney into
small pieces. Slice 2 medium onions. Slice ¼ pound fresh
mushrooms.
Use a 2-quart basin with an upper rim for a most authentic
pudding (check your mixing bowls if you don't have a pudding basin; or use a casserole if necessary). Roll the large
portion of suet pastry on a floured board, and line the basin
with it. Add, in layers, the beef, kidneys, onions, and mushrooms (about 2 layers of each). Mix 1 bouillon cube in 1 cup
boiling water. Add bouillon to come halfway up the filling

(about ⅔ cup).

Roll out the smaller portion of dough, and place on top of the pudding. Press the edges of top and bottom pastry together to seal. Cover the top of the pastry with a piece of buttered waxed paper. Cover this with a fine dish towel or several layers of cheesecloth so that it extends over the rim on the outside of the basin. Secure the cloth by tying with a string under the rim. Any long ends of cloth you can bring up over the top and tie in the middle. (This cloth will be used later to aid you in removing the basin from the steamer.) Steam the pudding for 6 to 8 hours. Serve from the basin. Serves 6.

If you don't have a steamer, use a blancher and set the basin on the perforated insert. Fill with water to come almost to the rim of the basin. Cover and steam; water should be at a steady slow simmer. If steam escapes at the top, set a weight on the lid. (We place the lid on the pan upside down and weigh it down with a brick.)

32
THE RIVER CRAB
St. Clair

Only a few establishments that are part of a larger chain are included in this book, because one of our objectives is to identify places with a special distinction. In the case of Chuck Muer's restaurants, though the menus are virtually the same in most of them, each retains its own individuality. We've described in detail only two of the Muer enterprises, one by the railway—the Gandy Dancer in Ann Arbor—and one by the river. The River Crab has a reputation for quality, a continuing popularity, and a fine setting where you can watch the lake vessels being navigated through the swift St. Clair River.

The decor is contemporary, with wooden archways and interesting fabric ceiling panels; it could use some refurbishing, but that's not so apparent when the place is populated with animated customers. And unless you're sitting right next to the windows, the view is less effective than at the other two riverside restaurants in St. Clair. If you have nautical interests, you should take time to look at the rowing shells hanging from the open rafters of the enclosed porch; both are from the Detroit Boat Club, which claims to be the oldest rowing club in the Western Hemisphere (and for which Chuck Muer once rowed). One, named the "Doc Raynor," is a 40-foot long shell weighing 175 pounds that was used by its crew to qualify for a slot in the 1956 Olympics at Melbourne, Australia, where the team won a silver medal. The other, the "Don James," a 60-foot long shell weighing 375 pounds, was used in competing for the Thames Cup in England in 1960.

Menus are fairly extensive and focus on seafood, but a limited number of other dishes are also offered. Smaller late evening "suppers" are available, and customers flock to the elaborate Sunday brunch (be sure to try the Bavarian apple dumplings). Many of the Muer specialties are on the menu: fisherman's catch, chowder, baked stuffed lobster Larry, cracked wheat bread, shellfish appetizers, and side dishes. For dinner you really ought to start with the selected hot *hors d'ouvre* (for two or more), which offers a taste of everything on the Boston Blue Plate entry except the fish. Charley's Bucket (of shellfish) and the Dungeness crab are two of the most popular entrées here, but about twenty other dinners are available, including the less frequently seen *paella* (a Spanish rice and seafood dish) and a daily special that's well worth your consideration. *Paella* can reach gastronomic heights; the best we've had was as guests of Juan Calvo-Costa. We'd love to get his opinion on this one. Dinners include a salad bar and vegetable, some at a slight additional charge. (See our notes on the Gandy Dancer for more ideas.)

If you're on a limited budget but still want to experience the best of the River Crab, come here for lunch or for the light dinners offered in the lounge. Many of the items served at dinner are available (often in smaller portions) at a considerably lower cost. And if you want something other than seafood, the beef kebab and lamb chops are especially good. The light menu in the lounge features seafood stews, pan-roasts (blends of seafood, cream, and spices), and Provençales—your choice of shellfish braised in a zesty tomato and garlic sauce and served with rice pilaf.

The wine list, as in other Muer restaurants, is presented in a delightful replica of the standard-sized U.S. passport. From forty to fifty wines are offered as well as a house carafe at relatively low prices. The cocktail lounge (where you can also snack on a number of appealing items during "off" or late evening hours) is cheerful and made especially pleasant by pianist Silas Walker, who plays soft jazz, contemporary music, and an occasional classical piece.

At times seating is a bit of a problem for those who want to enjoy the view or be out of the traffic pattern. It may be worth an extra wait if you're particular. (Table 56, seating four to six, is well situated in all respects.) There's ample parking with valets, or you can arrive by boat—the Crab has docking facilities and a gas pump. If any problems arise during your visit, call for help from Sam LeBlanc, the assistant manager. When "he" arrives, you'll find her to be an attractive and amiable young lady who appears to love her job and thoroughly enjoys making guests feel welcome and comfortable.

We've recommended three restaurants on the St. Clair River because of their special setting and the interest generated by passing lake vessels—not to mention fine food. In atmosphere and prices the River Crab fits nicely somewhere between the less pretentious Voyageur and the more sedate, formal St. Clair Inn. Here you can have a moderately expensive meal in one of Michigan's better known restaurants. Its popularity appears to be a good measure of its worth.

More Muer magic.

THE RIVER CRAB, 1337 N. River Road, St. Clair, MI 48079. Two miles north on M-29. Telephone (313) 329-2261. Hours: June-October, luncheon 11:30 a.m.-4:30 p.m., dinner 5-10 p.m. (Fridays and Saturdays till 11 p.m.), Sunday brunch, rest of the year open evenings only. Full bar service. Children's plates. Background music, entertainment Tuesday-Saturday 7-11 p.m., Sunday 5-9 p.m. Free parking. All major credit cards. Reservations recommended, especially on weekends.

STUFFED LOBSTER OR CRAB

One of our favorites at Chuck Muer restaurants is the stuffed lobster Larry. This is a stuffing recipe we devised years ago after enjoying several beautiful stuffed lobsters on the coast of Maine. It works well to stuff lobster or crab and can also be used as a filling for any number of baked fish (for example, red snapper, sole, or trout). Or you can bake it in a buttered casserole for 15-30 minutes in a 400-degree oven and serve it as an accompaniment to any shellfish or fish.

Melt 3 tablespoons butter or margarine, and place in a mixing bowl (or melt it in the bowl in your microwave oven). Mix in 1 cup coarsely crushed saltine crackers, the contents of a 7-ounce can of crabmeat, 1-2 tablespoons chopped parsley, and ½ teaspoon Worcestershire sauce. Add just enough light or heavy cream to hold the mixture together. If you like a more solid dressing, add a beaten egg yolk as well. The stuffing should be mixed just before using so it won't become soggy. Lobsters or crabs should be fully cooked; after removing the shell, fill the body cavity with the stuffing, sprinkle a few crushed saltines on top, and then drizzle on a teaspoon or two of melted butter. Bake about 15-20 minutes in a 400-425 degree oven.

33
A PICNIC IN PORT HURON

For a variation on eating out in restaurants in the Port Huron area, why not have cocktails with a view, followed by a picnic? We suggest stopping at the Fogcutter, on the sixth floor of the downtown bank, and enjoying with your before-dinner drinks what is probably the best view of the St. Clair and its river traffic. The decor is modernized Old English with a correctly banal red and black color scheme and a redundance of obviously synthetic coats of arms on tables and walls and matchbooks. But you'll be coming here for the view. (Stop early; men are required to wear jackets after 6 p.m.)

After leaving the Fogcutter, return to the main business

street (Huron Avenue) a block to the west, proceed for three blocks, cross the bridge, and turn right on Water Street. Go about six blocks to 1227 Water Street, where you'll come upon a charming blue building on the Black River, the C. E. Lixie Fish Company (open Monday-Friday 8-12 a.m., 1-5 p.m., and Saturday 9-12 a.m.). Pick up some smoked fish and return to downtown Port Huron, stopping for bread, beverages, and whatever else you think is essential for a picnic. Travel north through the business district to the well-kept city park on your right. Then go on to the river frontage, where there are ample parking spaces, spacious lawns, picnic tables, and riverfront walks. The closeup view of the Blue Water Bridge and the large lake vessels steaming by is fascinating. The current of the St. Clair River here is very swift as the water spills out of Lake Huron, and those boats and ships going upstream must use full power to make headway. The riverfront park offers comfortable surroundings, a great view, and nautical drama—all at a low price when you picnic here in Port Huron. **Blue water sojourn.**

34
THE CLARKSTON CAFE
Clarkston

Here is another gem that we almost hesitate to mention for fear that its already solidly established reputation will draw even more customers and drive out those of us who like to believe that it's our own discovery. Still, crowded or not, you'll probably have the same feeling that we do, of somehow stumbling upon a hidden treasure. From setting foot into the snugly warm lounge to seating yourself either here or in the homey, welcoming adjacent dining room to your first glimpse of the menu and chalkboard specials, we could almost guarantee that you'll forever after look back on the Clarkston Café with affection.

The building is obviously a lot older than it now looks after redecoration and expansion some nine years ago. Yet the American "main street" business front has taken on an agreeably publike and Victorian facade. Inside are worn and comfortable solid oak rustic armchairs, a pendulum wall clock and assorted odd plates. pictures, and agricultural implements on the walls. Over the bar is the original sign of the Clarkston Café of many, many years ago. And in the dining room, a glowing fire (get a table here on a wintry day), well-stocked China hutches, and converted hobnail milk-glass parlor lamps. Throughout are nuances of the early days in Michigan with the still clinging flavor of country living. Little touches are integral, such as the tiny bouquets of fresh daisies on the tables.

But the food is what will bring you again and again to the Clarkston Café. The luncheon menu offers omelettes, some standard but exceptionally well-prepared soups, salads, and sandwiches, as well as a few cafe specialties that win high praise: *crepes du jour*, chicken cassoulet, cheese fondue, and a Norwegian apple dish with Canadian bacon and onions. The appetizer list is brief but satisfying: French-fried crepe strips with lingonberry sauce, a crispy eggplant, escargots, and sauteed or deep-fried mushrooms. In the dessert category are strawberry shortcake, parfaits, chocolate mousse, and almond cheesecake—yes, yes, it sounds trendy, but wait till you taste the Clarkston Café's interpretation (a luscious, light confection dusted with cinnamon).

For dinner many of the same dishes prevail. But grilled steaks make a more commanding appearance, and the entrées are even more rewarding: among them, the very popular veal Madagascar (gently sauteed with brandy and green peppercorn sauce), braised pork chops, beef brochette, sliced tenderloin Bordelaise, chicken Daniel (chicken breast with ham, cheese, and bacon wrapped in pastry and served with Supreme sauce), whitefish, scrod, lake perch, frog legs, brook trout stuffed with crab and sauced with Hollandaise, crab legs, and scallops sautéed with mushrooms and onions. But no reservations are accepted in the evening, and by 8:30 or so you may need to wait for hours. Come early for dinner.

Daily specials at both the midday and evening meals are chalked on a blackboard. Look for it—some of Chef Greg Goodman's most enticing creations are described here. You

might, if you're lucky, see roast goose *au cerise*, chicken Estragon, *farci* of duck, or rack of lamb. There are always four or five of these daily specials, and they rank with some of the finest in the state. We hate name dropping, but the Clarkston Café, we've heard, is a favorite of Les Gruber; and if the owner of the London Chop House eats here (and we understand he's a fierce taskmaster), it might mean something.
A main street marvel.
THE CLARKSTON CAFE, 18 S. Main Street, Clarkston, MI 48016. About 10 miles northwest of Pontiac; in city center on M-15, south of I-75. Telephone (313) 625-5660. Hours: 11 a.m.-midnight Monday through Thursday (dinner till 10 p.m., sandwiches till 11); Friday and Saturday 11 a.m.-1 a.m. (dinner till midnight). Closed Sundays, holidays. Full bar service. Background music. Entertainment Thursday 8-11 p.m., Friday and Saturday 9-midnight (piano, light music, folk). Free parking in rear. Credit cards: AE, MC, V. Reservations taken for lunch only.

THE CLARKSTON CAFE'S
SOUFFLE AU GRAND MARNIER

Chef Goodman kindly parted with the café's house holiday dessert. If you've never ordered this in a restaurant, plan to in the future (usually you must request it when you first order so that it'll be ready for you at dessert time; soufflés don't like to wait). Fortunately if you make it at home, the problem is more easily solved, but good planning is necessary.
Heat ¼ cup confectioners sugar and 5 egg yolks in a saucepan. Stir in 3½ tablespoons flour. Add 1¾ cups hot milk, and cook, stirring rapidly, until the mixture is smooth and has thickened. Don't let it boil. Remove from heat, and add 1 tablespoon butter. Let cool. Stir in 3 tablespoons Grand Marnier liqueur. Preheat over to 400 degrees. Beat 6 egg whites with a pinch of salt until stiff, and fold into the egg yolk mixture. Butter a 6-cup soufflé dish, and sprinkle with a little granulated sugar. Pour in the souffle mixture. Place in the hot oven, and immediately reduce the temperature to 375 degrees. Bake 30 minutes. Sprinkle the top with 1 tablespoon

granulated sugar, and continue to bake 10 minutes more. Serve immediately.

35
THE NICKELODEON
Clarkston

For truly fine dining, nothing in the village of Clarkston can surpass the Clarkston Café in the center of town. But for the family who wants a quick lunch or for the college crowd with a taste for beer and a case of the munchies, the Nickelodeon is the place to go. Here you can have a casual, informal meal at moderate prices. The menu focuses on sandwiches, snacks, a few dinners (and yet another salad bar). The place is very popular locally, especially with a younger clientele, and we think it's fine for families on a budget—there are lots of things here that kids like.

The restaurant tries, with mixed success, to achieve a turn-of-the-century atmosphere, with tile and wooden floors, assorted old-fashioned chandeliers (Victorian and imitation Tiffany), a pot-bellied brass stove, antiques, and an authentic nickelodeon in the lounge that sometimes works. A modern stainless steel kitchen somewhat incongruously is open to view in the main room. At the rear on a lower level the sun-washed solarium—with its lime green wrought iron chairs, cactus, cascading greenery, and small tiled pool—attracts most of the customers, especially in the daytime. The table settings in both areas are plebeian: paper mats printed with the menu, heavy utilitarian crockery, plastic water glasses, and naked mustard and catsup bottles. But the total effect is pleasant enough.

The sandwiches are large and tasty and include such favorite American varieties as ground round, Reuben, roast beef or ham, pastrami, Kielbasa, hot dogs, and the like. Especially good is the big and spicy homemade pork sausage patty on a toasted onion roll. There are three weekly specials; on Wednesday it's beef stew, on Thursday knackwurst and sauerkraut, and on Friday Fisherman's Chowder. Assorted side dishes and appetizers might be ordered, but probably shouldn't be.

Only beer and wine are sold here, no cocktails or spirits. But the choice will appeal to beer drinkers. On tap and available by the mug or pitcher are various beers from the United States, Canada, Germany, and Ireland. And by the bottle, you'll probably rarely see such choices: beers of the world—Mexico, England, Czechoslovakia, the Philippines, Japan, Australia, and many others. The wines are pretty limited. However, it's not a problem—beer goes best with the sort of food served at the Nickelodeon.

A sprightly sandwich spot.

THE NICKELODEON, 10081 M-15, Clarkston, MI 48016. About 10 miles northwest of Pontiac; 2½ miles north of I-75. Telephone (313) 625-4833. Hours: 9 a.m.-11 p.m. (till 1 a.m. Fridays and Saturdays), Sundays 10 a.m.-9 p.m. Closed Mondays, most legal holidays. Beer and wine. Deli takeouts. Background music. Free parking. Credit cards: AE, MC, V. Reservations not accepted.

36
THE HOLLY HOTEL
Holly

We were tired, enormously hungry, and feeling the first rippling waves of irritation. We arrived at the Holly at 6:50 and were seated at 8:50. Our dinner began with a large, warm wedge of steaming dark rye bread served with decoratively pressed butter. The soup was a fine mushroom and celery, well seasoned and bubbling hot. As for the salad, we liked the garlic better than the house dressing (mustardy and a bit too acidic). An hour later (!) our main course arrived. But, believe it or not, it was worth the seemingly endless wait: the veal Estragon was superb; the mixed vegetable accompaniment artistically presented; the *gaufrette* potatoes, as Molly Abraham of the *Detroit News* has written, "marvelously light and crisp" and worth driving 100 miles for; and the stuffed sole with lobster sauce the best we've ever tasted.

The Holly Hotel isn't a hotel at all but a fine restaurant

that retains the original name of the historic building in which it is housed, a restored turn-of-the-century railroad hotel. The lounge is unadulterated Victoriana: a nostalgic old bar labeled the "Dispensing Department," high-backed red plush chairs, floral carpeting, embossed metal ceiling, marble tables, and the obligatory reclining nude on the backbar (two-dimensional and framed, of course). This is also the waiting area for dinner customers, who from our experience sometimes do wait quite a long time.

Two tiny rooms for dining are the Depot Room, with brick walls, cascading ferns, and ceiling fan, and the nearby Dining Car, where patrons are seated on old train seats with luggage racks overhead. But the third and main dining room is by far the most appealing and gracious, with a Victorian decor similar to that in the lounge. The tables for two hugging the walls might seem attractive for *tête-à-têtes*, but the plushy low chairs that were fine for cocktails earlier are a little impractical at a dinner table. The tables for four have far more suitable chairs. And we like the table settings at the Holly: glowing candles and appropriate old-fashioned bouquets of silk flowers.

Chef Tom McKinnon, who hasn't yet reached the ripe age of 25, and his young staff are to be highly commended for the execution and presentation of some of the state's most extraordinary culinary offerings. The chef spent over a year working in restaurants in France and in a Belgian pastry shop. If those sole and veal dishes are any indication, just imagine what he'll be doing with more experience. There's dedication here—the staff even makes its own ice cream. Our undue wait isn't the fault of the kitchen, but probably a result of an exasperating reservations policy (they're not taken after 6:30) and the justifiable popularity of the place. Take special care to visit when the Holly Hotel isn't overcrowded or overcommitted. Arrive early, or phone ahead.

On the luncheon menu are such appetizers as *farci* of duck, shrimp-stuffed mushrooms, and *escargots*; salads and soups; omelettes; fairly standard sandwiches; four creditable entrées—London broil sauced with Bordelaise, *ratatouille*, sautéed chicken, and sole Hollandaise—and two desserts—a fresh fruit Bavarian cream flan in a walnut crust and marble cheesecake with chocolate sauce. The dinner menu, too, is small but by no means inadequate. The same appetizers as on the luncheon menu appear, as well as two soups (onion and *de jour*). Entrées regularly comprise, among others, veal Estragon with wild rice, filet of beef Wellington, tenderloin of beef with morel mushrooms, poached brook trout with watercress sauce, breast of chicken with green peppercorn sauce, and broiled New York sirloin steak. Specialties are also offered, including such interesting dishes as roast goose with sour cherry sauce, *bouillabaise en croute*, roast elk with gooseberry sauce, and stuffed fillet of sole Nantua. Desserts include the flan and cheesecake as well as Galliano grapes and special daily creations. Prices, for this quality, are fair.

Slightly more than thirty wines are offered—from France, America, Italy, and Germany. There aren't any great wines on the list, but it's a varied offering, and the Holly appears to be keeping the prices tolerable. You'll find a decent wine (for example, a Chassagne Montrachet and a Chateau Greysac), but if you're looking for something unusually good to match the outstanding food, you'll be disappointed.

Worth driving to, worth waiting for.

THE HOLLY HOTEL, 110 Battle Alley, Holly, MI 48442. South of Flint, west of I-75; just off the main street of Holly. Telephone (313) 634-5208. Hours: luncheon 11 a.m.-3 p.m., Monday through Saturday; dinner 5-10 p.m., Monday through Thursday (till midnight Friday and Saturday); Sunday dinner noon-8 p.m. Full bar service. Free parking. All major credit cards. Reservations accepted only until 6:30 p.m. or for groups of 8 or more.

POTATOES GTO

We have no recipe from the Holly Hotel but won't even attempt to duplicate the *gaufrette* potatoes. But the recipe we do include here is another nice change of pace for the potato. First, bake or parboil Idaho potatoes till just almost tender (or cook in a microwave oven on high setting about 4 minutes). Peel, dry on toweling, and slice into ¼-inch crosswise rounds. Dip first into beaten egg (with a little cream or milk added), and then into dry seasoned bread crumbs.

Deep fry at 375 to 400 degrees until golden brown. Vary the seasonings in the crumb mixture, or use a purchased breading mix, if you wish. Another possibility is to dip the potatoes into beer batter instead of using eggs and crumbs (see the index in this book). One large Idaho baking potato will serve 2.

37
LITTLE JOE'S
Grand Blanc

Here is a tavern atmosphere with style, as well as delicious pizza, ribs, and fish; frothy pitchers of beer and soft drinks; and relaxed, informal dining. If this is what you're after, especially when out with the family, Little Joe's of Grand Blanc will more than fill the bill. The bustling tavern has a long tradition as a local gathering place. It started as a grocery store in the mid-1930s, and later Joe Dewey (the Little Joe in the name) started up the tavern and began to serve sandwiches. For years the village's oldtimers played euchre here in their free hours. And today, under the able management of Pat Hughes, it has come into its own as a cheerful, noisy magnet for all age groups.

There's a late nineteenth-century flavor, with leaded windows, Tiffany lamps, walls of shake siding, bentwood chairs, and pseudo-slate tables. The main dining room is the center of activities, and on Friday nights it really swings when Linda Milne plays ragtime piano on the small dais along the wall or when the Dixieland band plays its monthly gig. Through the arched doorway is another smaller eating area, the Sports Room, decorated with photographs of high school teams: any Grand Blanc High School varsity team that wins in the league is treated to a pizza dinner, on the understanding that a team picture will be donated to the Sports Room.

Our MSU students are very appreciative of Little Joe's, as we are. The menu is smallish but versatile: excellent pizzas (you can order a thick crust, if you prefer); some other Italian favorites—lasagne, veal Parmigiana, and spaghetti—all three sold in full or half portions; a good antipasto salad; sandwiches; steaks; deep-fried seafood (cod, shrimp, and clams); and for a special treat, zesty barbequed ribs in four cost categories—full and half dinner portions with salad and potato or by the pound and half pound for the real aficionados. And the prices are, for these days, astonishly paltry. The most expensive item on the menu, excluding the largest super pizza, is $7.90, with most in the $3-6 range. Seat yourself. Casual dress is the rule.

Light hearted, low prices.

LITTLE JOE'S 11518 S. Saginaw, Grand Blanc, MI 48430. South of Flint, in city center. Telephone (313) 694-8391. Hours: 10 a.m.-12:30 p.m. Full bar service. Background music. Entertainment Friday evenings and first Saturday of the month. Free parking in the rear (almost everyone uses this entrance). Credit cards: MC, V. Reservations only taken during the week for large parties.

LITTLE JOE'S STRAWBERRY COLADA

Try this one for dessert, too. Combine 1½ jiggers (2¼ ounces) Cream de Strawberry, 1 jigger (1½ ounces) Coca Casa (cream of coconut), 3 jiggers pineapple juice, and 1 jigger cream. Pour over ice in a large glass. Garnish with a chunk of pineapple and a Maraschino cherry or fresh strawberry when in season. Serves 1.

38
D'AGOSTINO'S
Lapeer

In business since January 1979, D'Agostino's features an Italian/Continental menu that fairly overwhelms the mind and sends the palate trembling in anticipation. Some 76 entrées are offered at dinner, each accompanied by soup, salad, vegetable, and beverage. Almost defying description are the numerous variations of pasta (fettucine, spaghetti, cannelloni, manicotti, tortellini, ravioli) as well as risotta, gnocchi, fritto misto, polenta, eight classic veal dishes, eleven French and

Italian chicken concoctions, the customary steaks and chops (but treated imaginately), several seafood entrées, and even more unusual dishes such as roast or sautéed pigeon, stuffed breast of veal, sweetbreads prepared in two styles, and a steak and quail combination. Even the pasta is made on the premises, and the two partners, along with Mr. D'Agostino's mother, supervise the kitchen carefully and aid in the production of this culinary galaxy. Most popular are the steak and quail, the pasta dishes, and seafood. We also especially recommend the stuffed veal chops, Ripieni or Pollo.

The luncheon menu is much less extensive but very appealing, with assorted pasta dishes and some intriguing sandwiches, quiches, crepes, omelettes, and frittatas. D'Agostino's Sunday brunch is a treat. You have a choice of omelette, frittata, or crepe and a choice of meat, complemented by juice, fruit salad, hot muffins, potatoes, and beverage. But the flamboyance of it is almost as rewarding as the food, as the chefs create flaming specialties in the dining room.

The new restaurant is decorated handsomely in a French-Italian style with deep red draperies and velvet upholstery, dark wood furniture, and crystal chandeliers. In the main dining room we prefer the booths, especially booth 6, or table 22 for privacy and comfort. The terrace, off the bar, seats up to twenty and is more suitable for a large party. The wine list includes Bordeaux, Burgundy, Loires, and Italian, American, and German wines, mostly of recent vintage. And, if you're lucky, there may still be a bottle left of Lafite-Rothschild 1971.

Prices are very good, even for wine, considering the variety and quality of offerings. We give no end of credit to the D'Agostino family and the visionary *chef de cuisine*, Ron Walker, for providing Michigan with this delightful new companion to the more boisterous Lapeer Family Inn. D'Agostino's is an ambitious undertaking, and we hope that the investment in time, effort, and money pays off. If it becomes a success (and it certainly deserves to), it may well become one of the state's finest country Italian restaurants.

Classic Italian in every way.

D'AGOSTINO'S, 325 E. Imlay Road, Lapeer, MI 48446. On Route 21 east of the central business district, at the rear of the Lapeer Family Inn; 16 miles east of Flint. Telephone (313) 664-9804. Hours: 11 a.m.-11 p.m. or later, Sunday brunch

11 a.m.-2 p.m. Closed Mondays. Full bar service. Children's portions. Dancing and accordian music on Fridays and Saturdays after dinner. Free parking. Credit cards: AE, MC, V. Reservations recommended Friday and Saturday evenings.

D'AGOSTINO'S VEAL SCALLOPINE PIGNOLI

Pound 1½ pounds veal very thin, and cut into 4 x 3-inch scallops. Mix together ¼ cup ground pine nuts, ¼ cup flour, and salt, pepper, and basil to taste. Stir in 1 tablespoon Parmesan cheese. In a second shallow bowl beat together 2 eggs and 1 tablespoon water. Dip the first first into the egg wash and then into the flour mixture. Refrigerate 10 minutes.

Heat 4 tablespoons butter and 2 tablespoons vegetable oil in a skillet. Quickly brown both sides of the veal scallops. place them on paper toweling, and keep them warm while preparing the sauce. Add 2 tablespoons butter to the skillet, and sauté 2 mashed cloves garlic and ¾ cup chopped onion until wilted, but not brown. Add 2 cups dry white wine, and simmer until the liquid is reduced by one half. Add 1 cup chicken stock, and again simmer till reduced by one-half. Add ½ pound sliced fresh mushrooms and 1 teaspoon dry (or 1 tablespoon fresh) basil. Simmer 2 minutes. Remove from heat. Add ¼ cup whole pine nuts, 1 cup Béchamel sauce, and the juice of 1 lemon. Add salt and white pepper to taste. Arrange scallops on a hot platter, and spoon on some of the sauce. Serve the remaining sauce separately at the table.

Hints from the Winters: If you have trouble finding pine nuts, try an Italian or Mexican food store or a health food store. Use your own recipe for Béchamel, or try this: heat 2 tablespoons butter. Add 1½ to 2 tablespoons flour for a *roux*. Cook 2 minutes on very low heat. Add gradually 1 cup milk (or ½ milk and ½ chicken stock). Add 1 small onion studded with 2 whole cloves and ½ small bay leaf. Cook, stirring, until thickened. Set in a 350-degree oven for 20 minutes (or simmer in a microwave oven 6-7 minutes). Strain and season to taste with salt and white pepper.

39
THE LAPEER FAMILY INN
Lapeer

"Family inn" is a mundane but most appropriate name for this informal, crowded, noisy, animated restaurant. On our last visit we saw at least six or seven grandmothers and a veritable host of small, wriggling, happy children—and just about everything imaginable in between. We arrived at 7 p.m., and the little ones were still struggling with their pizzas, dropping napkins, playing television games, or watching the large screen at one end of the dining room showing cartoons and and old movies (all rated "G," of course). We could, however, visualize the later college crowd enjoying pitchers of beer and deep-dish pizzas at perhaps the same or even greater noise level.

When you enter the Family Inn, you'll first notice the hanging ferns, brick walls, wooden booths with red tables, and large metal chandeliers. But don't wait for the nonexistent host or hostess to seat you—walk right in, stake out your booth, and go to the "Order Food Here" sign to pick up a menu. If you want a cocktail before dinner, you might also stop at the "Pick Up Drinks" sign and carry them to your booth so that you can whet your palate while studying the extensive bill of fare. We should note, though, that cocktails aren't a very good idea here (no ice cubes, no olives, no expert bartender during our visit). Your best bet is to emulate the knowledgable regular clientele, most of whom tote pitchers of beer or water or soft drinks to their tables. When you've placed your order, a loudspeaker (yet more noise) will let you know when to pick up your food (and paper plates).

The American-Italian menu features three varieties of pizza: the Round House Special, a soufflé-like creation made with two layers of dough like a pie; the Regular Round, with a nice thin crust and your choice of 22 different toppings (we recommend the Lapeer Special); and the Italian-style Deep Dish Pizza (again, try the Lapeer Special). If you're having pizza, let the kids watch at the kitchen windows where they're prepared and baked in large wall ovens. Also on the menu are several pasta dishes (and the pasta is homemade, a treat), veal

Parmesan, chicken, steaks, seafood, some very appealing sandwiches, minestrone, salads, desserts, and assorted deep-fried side orders. We like the pizza and pasta, but for our taste the batter on the fried onions and peppers is a trifle too thick and soggy—but we imagine that teenagers would adore it.

The most popular items on the menu, besides pizza, are the lasagne, ribs, spaghetti, and chicken, the last two at really low prices. In fact, if you order the right thing (and there are half orders and special plates here for children), the place is a bargain. The hard wooden booths are surprisingly roomy and comfortable. Don't look for privacy or the best table; don't expect any niceties. Just enjoy the food and marvel at the generational melting pot.

We must mention that the Lapeer Family Inn is not to be confused with the second restaurant in the same building at the rear, D'Agostino's. In fact, if you're with the family and a child old enough to look after the smaller ones, you might consider letting the kids eat at the Family Inn while you splurge on some gourmet Italian dishes next door at the more stylish D'Agostino's. Ideally, if you're in the Lapeer area, you should try both, for the best of two very different worlds. The restaurants are under the same management, and we would guess that this is the most unusual restaurant combination in Michigan (or in the world, for that matter).

Family fun, Italian bargains.

THE LAPEER FAMILY INN, 325 E. Imlay City Road, Lapeer, MI 48556. Sixteen miles east of Flint, on route 2I east of the Lapeer central business district. Telephone (313) 664-5983. Hours: 11 a.m.-2 a.m. (Friday and Saturday till 3 a.m.). Closed Easter and Christmas. Full bar service. Free parking. Credit cards: MC, V. Reservations not accepted.

LAPEER FAMILY INN SPAGHETTI SAUCE

In a large pot heat 2 tablespoons olive oil and 2 tablespoons butter. Sauté until wilted: 4 ounces chopped carrot (1 medium carrot), 8 ounces chopped onion (1 medium), 1 chopped rib of celery, ½ green pepper (chopped), and 4 chopped cloves of garlic. Add ¾ pound of chopped beef (or combined beef and pork) and ¼ pound seasoned sausage. Cook until color changes, stirring constantly. Add 1 cup dry red wine (preferably Barolo or Chianti) and cook 4 minutes. Add four 30-ounce cans of whole tomatoes (chopped, with juice), 1 tablespoon dry basil, 1 teaspoon pepper, 2 tablespoons sugar, 1 teaspoon dry oregano, and 1 teaspoon dry rosemary (chopped together). Simmer 1 hour. If liquid reduces too quickly, thin with chicken or beef stock. When sauce is done, it will have a smooth appearance; do not overcook , or it will taste too acidic. When done, stir in 2 small cans of tomato paste and salt to taste (about ½ to 1 tablespoon). Serves 8-12.

Hints from the Winters: You'll find this sauce somewhat different in texture and flavor from the all-day, slow-cooked version many Italians make. Until we tried this one (and the very good fresh tomato sauce of Craig Claiborne), we had always relied on the excellent recipe by Marion Capecci that she somehow keeps improving each year and on Sylvia Flint's Roman sauce with its rich basil flavor. But we find the Lapeer sauce a nice change.

Cut the recipe in half if you wish—it'll be just as good. Incidentally, we simmered it about 1½ hours or slightly longer and didn't notice an appreciable increase in acidity. If you prefer a softer, less tart sauce, you should remove the seeds from the tomatoes before adding. And no matter what your preference, don't omit the sugar—it won't make the sauce sweet.

40
DAVISON

THE HOME BAKERY

This one's for the night owls and the sweet-toothed. The Home Bakery in the little town of Davison attracts a faithful following from miles around who might be returning late after an evening out and decide that, yes, dessert is finally in order. The bakery (the only one in town; you can't miss it) opens its doors at 9:30 p.m. and stays open till 6 the following evening. Takeout coffee and steaming baked goods fresh from the oven as well as doughnuts and a variety of holiday specialties (in season) are available daily—and nightly. The spicy aromas are irresistible; and the phone is constantly ringing: "When are the glazed doughnuts coming out?"

The Fortner family have been bakers in the area for four generations, starting in the early 1900s in Clarkston. An uncle, Dude MacArthur, continues to run the Flushing bakery, started after the crash of 1929. The Davison establishment opened some 33 years ago. Young Fred Fortner took over the business from his father in 1976, and the old family recipes are still used. There's a full line of superlative, yeasty breads—white, rye (sourdough, light, caraway), French bread, onion rolls, whole wheat. Among the sweets are cakes made from "scratch" (and you can tell the difference), delicate puff pastries and eclairs, chewy baked chop suey rolls (with chopped fruit and coconut), downright ethereal cream rolls, and usually only on Saturday the Fortners' own chocolate raised doughnuts. At Christmastime the bakery features such treats as sour cream molasses cookies, stollen, fruit bread and cake, fudge, and—from a recipe of Fred's great-grand-father—peanut brittle, a crunchy confection that sells some 400 pounds a year. For those who care, no preservatives or emulsifiers are used. You might ask, if the place isn't too busy, for a tour of the bakery, too.

Sugar and spice, and everything nice—even at 2 a.m.

THE HOME BAKERY, 331 N. Main Street, Davison, MI 48423. Seven miles east of Flint. Telephone (313) 653-6048. Closed only 3½ hours a day, from 6-9:30 p.m.; also closed Sunday, Monday, for one week in summer (usually end of July or first of August) and between Christmas and New Years. Call ahead to be certain—and to ask if the glazed doughnuts are out.

BON APPETIT

Just south of the bakery on Main Street is the Bon Appetit, a little place that's just made a beginning and shows great promise. The young chef, related to the Fortner family, is a graduate of the Culinary Institute of America. The storefront restaurant, with its bare floor and fluorescent lighting, is rather stark and plastic. But, as for our first impression, this was less important than the reassuring sight of two books propped up in the window: *Larousse Gastronomique* and *Escoffier*. There are only seven tables, seating about 25 at most, and three meals a day are served.

The breakfast menu features omelettes. Luncheon entrées include crepes à *la reine*, quiche Lorraine, eggs Benedict, mushroom crepes, three salads and a few conventional sandwiches. The salad is nice—romaine lettuce and good dressings. Entrées are served attractively, as are the vegetable side dishes. Desserts include chocolate mousse, ice cream, and a dessert of the day (on our visit we were offered bananas Foster). The dinner menu, too, is small—soup *du jour*, two salads (Caesar and spinach), and just seven entrées: steak Bon Appetit (tenderloin slices with mushrooms, Dijon mustard, and *demiglace* sauce), steak *au poivre*, breast of chicken Valoise (sautéed and topped with Swiss cheese and Supreme sauce), shrimp scampi (with garlic and white wine sauce), crepes *au fruit de mer* (seafood in a sherry sauce and topped with Mornay sauce), and veal à *la creme* (white wine, cream, and mushrooms). Prices are fair for the quality of the food; entrees include potato, salad, vegetable, and roll).

A newcomer in French fare; bears watching.

BON APPETIT, Main Street, Davison. Hours: breakfast 7-11 a.m., luncheon 11 a.m.-5 p.m., dinner 5-9 p.m. No alcoholic beverages.

41
MAKUCH'S RED ROOSTER
Flint

Tableside cookery is billed as a specialty, but at the Red Rooster it's done as it should be done, not just to impress the naive nor to intimidate the timorous nor to provide mere entertainment, but to bring the diner into closer contact with the pleasures and rewards of cooking. The Makuchs like to cook and enjoy sharing their own enthusiasm in creating exciting dishes for their guests. In business for twenty years, this is another admirable family operation. Arthur senior and his two sons Arthur and Kenneth own and manage the Red Rooster; Kenneth is also the chef and tableside wizard; young Arthur's wife Avis attends to the office; and Kenneth's wife Suzy also cooks—her cheesecakes are the stuff of dreams.

There are lots of inviting nooks and crannies, banquettes and booths, for semisecluded dining. The red and black decor is warm, enhanced by barnwood, soft lighting, and paintings by local artists (on sale). The table settings are tasteful and attractive—pewter service plates, fresh flowers, red and white linens. Another small room has recently been added at the rear of the main dining room, and we assume it will have an appeal for large groups who want to be out of the traffic pattern. While at the Red Rooster, take a look at the well-designed backbar in the lounge, serving as the wine storage area.

It's especially crowded for lunch here; in fact, reservations are necessary for the midday meal. The menu is a typical roster of American favorites: steaks, shellfish, salads, sandwiches, several entrée combinations, and three daily specials. It amounts to a good choice of hearty food to satisfy the hungry auto workers who fill up the restaurant at noon. But the dinner menu is what most appeals to us. The appetizers include three shrimp and three oyster preparations. Other starters are an onion soup, gratinéed and crusted with a delightful blend of four cheeses, and the ever-popular Caesar salad. Entrées on the regular menu consist of commendable steaks and seafood, but we prefer the chef's specialties: a creamy veal scallopine, Gaucho steak, *tournedos Lyonnaise*, pepper steak *au bleu*, or sauteed shrimp with mushrooms. Among the tableside cookery choices are pepper steak with brandy and wine sauce (Kenneth takes justifiable pride in this), steak Diane, crab-stuffed filet with Vermouth, and skillet of crab. Some half-dozen specials are also offered each evening—these, too, are standouts.

On Monday evenings a special six-course Continental-style dinner is prepared, at a good price for this sort of offering ($15.95). More elaborate entrées such as beef Wellington, steak Choron, or steak with morels might appear on this occasion. Kenneth also flames a few desserts: bananas Jamaica (like Foster, but with a dark rum sauce), crepes Suzettes, cherries Jubilee, crepes Fitzgerald (filled with Grand

Marnier-flavored cream cheese and topped with strawberry sauce), and banana strawberry Royale. Other possibilities include that great cheesecake of Suzy's, toasted almond ice cream pie, crepes Kirsten, three coffee concoctions, and a liqueur parfait.

The wine list emphasizes Californian, but there are also four of the five *premiers grands crus* of Bordeaux (no Haut Brion); the Burgundies, however, are thin. California chablis, rosé, and Zinfandel (a good selection for a house wine) can be ordered by the glass. And you might also wish to see the private list.

Très bon, le rouge chanticleer—Flint's finest.

MAKUCH'S RED ROOSTER, 3302 Davison Road, Flint, MI 48506. One mile northwest of I-69, Center Road exit. Telephone (313) 742-9310. Hours: 11 a.m.-10 p.m., Saturday 5:30-11 p.m. Closed Sundays, major holidays. Full bar service. Background music. Free parking. Credit cards: MC, V. Reservations recommended for lunch, on weekends.

THE RED ROOSTER'S SCALLOP-STUFFED FLOUNDER WITH LOBSTER SAUCE

This is just one of Chef Kenneth Makuch's extraordinary interpretations of a classic dish. The recipe serves eight, and you'll need 5 ounces (about 3 pieces) per person of fresh flounder fillets. For the stuffing, poach 1 pound tiny bay scallops (or sliced or chopped larger ones) in water with a dash of salt, about 7 minutes. Drain scallops, and blend with 1 cup fine bread crumbs and 2 eggs. Saute ¾ cup sliced or chopped mushrooms in garlic butter and 1 ounce Vermouth. Add to scallop mixture along with 1 teaspoon nutmeg, 1 teaspoon ground thyme, 1 tablespoon tarragon, 1 tablespoon seasoning salt, and 1 teaspoon freshly ground pepper. Mix thoroughly.

Lay one flounder fillet on a pie tin with a little water in the bottom, and add a generous amount of the stuffing. Cover with two more pieces of flounder. Season with salt and pepper and fresh lemon juice. Continue with remaining fillets. Bake at 375 degrees for 30 minutes.

For the lobster sauce, saute ½ medium onion (minced fine)

in ¼ pound butter, about 2 minutes. Add 1 cup flour, and cook about 7 minutes on very low heat. In another pot, heat 2 cups clam juice with a 4-ounce lobster tail (with shell) until cooked. There is a lot of flavor in the shell. Remove the lobster, and discard the shell; dice lobster meat. Add 2 cups milk, 1 tea-spoon salt, ¼ teaspoon white pepper, dash Tabasco sauce, ¼ teaspoon mace, ¼ teaspoon nutmeg, ¾ cup cream sherry, and paprika to color (about 1 tablespoon). Heat until almost boiling. Add this mixture to the *roux* with onions, and stir over heat until thickened.

Hints from the Winters: Sole or another flat fish may, of course, be substituted for flounder. Bottled clam juice is avail-able at grocery stores (we've found it occasionally with the condiments at the liquor counter). Another substitution you might want to make to cut costs or for convenience is the use of crab legs instead of lobster—it'll change the flavor, but you'll like it, too (remember to cook it in the shell). Our only other suggestion is to go easy on the paprika, especially if you buy the sort that most stores carry; Hungarian paprika is milder than the Spanish and preferable in this dish.

42
THE PX BARBEQUE
Flint

Some of the most memorable moments of our lives were spent savoring spicy, crusted ribs in Georgia and the Caro-linas. In the South the barbeque is an event, a spectacle, a social occasion, a feast for crowds from all walks of life: the pit glows red with hickory or oak coals and sends up puffs of aromatic steam as it meets the juices from the pork above it, and all the while the smoke and heat are transforming a sow's ear into a silk purse. We especially recall the little place in Georgia where we stood transfixed over the crackling hot pit and learned how to make "hash," and Earl Duke's in Cameron, South Carolina, where our Golden Retriever was nearly done in by the August sun, while we feasted on ribs, chopped pork barbeque, homemade slaw and pickles, and spongy white bread.

Barbequed pork has more than a century-old history in the South, but in Northern cities the pit barbeque has generally been supplanted by ceramic and electrical contrivances, and more barbequeing is done at home than with groups. Fortunately Michigan can boast a few authentic barbeque establishments where the skill and sauces equal (well, almost) the great tradition of its sister states below the Mason-Dixon line. The PX may well be one of them. There's been a PX Barbeque in Flint for more than thirty years.

Since 1961, Donna and Alex Meyer, who earlier had a rib place in Memphis, have been managing the perennially popular restaurant. Alex is an ex-owner of a minor league football team, the Flint Sabers. He might have worried about damaged ribs then, but now he and his wife specialize in roasting them to glazed perfection. If all goes according to plans, by the time this book is published, the Meyers will have moved the barbeque to a new location (possibly near the Flint airport). As of this writing, the restaurant is located on a busy thoroughfare and, with its mirrored walls and splashes of red, is comfortable enough—but when the ribs are turning out back and when the heady fragrance reaches the dining room, who cares about decor?

The specialties of the PX are rotisserie-roasted barbeque (pork spareribs, chicken, beef, and ham), steaks from a ceramic broiler, and a fine spaghetti with a choice of four sauces. À la carte appetizers include assorted portion sizes of antipasto and Italian salad among others. The ribs are as popular as the steaks, and both may be ordered with either potato or spaghetti. Rib dinners come in two portion sizes, and a third appetizer portion is worth thinking about if you want to try one of those delicious steaks. The same sauce is used on all the barbequed meats. It's a mild sauce, but a hotter one is available by request. Extra sauce is served at the table and, by the way, can be purchased by the pint or quart. The wine list is small, but our own preference with the zesty ribs is ice-cold beer.

Down home goodness.

PX BARBEQUE, 5220 Clio Road, Flint, MI 48504. (Again, check if the location has changed.) Telephone (313) 787-4511. Hours: 5-11 p.m. Closed Mondays, Tuesdays, most major holidays, the week of Passover, and the first two weeks in July. Full bar service. Children's plates. Takeouts. Free parking. Credit cards: MC, V. Reservations recommended for parties over 4 persons.

BARBEQUED BACK RIBS

We found no way into the inner sanctum of the PX, when it came to a recipe. So, instead of a PX production, we present here one of the hundreds of barbequed rib recipes we've been testing over the years. We're still testing; like all the fanatical barbequers we know, we're still looking for the Ultimate Rib. This one, however, is very tender, meaty, and flavorful.

Depending on your dinner plans, purchase ¾ to 1¼ pound pork back ribs per person. Be sure they're back ribs; don't confuse them with spareribs or "country" ribs. The small portion is adequate if you're having appetizers, soup, salad, and dessert. If the ribs are the important thing, plan on the larger portions, or 6 to 8 ribs per person. Place ribs, bone side down in a shallow roasting pan, and add about ¼ inch water to the pan. Cover with lid or aluminum foil, and bake at 250 degrees about 3 hours or until very tender. (You can cook the ribs for 2 to 2½ hours the night before, refrigerate, and finish baking the next day.)

While ribs are baking, prepare the sauce (this, too, can be done ahead). In a 1-1½-quart saucepan, sauté ½ cup chopped onion in 2 tablespoons oil until onion is transparent, 2 to 3 minutes. Add 4 medium cloves garlic put through a press, and cook 1 minute more, without browning either onions or garlic. Add 1 cup water, 1 cup catsup, 1 cup chili sauce, ½ cup red wine vinegar, ½ cup fresh lemon juice, ¼ cup brown sugar, 3 tablespoons horseradish, 2 teaspoons prepared mustard (preferably Dijon), 1 teaspoon liquid smoke seasoning, 1 teaspoon salt, 1 teaspoon pepper, ½ teaspoon ground cumin, and ¼ teaspoon Tabasco sauce (or more to taste). Simmer 20 to 25 minutes. Makes about 3 cups sauce (plan on ¼ cup sauce to 1 pound back ribs).

When ribs are very tender, pour off liquid in bottom of roasting pan. Turn oven temperature to 350 degrees. Spoon sauce on both sides of ribs to coat well. Return ribs to upper rack of oven, bone side down. Bake at 350 degrees for 15-20 minutes. Turn on the broiler, and broil 3-4 inches from the heat or until sauce becomes slightly charred.

43
THE BEECH TREE
Flint

Disco and dining—at first the combination seemed to us as likely as a merger between RCA and Sara Lee. But, then, we hadn't seen the Beech Tree in Flint (absolutely no relation to our publishing company, by the way). Located in a shopping mall, in itself a deterrent, the restaurant is fast acquiring a magnetic appeal, probably attributable to that very unusual juxtaposition of attractions. If it hadn't been done well, one can imagine the consternation of both sets of clientele— eager dancers in fluorescent attire trying to avoid tray-laden waiters on their way to the strobe lights, eager diners trying to concentrate on a broiled lobster tail to the beat of a sizzling Donna Summer number. But the Beech Tree has avoided all possible horrors. The restaurant has combined the best of two different worlds, tastefully and with style.

Here there are no garish colors or flamboyant, glitzy furnishings. The dining room, well separated from the disco in the lounge, is airy and light, part of it suggesting a sunny outdoor patio, with elaborately scrolled rattan and Philippine *buri* hood chairs, light woods, masses of greenery, and a high open ceiling. The lounge is large with very comfortable seating and a friendly, clubby atmosphere. There's an "in place" feel to it, yet it seems to be "in" with all age groups, unlike the the typical discotheque. As for dining, the food is geared to popular tastes for steaks, lobster, prime rib, seafood, and the like (complete with the ubiquitous salad bar), though there are a couple of imaginative vegetable selections. The food isn't innovative, but it's tops in its category. And if the menu is familiar, the surroundings are far from it.

Hustle to the Beech Tree.

THE BEECH TREE, G-3503 Beecher Road, Flint, MI 48504.

Ten miles from the Flint city center, ¼ mile from I-75. Telephone (313) 733-5590. Hours: breakfast 7-10:30 a.m., lunch 11 a.m.-4 p.m., dinner 4-11 p.m. (Sundays till 9 p.m.). Closed Mondays. Full bar service. Background music; piano bar 5-8 p.m., disco-dancing 9 p.m.-1:30 a.m. Free parking. Credit cards: AE, MC, V. Reservations recommended. Casual dress acceptable, but you'll see lots of jackets.

44
WALLI'S SUPPER CLUB
Flint

Walli's, which gradually over the years has grown from a root beer stand to a small restaurant (on the present site of the lounge) and finally to a dining establishment that serves up to 500 people at a time, specializes in only one kind of "supper": the smorgasbord. It has an understandable attraction for the many students who recommend it, though we much prefer to be served when we dine out. We don't care for picking and choosing from dozens of mayonnaise-based salads and gelatin molds or facing the choice of either scooping out the last, drying spoonful of a casserole or calling for the management. Yet we can appreciate the persistent appeal of the buffet to those with lumberjack appetites or to self-deceivers who think they're getting something for nothing.

Walli's, however, is much more elaborate and satisfying than the typical and more familiar smorgasbord chains—in decor, variety of offerings, and the addition of live entertainment. The spacious dining room is characterized by the restauranteur's version of Victorian opulence: large crystal chandeliers, flocked wallpaper, near-matching red printed table linens, and upholstered captains' chairs.

As "bounteous buffets" and "fantastic salad bars" go, this is at their most bounteous and fantastic. At least sixty salads make an appearance, along with such ever-popular wholesome entrees as baked and fried chicken, roast beef, baked ham, whole poached salmon, spareribs, spaghetti, and lasagne. There are a few authentic Scandinavian dishes, too—notably Swedish meatballs and a herring and beet salad. One favorite regular offering is the shrimp cocktail. Among the breads are French, pumpernickel, stollen, dinner rolls, and garlic toast. A second buffet table is laden with numerous desserts: cream pies, fruit, cakes, mousse, cookies—all made in Walli's kitchen. No soups, we're sorry to say.

The restaurant is a family operation. Arne and Fran Walli have been in business for some thirty years. But we must note that, if you want the smorgasbord, don't be confused by the two other Walli's restaurants in Flint—each run by a Walli son, Ken and Bob, as well as Walli's Scandia Hall, a private banquet hall. Be sure to head for the Supper Club. On Fridays and Sundays in the evening Mrs. Walli's sister has been playing the organ for twenty years. And on Saturday nights there's a band and dancing. A luncheon buffet is also served, offering fewer dishes and no dessert.

Probably the best smorgasbord in Michigan.

WALLI'S SUPPER CLUB, G-5432 N. Saginaw Road, Flint, MI 48505. Five miles north of the city center (in Flint the "G" prefix indicates greater distance from the downtown; so if you find a 5432 without the "G," keep going farther north, and you'll eventually get there.) Telephone (313) 785-5511. Hours: luncheon buffet 11 a.m.-2:30 p.m. Tuesday through Friday; smorgasbord 5-9:30 p.m. Tuesday, Wednesday, Thursday; 5-10 p.m. Friday; 4:30-11:30 p.m. Saturday; noon-9 p.m. Sunday. 1979 prices were $4.75 at noon and $9.25 for the smorgasbord. Full bar service. Children's prices. Background music, entertainment on weekends in the evening. Free parking. Credit cards: AE, MC, V. Reservations recommended, especially on Saturdays.

45
GRACIE'S COUNTRY INN
New Lothrop

An old brick building once occupied by a bank (the safe's still there) and an antique store on the main street of New Lothrop is now painted firehouse red and black and is the home of one of the best-known steak houses in the area.

Rural charm has been forefeited to a modern utilitarianism, so don't expect "country inn" to carry the usual connotations. Gracie£s is not for the epicurean, the gourmet, or the connoisseur, but simply and unpretentiously caters to those who want good steaks at good prices and a generous salad bar with no fewer than 26 choices (half-price for children). On Saturday nights the waiting line stretches into the street, and most people leave here with doggie bags.

On Mondays through Fridays from 11 a.m. to 2 p.m. Gracie's features an all-you-can-eat luncheon buffet in addition to a simple sandwich menu. The most popular dinner steaks are the 3-pound sirloin for two persons and the Delmonico. Six other steaks are listed as well as steak and ground sirloin sandwiches. You might also consider the barbequed beef ribs, another specialty and one that sells out early. The family-style pan-fried chicken dinners are a bargain, too. The wine list is modest; carafes are available.

Don't plan on an evening at Gracie's. The bar is used mainly for eating; there's no music (except an occasional jukebox selection) and no entertainment. We include Gracie's as a special place, not for its decor, not for its inventive menu— but because, relatively, it's a bargain and is extremely popular with students and other people from the immediate area. **A country American bargain.**

GRACIE'S COUNTRY INN, 9483 Genessee Street (Easton Road), New Lothrop, MI 49460. About 20 miles northwest of Flint; 2 miles west of M-13 in village center. Telephone (313) 638-5731. Hours: luncheon 11 a.m.-2 p.m., dinner 3-10 p.m. (Fridays and Saturdays 10 a.m.-midnight), Sunday noon-10 p.m. Closed Labor Day, Christmas, New Years Day. Full bar service. Free parking. No credit cards. Reservations recommended for Friday and Saturday evenings.

46
THE BAVARIAN INN
Frankenmuth

The Bavarian Inn, along with its near relative across the street, Zehnder's, is practically an institution in Michigan.

In a village fairly overflowing with colorful Bavarian motifs and tourist attractions, the two restaurants amiably compete for customers who may have driven miles for the sole purpose of treating their families and friends to the generous chicken dinners featured here. As for choosing between the two, it's mainly a matter of taste in decor or offerings *other* than chicken on the menus. The Bavarian Inn's five dining rooms and Koffee Haus are expectedly German in theme, and the menu here includes such Bavarian entrees as *wiener schnitzel*, *sauerbraten*, *kasseler-rippchen* (smoked pork loin), and German sausages.

You may also order the weekly or monthly special from the à *la carte* selections, as well as several seafoods and sandwiches, all at quite modest prices. Everything is prepared and cooked on the premises, and you'll find some excellent breads, soups, and desserts—our favorite is the apple strudel, topped with whipped cream and caramel sauce. During the Frankenmuth Bavarian Festival in the second week in June, there is also outdoor dining in the rear.

The famous family-style, all-you-can-eat chicken dinners comprise soup, relishes, breads (try that fragrant dark rye), *krautsalat*, heaping bowls of noodles and mashed potatoes and gravy, beverage, and ice cream. There's a very limited wine selection, none distinguished—not even the German. But probably the most popular drink is beer; we suggest one of the beers brewed right in Frankenmuth, Carling's or, our own choice, Geyer's.

The Bavarian Inn was founded as a boarding house in 1883 and, aside from its German-American cooking, has become well known for its Glockenspiel, a 35-bell carillon that plays daily at noon, 6 p.m., and 9 p.m., followed by a figurine movement portraying the legend of the Pied Piper of Hamelin. With bells from Holland and mechanism from Germany, the intricate device is housed in the clock tower rising above the parking lot. It draws milling crowds, and kids seem to love it. On our visit last fall, the Mayor refused to come out of the Glockenspiel. But that's the only thing that didn't work, as far as we could see, at the Bavarian Inn.

We were fortunate to tour the working part of the inn with Bill Zehnder, son of the owner, as our guide. This is a spectacular, large-scale restaurant operation, of which the thousands of tourists who visit here are probably unaware. Efficiency, cleanliness, and quality control are predominant. The chickens, we found, are superchickens—weighing 3¼ pounds each at the age of only 7 or 8 weeks. On a busy day the Bavarian Inn uses 1,500 of these chickens and serves 5,000 diners. In an average year it cooks 250,000 chickens, weighing 600,000 pounds (or 300 tons). Little is wasted. Even the leftover grease from deep frying is used in making laundry soap—Oscar, retired and aged 79, has been attending to this for twelve years now—which in turn is used in the Bavarian Inn's own laundry (also servicing the linens at Zehnder's). For the past year or so an elaborate electronic liquor-dispensing machine has been in use, assuring control of quality and measurement—and, yes, you can ask for your personal variations; the computer handles nearly any request. All in all, both the Bavarian Inn and Zehnder's provide fine quality and fine food; you can expect to get your money's worth here. **Always gemutlich.**

THE BAVARIAN INN, 713 S. Main Street, Frankenmuth, MI 48734. Between Saginaw and Flint on M-83, 7 minutes from I-75; in the city center. Telephone (517) 652-9941. Hours: 7 days a week April through December, 11 a.m.-10 p.m. Closed on Mondays January through March. Full bar service. Children's plates. Background music. Free parking. Credit cards: AE, MC, V. Reservations accepted any time Tuesday through Thursday.

THE BAVARIAN INN'S
CRANBERRY-ORANGE RELISH

Sort 6 pounds cranberries, removing any bad ones. Core 6 pounds apples and 6 seedless oranges (or 7 or 8 if small), leaving on the peel. Grind the apples, cranberries, and oranges with the medium blade on the grinder. Mix well. Add sugar to taste (about 3 pounds) and 1 tablespoon red food coloring. Refrigerate; this keeps well. Serves 12-15. The recipe can be increased or cut quite easily. No hints from the Winters—this is one of those simple things that can't be improved upon by any amount of elaboration.

47
ZEHNDER'S
Frankenmuth

Rumor has it that both Zehnder's and the Bavarian Inn are under one management and that waiters bear their enormous burdens of steaming, crusty chicken from a kitchen located under Main Street that serves both restaurants. In truth, the two establishments are each separately managed, although owned and operated by the Zehnder family, and related mainly by the fact that both specialize in the chicken dinners for which Frankenmuth is noted. It is estimated that 2 million tourists visit the American/Bavarian community each year and that at least 1,500,000 of them order the celebrated family-style chicken dinners. The chief difference between the two restaurants is in decor and the additional menu offerings.

At Zehnder's the theme is colonial American. Unlike those at the Bavarian Inn, the accompaniments to the chicken include old-fashioned fruit bread, poultry dressing, chicken livers, and cabbage salad. The dessert specialty here is, predictably, homemade pie. Other entrées are grilled steaks, prime rib, ham, duckling, pork chops, barbequed spareribs, and some seafood. In addition, soups and sandwiches and weekly lunch and dinner specials are available in the Coffee Shop; lighter appetites and tighter budgets might prefer this room (although all prices are moderate). The wine list is much the same as the Bavarian Inn's.

Zehnder's is an outgrowth of the Exchange Hotel, built in 1856, and it's about 34 years older than the Bavarian Inn. It accommodates 1,200 visitors at a time and serves more than 4,500 meals every Sunday—about 80 percent of them the famous chicken dinners. There are seven dining rooms, each furnished in early American and each with its own atmosphere; you might, if it's not too busy, visit each room and decide which appeals to you before asking for a table. The "Original" dining room is a century old and located in the center of Zehnder's, where the old Exchange Hotel once stood. You might wish to have cocktails (or eat) in the quaint and nostalgic Tap Room, where the early history of Frankenmuth is depicted on the walls in rustic photographs. But Zehnder's, like its neighbor across the street, is generally packed and requires your patience if you want much choice in dining area.

Both restaurants in Frankenmuth have gift shops and bakeries, and the wine cellar in Zehnder's, which is fun to visit, is cleverly arranged as a maze to give you the impression of visiting a real and larger vineyard cellar. And there are plenty of other things to see and do in Frankenmuth, so you might plan a day's outing. Pick up a brochure in one of the restaurants, and take your choice—the art gallery; the Schnitzelbank Shop, where you might even see Georg Keilhofer or one of his students carving wood; Bronner's, where you can stock up on Christmas decorations; the Chippewa cemetery; and either of the local breweries, Carling's and the smaller and, we think, more interesting Geyer's, brewers of Frankenmuth Bavarian dark beer. Geyer's is well over a hundred years old and, unlike most of its bigger competitors, adds no sugar to its beer and lets it age naturally. It employs only six to sixteen people, but does an impressive business, some 33,000 barrels each year. Call the brewery ahead to check on tours. North of Geyer's is the Star of the West Milling Company, dating from 1845 and one of the very few flour mills in the state.

18th-century flavor with 20th-century amenities.

ZEHNDER'S, Main Street, Frankenmuth, MI 48734. On M-83, 7 minutes from I-75. Telephone (517) 652-9925. Hours: 11 a.m.-10 p.m. daily (Sundays and holidays 11 a.m.-9:30 p.m.), lunch available till 4 p.m., dinner available any time, breakfast in the Coffee Shop 7 a.m. Closed Good Friday, last Tuesday in November. Full bar service. Background music. Free parking. Credit cards: AE, MC, V. Reservations never necessary, though there might be a waiting line. Reservations taken Mondays through Saturdays depending on availability; not taken on Sundays and holidays.

ZEHNDER'S CHICKEN,
CHEESE, AND BROCCOLI QUICHE

Bake 1 pie shell, using your favorite short pastry recipe

(or see index in this book). Mix 4 beaten eggs and 1 cup cream. Pour into the pie shell. Add ¼ cup diced cooked chicken, ¼ cup diced Cheddar cheese, ¼ cup diced cooked broccoli, 1 teaspoon Frankenmuth Seasoning (or substitute seasoning salt). Bake at 325 degrees for 35 minutes or until cooked in the center. Remove from oven, and let stand 5 minutes. Cut and serve immediately. Serves 4-6.

Hints from the Winters: As in many restaurant recipes, the oven heat and timing might not agree with what's possible in the home oven. We suggest a higher temperature; thequiche will probably take closer to 45 minutes.

ZEHNDER'S RHUBARB CRUNCH

Mix 3 slightly beaten eggs, 1½ cups sugar, and ¼ cup flour together. Add 4 cups sliced rhubarb, and pour into a 9 x 13-inch baking pan. Mix crunch topping: combine 1 cup brown sugar, 1 cup flour, 1 cup oatmeal, and ½ cup soft butter. Spread this over the rhubarb mixture. Bake at 375 degrees 35-40 minutes. Serve with whipped topping.

48
TERRY AND JERRY'S O SOLE MIO
Bay City

Benvenuto to Terry and Jerry's, and that's exactly how you'll feel—welcome. A family-owned restaurant for nearly thirty years in downtown Bay City, O Sole Mio has a faithful clientele of regulars who enjoy its special cheerfulness and well-worn comfort as well as Chef Jerardo's memorable assortment of Italian specialties. If the restaurant's name puzzles you, you should know that Terry and Jerry (Teresa and Jerardo) were musical and comedy entertainers before turning to entertainment of another sort.

The decor is an attempt at classical Italian, but decor isn't really important to management or guests. The table settings? When we last visited, along with paper mats over a bandanna-printed oilcloth were a red Victorian pressed-glass sugar bowl and a Perrier bottle with a fresh daisy in it. The lounge is primarily a waiting room for hungry customers and a center of activity by red-checked-skirted waitresses picking up drinks for the dining room. The dining room adjacent to the bar and kitchen has an awkward traffic pattern, and we strongly urge you to reserve a table in La Vinezia, away from the salad bar and entryway.

Dinner, if you don't order a pasta dish, includes entree, soup, salad bar, and a spaghetti course. The salad bar, unlike many, is small but perfectly adequate and includes only two dressings, Italian and tarragon, plus a few appetizers (excellent olives). We had a tasty and hot seafood chowder and ordered at an extra charge (well worth it) a small loaf of delicious homemade garlic bread. There is a choice with the spaghetti of the familiar meat sauce or a spicier *pomidoro*, a mushroom-tomato sauce redolent of basil. Especially popular entrées are the beef tenderloin with parsley sauce, the scampi dishes, and various pasta *speziale*, including ravioli, spaghetti Caruso, manicotti, and a tantalizing *calimari* (squid stuffed with shrimp and simmered in a *pasta con sarde* sauce Sicilian). Daily specials from Chef Jerardo are also available. There's a limited wine list, and though one can visit the wine "cellar," connoisseurs will be disappointed. But the prices are fair; different-sized bottles are on the list; and you can order Californian and Italian wines by glass or carafe.

One warning—go to O Sole Mio hungry. You'll be served enough food to please the most famished longshoreman. And you might even have room for the cappuccino, made with your choice of Chocolate Mint, almond liqueur, or Amaretto. (Take home your cup as a souvenir.) Presently Terry and Jerry's is undergoing a change in ownership and management. But it's within the family and involves those familiar with the business. Because of this we expect it to continue as one of Michigan's restaurants offering good values. *Buon appetito.*

Let them entertain you.

TERRY AND JERRY'S O SOLE MIO, 1005 Saginaw Street, Bay City, MI 48706. In city center. Telephone (517) 893-3496. Hours: 5-10:30 p.m. daily, 4-9 p.m. on Sundays. Closed Mondays and most holidays. Full bar service. Children's menu. Background music. Free parking after 5 p.m. in adjacent lot. Credit cards: AE, MC, V. Reservations recommended.

TERRY AND JERRY'S
FRAGOLI UMBRIACOTTO

Literally, this means "drunken strawberries"; you'll be able to guess why. Clean 1 quart of strawberries. Reserve 4 whole berries for garnish, and cut the remainder in half. Toss berries in a bowl with 1 tablespoon light brown sugar till all are coated. Add 1 ounce Grenadine syrup, 1 ounce Triple Sec, 2 ounces Bacardi dark rum, 2 ounces Galliano (or Florentino, Napolitano, or Allegro—all imitations). Marinate in refrigerator 2-3 hours. Pour berries and marinade into 4 wine glasses to serve. Float 1 tablespoon Sicilian Gold Wine on top of each serving (optional). Top with whipped cream and the reserved berries. Vary by adding one of the following to the berry mixture: 2 ripe peaches, 1 pineapple, or 1 ripe papaya (each peeled and cut the same size as the berries). 4 servings.

49
BINTZ APPLE MOUNTAIN
Freeland

Primarily a ski resort, Bintz Apple Mountain is a spacious, attractive A-frame "chalet," part of a larger complex including a ski lodge and shop, cider mill, bakery, and gift store—all set in the midst of an extensive fruit farm and orchard on the west bank of the Tittabawassee River valley that provides a bluff for a ski slope. The main dining room in the steak house seats about 140 and offers views in two directions, one of the slope and one of the lawns by the entryway. We suggest that you try to be seated in the west part of the dining room closest to the windows. The room has specially designed carpeting and several interesting metal sculptures in an apple motif, the latter the work of Max Heiderer, brother-in-law of John Bintz, who with his father in 1949 planted 1,300 apple trees in what was once a cornfield here. If at all possible try to visit the resort when the apple blossoms are in bloom.

Dinner is price fixed depending on entrée and includes a wide variety of steaks (choose your own from the steak counter), charcoal-broiled lobster tails, or steamed Alaskan King crab legs accompanied by baked potato, a copious salad bar, homemade cider bread, apple ice cream, and beverage. The only *à la carte* item on the menu is apple pie at an additional charge. The wine list is quite satisfactory, comprising about fifty selections—a Chateau d'Issan of a fine year, a Vosne Romanée shipped by Bouchard, and when we visited, a special Chianti Classico for only $7. Californian carafe wine is also available. Cocktail specialties include the Apple Knocker (cider and vodka) and for dessert, especially, Keoki Coffee, a blend of Kahlua, Creme de Cacao, brandy, and whipped cream.

Would you believe a ski chalet in an orchard?

BINTZ APPLE MOUNTAIN STEAK HOUSE, 4535 N. River Road, Freeland, MI 48623. About 10 miles northwest of Saginaw; take 675 to Tittabawassee Road, then west on Tittabawassee, following signs. Telephone (517) 781-0030. Open for dinner only 5 p.m. Monday-Saturday, 1 p.m. Sunday. Closed Christmas Eve and Christmas (call about other holidays). Full bar service. Background music, pianist in lounge Tuesday through Saturday, band and dancing Friday and Saturday (except in December, dancing 6 nights a week, in July and August on Saturday only). Credit cards: AE, MC, V. Reservations highly recommended, essential on weekends.

BINTZ APPLE MOUNTAIN'S
PEAS AND PEANUTS SALAD

Here is a rather simple recipe from the salad bar given to us by the manager. It is supposedly one of the most popular items on the salad bar. Mix equal parts of salted Spanish peanuts and frozen green peas. Blend together equal parts of Miracle Whip (Kraft) and sour cream. Add to the peas and peanuts to sufficiently coat them.

JAN'S APPLE PIE

We wish we'd been given a recipe more interesting and more appropriate to the theme of Bintz Apple Mountain. Fortunately, we're able to offer a recipe for one of the best apple pies we've tasted, a specialty of Dr. Janet Alleman-Brooks, Professor of Education at Michigan State University, world traveler, and pastry expert.

For the crust, blend together 1 cup flour, ⅓ cup shortening (Crisco is good), and ¼ teaspoon salt. Place 3 tablespoons ice water in a separate bowl. Blend in a small amount of the flour mixture till a paste is obtained. Add the rest of the flour mixture, and blend lightly till the dough holds together. (Don't overwork the dough.) Form into a ball, wrap in waxed paper or plastic film, and refrigerate 15 minutes or longer. Roll out on a lightly floured board, and line a 9-inch pie tin or plate.

For the filling, pare and slice 8 tart apples (Jan uses Paula or Sloan). Mix together ½ cup brown sugar, ⅛ cup white sugar, 1 teaspoon cinnamon, 1 tablespoon flour, a dash of salt, and a "titch" of nutmeg. Blend this mixture into the apples slices, and fill the pie shell. For the topping, mix together ½ cup sugar and ¾ cup flour. Cut in ⅓ cup butter till mixture is crumbly. Sprinkle over the filling in the shell. Bake in a preheated 400-degree oven for about 40 minutes or until done—the top with be browned, and the crust golden in color. Good warm or cool. You might want to top the pie with ice cream or nutmeg-flavored, sweetened whipped cream.

50
CAPTAIN NEMO
Midland

The name "Captain Nemo" reflects here the decor more than the cuisine; except for the excellent clam chowder, the restaurant doesn't particularly specialize in seafood. But there is a plush Victorian atmosphere with red velvet upholstery, flocked metallic wallpaper, dark wood, and smoky mirrors of which the captain of the Nautilus would highly approve. You can dine in the Victorian Room for breakfast or dinner and in the Drawing Room for luncheon and dinner. The latter is an uncommonly charming array of semiprivate booths that are intimate, mostly comfortable, and—some say—romantic (each booth with drawable draperies), though others might find all this a bit flashy. We think Captain Nemo would have been enchanted. The Drawing Room is especially conducive to good conversation and relaxed dining. Indulge in make-believe for an evening.

Interestingly the luncheon menu with four different special offerings daily is in some ways more appealing than the standard fare, nice as it is, offered in the evening. These require some chef preparation and inventiveness. Aside from the specials the most popular item for lunch is the Hot Brown, an open-faced turkey, mushroom, and cheese sandwich. At dinner shrimp à la Nemo and the Captain's Sword (tenderloin steak kebab) are the most frequently ordered dishes. Some twenty wines are available, none of them distinguished, but you'll find something adequate. Carafe wines are also on hand.

It's more important to make reservations by table number here than at most restaurants. If at all possible, get booths 4, 5, 7, or 8—ideal for two and suitable for four. Or, for a party of four to six, we strongly recommend booth 6 and, for eight to ten, the Captain's Table in a small private room. We also suggest that you stop in at the Library Lounge either before or after dinner (don't confuse it with the Lobby Bar downstairs). The Library, overlooking the pool, is an intimate and warm room decorated as you can imagine (but even better) with tufted Victorian sofas, reproductions of famous paintings, wood paneling, and shelves of books. And that view of the pool isn't so incongruous, if you recall the luxurious library on Captain Nemo's Nautilus in Jules Verne's *20,000 Leagues Under the Sea.*

Plush Victoriana.
CAPTAIN NEMO, in the Ramada Inn, Midland, MI 48640. On Midland Road off Route 10. Telephone (517) 496-3130. Hours: breakfast 6-11 a.m. (till noon Saturdays and Sundays) in main dining room (Victorian Room); luncheon 11:30 a.m.-2 p.m. Mondays through Fridays, dinner 5-11 p.m. daily. Full bar service. Background music. Free parking. All major

credit cards. Reservations required for booths in the Drawing Room.

RAMOS GIN FIZZ

There is something at Captain Nemo far removed from the twentieth century. This is our own recipe for a most romantic cocktail that seems suitable to the ambience of the restaurant. Place in a blender container 2½ tablespoons bar sugar (superfine sugar), 2 teaspoons orange flower water, 2 tablespoons lemon juice, 2 tablespoons lime juice, 1 to 2 egg whites, 3 jiggers gin, 3 jiggers heavy cream, ½ teaspoon vanilla extract, and 6 cubes of ice. Blend on high speed, and strain into large stemmed glasses. Serves 2.

51
THE SHANGHAI PEDDLER
Midland

The exterior of the Shanghai Peddler is deceiving—located in a supermarket shopping area and giving the impression of a typical Chinese-American restaurant. But you'll be delighted to find such a comfortable and inviting interior. Oriental murals, cane-backed chairs, potted bamboos, wooden railing and trim in Mandarin red, a collection of Chinese porcelain and scuplture in the lounge, and a large Buddha from San Francisco comprise one of the most appealing Chinese restaurants we've seen.

But most noteworthy are the several small semiprivate rooms flanking the main dining room, three that seat four people, two for six, one for groups of eight or ten (the Moon Room with a circular doorway), and a larger glassed-in small banquet room that will seat up to eighteen. These rooms are available at a slight extra cost ($6 for the small banquet room, $4 for the Moon Room, and $2 for the others), and they are well worth it for intimate and ambient dining. But if you're unable to reserve one, we suggest instead one of the three booths in the lounge, more of a dining room than the name suggests: the small bar seats only four persons and most beverages are consumed at the dinner table. The menu features the various cooking styles of China, with each dish labeled according to origin (Hunan, Shanghai, Cantonese, Szechwan, Mandarin) and with hotly seasoned dishes marked in red. Items on the dinner menu that we haven't seen often in restaurants include the shark's fin soup, Mongolian fire pot dishes, tea-smoked duck, and a succulent velvet chicken, as well as more than 100 other items. Dinners for two to six persons may also be ordered. The house specialty is No. 77, stir-fried beef with a ginger sauce, a hot and spicy creation from Szechwan.

The luncheon menu is less elaborate, and of special note is the Tuesday buffet, served from 11:30 a.m. to 2 p.m. with offerings changing weekly. The wine list is the best we've seen in the Saginaw Bay area and includes a Chateau Greysac at a good price, a Margaux 1975, Latour 1973, and many more fine offerings. In operation since 1977, the Shanghai Peddler is still proving itself, but all the signs are promising. The quality is high and the facilities excellent. With this combination, Mrs. Chow, the accommodating manager, should read only successful prophecies in her fortune cookies.

Get "Shanghaied" in Midland.

THE SHANGHAI PEDDLER, 1908 S. Saginaw Road, Midland, MI 48640. Near intersection with Route 10, in shopping plaza. Telephone (517) 835-7726. Hours: 11:30 a.m.-(:30 p.m. Mondays through Thursdays, 11:30 a.m.-10:30 p.m. Fridays and Saturdays, noon-8 p.m. Sundays. Full bar service. Children's menu. Carryouts. Chinese background music. Free parking. Credit cards: AE, MC, V. Reservations recommended, especially on weekends; required for private rooms.

THE SHANGHAI PEDDLER'S CHUNG KING PORK

Once you get started on Chinese cooking, you can become carried away. For example, our friends Ev and Mike Roberts are a two-wok family, and the Wangs, a two-kitchen family (one gas for Chinese and one electric for American). The best hint we can offer on Chinese cooking is to read through the recipe carefully and plan to prepare all ingredients ahead so that you won't be in the midst of stir-frying and suddenly need to stop to slice up the water chestnuts. This dish from the Shanghai Peddler is also described as double-cooked pork slices.

Simmer 1⅓ pounds pork hind leg (fresh ham) or substitute the loin or another lean cut) in water for 30 minutes. Remove and drain. Slice thinly into pieces about 3 by 2 inches. Remove the stem and seeds from 3 green peppers; then slice. Cut 2 garlic stems into sections. Stir-fry the pork in 3 tablespoons peanut oil for 1 minute. Add 1 tablespoon hot soybean paste, 1 tablespoon sweet soybean paste, 2 teaspoons sugar, ½ tablespoon sherry wine, and 1 tablespoon soy sauce. Stir-fry quickly over high heat for less than 1 minute. Remove and serve. Serves 2 to 4, depending on number of dishes being served. A large clove of garlic can be substituted for the stem. All these ingredients are sold in Chinese or specialty food stores.

52
LIXEY'S
East Tawas

Though its full name is Lixey's China House, the restaurant is an unusual combination of the Chinese and American with which we're all familiar. Unlike most, the American here is as popular as the Chinese. And by American we refer specifically to the freshly caught, well-prepared lake perch served at luncheon and dinner at a very attractive price. The most frequently ordered item on the menu, it's deep fried in a delicate breading that combines ground toast and almonds. Yuk Lum, one of the owners, tells us that some of her customers leave when the perch supply is depleted.

Lixey's Chinese food, too, draws its share of enthusiasts. Occasionally crowds of up to 30 students commandeer the rear of the restaurant and regale themselves with Chinese specialties. To our tastes, the egg rolls and fried rice are nothing to become excited about. But the ribs, barbequed in a fine sweet and sour sauce, are very meaty and tasty, and the soups and sauces with some of the stir-fried dishes are based on a rich, flavorful chicken broth. The combination platters, the Lichee shrimp, and Gum Lo Wonton (no. 25 on the menu, an imaginative sweet-sour mix of shrimp, barbequed pork, chicken, and wonton) are worth trying. Mainly Cantonese dishes are prepared here (the subgum is a favorite), though there are two spicier, hotter Mandarin items (nos. 6 and 7, Kung Po Gai Ding and Kung Po Char Shu Ding, a chicken and pork dish, respectively) and a spectacular Volcano Steak, subtly seasoned with ginger and served with a flaming wine sauce. Other American offerings are available—sandwiches, steaks, chicken, and seafood to suit most tastes. But what we think is special about Lixey's is the perch and the Chinese ribs.

It's not a fancy place; no attempt is made at creating an atmosphere. This looks like a plain American "cafe" with only a few hints of its Chinese proprietorship. Lixey's in the name, by the way, is a holdover from the past; Bing and Yuk Lum simply didn't get around to changing it. Bing Lum, who came from Hong Kong in 1948, must be surprised that the restauant is better known for its fried perch than for its Oriental offferings. You might try the crumb and almond mixture on your own perch next time, or think about a Chinese dinner featuring Lixey's Chow Steak Kew (see recipe below).

The prices are moderate, and there are a few bargains on the menu. Dress is casual. If you like live fish, too, stop in at the lounge on your way out and see the 55-gallon aquarium.

Splendid lake perch—the Chinese way.

LIXEY'S CHINA HOUSE, 600 E. Bay Street, East Tawas, MI 48730. Two miles north of Tawas City on U.S. 23. Telephone (517) 362-5201. Hours: luncheon 11 a.m.-2 p.m., dinner 5-10 p.m. in winter (till 11 p.m. in summer). Closed holidays. Full bar service. Children's menu. Background music. Free parking. Credit cards: MC, V. Reservations recommended on weekends.

LIXEY'S CHOW STEAK KEW

This is no. 4 on the Chinese menu at Lixey's—a good Cantonese dish with a crunchy contrast of fried noodles. First, deep fry 1-2 ounces Chinese vermicilli noodles till crisp, and drain well. Set aside. Slice ½ pound beef tenderloin thin-ly. Prepare vegetables: slice 1 small onion thinly (about ¼ cup); slice ½ green pepper thinly (¼ cup or more); slice ¼ pound water chestnuts and ¼ pound snow peas. Mix sauce: combine ½ cup chicken broth and 1 tablespoon soy sauce. Soak 5 large dried Chinese mushrooms in warm water ½ hour or more till softened. Cut in small pieces. Finally, mix 2 tea-spoons cornstarch with 1 tablespoon chicken broth (or wa-ter).

To cook, heat 2 tablespoons peanut oil in wok or skilllet. Add onion and green pepper, and cook about 2 minutes till slightly wilted. Remove from pan. Add beef (and more oil if necessary). Sprinkle with garlic powder and cook just till meat loses its pink color. Remove. Add vegetables and mush-rooms. When bubbling hot, return meat, onions, and peppers to pan. Stir-fry till peapods are tender-crisp. Add sauce mix, stir well. Add cornstarch mixture, and cook till thickens. Place in serving bowl, and top with fried noodles. Serves 4-6.

Hints from the Winters: For very thinly sliced beef, slice when it's slightly frozen. Exact quantities are not important. Add more or less of the vegetables, depending on what you like best. Button mushrooms are good in this, too. The chicken broth for the sauce may be canned or made from a bouillon cube, but homemade is much better. Noodles also may be the canned chow mein noodles, but the freshly fried Chinese vermicilli makes a difference.

53
THE SPRINGPORT INN
Harrisville

From our experience, there are hardly any special places for eating on the northeast coast of Michigan. Two notable exceptions are near Harrisville, and both offer fine, home-style cooking. One is a higher-priced, immaculate lodge on the shore of Lake Huron (see Big Paw Resort), and the other is a large, old Victorian house south of town. The Springport Inn will have its greatest appeal to the nos-talgic. For us, it pleasantly recalls one of our favorite bed-

and-breakfast spots in Ireland (in fact, there are ten low-priced rooms here for an overnight stay). The small "front parlor" with wicker furniture serves as a waiting room; and the dining room, seating about thirty, boasts an especially inviting table for twelve in front of the fireplace. The furnishings are from decades ago, and the old building has a musty aura faintly reminiscent of Miss Havisham's house in Dickens' *Great Expectations*.

If you visit the Springport Inn, we hope you'll have the chance to speak with its white-haired owner, Kathleen Wyman, who came to the United States from the Irish Midlands in 1923 but glows with the graciousness and charm of Eire. Her tales of the "old days" and of her growing up in the area are fascinating. Today her sister, daughter, and two grandchildren cook the "home dainties," but Kathleen's gentle influence is still apparent.

The luncheon menu at the Springport features a daily special plate lunch, homemade soup, sandwiches of the customary variety, and freshly baked pie or ice cream for dessert. But what impresses us most is the family-style dinner specialty of Irish stew, with "dumplings so light you'll need two forks—one to eat them with and one to hold them on the plate." Second in popularity with us and other customers is the pan-fried chicken; and we recommend that you order with it (at a slight extra cost) those marvelous dumplings. Other successful entrées are the baked ham, sautéed chicken livers, pork chops with applesauce, pan-fried whitefish, and fried shrimp. Luncheons and dinners are reasonably priced and include a relish bar, potato, vegetable, chicken soup, and a freshly made variety bread basket.

An authentic Irish hostelry—and a bargain.

THE SPRINGPORT INN, U.S. 30, Harrisville, MI 48740. Between Alpena and Tawas City; 1 miles south of Harrisville's city center. Telephone (517) 724-6308. Hours: luncheon noon to 2 p.m., dinner 5-9 p.m. daily. Closed October 15-Memorial Day. No alcoholic beverages. Half-servings for children. Background music. Private beach. Free parking. No credit cards. Reservations recommended, especially for large parties.

IRISH SODA FARLS

Mrs. Wyman has given us—no, sadly not the prized dump-
ling recipe (Peggy wouldn't even let us see her cooking them
in the kitchen)—a family recipe for Irish soda bread (*Aran
Crojc*). This you won't see on the Springport menu because,
as Mrs. Wyman told us, it's too difficult to keep perfectly
fresh. Sift ½ pound flour (2 cups). Add 1 teaspoon bicarbo-
nate of soda (baking soda), ¼ teaspoon salt. Stir in ¼ pint
(½ cup) buttermilk or sour milk (buttermilk is better), and mix
to a soft dough, kneading very lightly. Turn onto a floured
board, and shape into a round about ¼-inch thick. Cut into
fourths. Bake on a floured griddle, turning, about 4 minutes.

Hints from the Winters: Baking on a floured griddle is a
bit tricky. When we first tried this recipe, the bread wasn't
done in 4 minutes. We find the results more satisfactory if
the bread is shaped so that it's 1 inch thick. Cut into wedges,
and place on a lightly oiled iron skillet, and bake about 10
minutes a side in a 375-degree oven. Serve immediately.

54
THE BIG PAW RESORT
Harrisville

Here is home-style cooking as good as you'll find in a beautifully kept, simple rustic dining room overlooking the shore
of Lake Huron. The resort—nestled amid 70 acres of pine
forest and reached after an adventurous drive down a narrow,
winding old logging road, now blacktopped—has been in
operation since 1940, and three generations of Yokoms work
here. For the last seven years Ron and Nancy Yokom have
managed the place, but their parents Emily and Chuck and
children Sandy and Steve all contribute to making the Big
Paw ideal for quiet relaxation and seclusion in the charming
log cabins and for superior home-cooked meals in the small,
immaculate lodge.

The kitchen at the resort is much like your own at home,
with the addition of a ten-burner gas range. The spotless
dining room has three large windows facing the lake and

woods nearby. To take full advantage of all the Big Paw's meals and activities, you might want to stay overnight (or longer) in one of the cottages, each with its own fireplace, small fridge, and private paths to the lodge and beach. Aside from the swimming beach and boating, there are lighted tennis courts, lawn sports, and a game room for inclement weather. The Big Paw is one of only 24 state resorts and hotels chosen to receive AAA's four-diamond accommodation rating, along with such notables as the Dearborn Inn and Mackinac Island's Grand Hotel.

But the fine food is the main attraction for us. A single menu is offered for breakfast and dinner, the latter including juice, entrée, potatoes, vegetable, salad, freshly baked bread or rolls (see the muffin recipe that follows), dessert, and beverage (no wine). Particularly popular is the unusually tender pan-fried New York strip steak, and for dessert you might be lucky enough to be served deep-dish apple pie or an uncommonly good chocolate fudge cake. Other main dishes are likely to be baked chicken, Swiss steak, or roasts. On Sundays the Yokoms host a weiner roast on the beach (what makes it special is that they bake their own hot dog buns). Meals are served family style and are price fixed at one rate; and since the menu is determined on a daily basis, you might wish to call ahead for information on what's cooking. You must either be an overnight guest or make reservations well in advance to eat at the Big Paw. But the lack of selection and the bother of advance planning are minor problems if you consider the quality of food, hospitality, and pleasing surroundings. If you're only passing through the area and the Big Paw can't accommodate you, try the Springport Inn nearby—a very different kind of spot with fine home cooking, also.

Genuine food, genuine hospitality.

THE BIG PAW RESORT, Route 23, Harrisville, MI 48740. Between Alpena and Tawas City on Lake Huron; 1½ miles north of town. Telephone (517) 724-6326. Hours: breakfast 8:30-10 a.m., dinner 6 p.m. only. Closed November 1, open again on Memorial Day weekend. No alcoholic beverages. Background music. Free parking. Credit cards: MC, V. Reservations required.

BIG PAW'S SOUR CREAM MUFFINS

Combine ⅓ cup sugar, 1 teaspoon baking powder, ½ teaspoon baking soda, 1 teaspoon salt, and 1¼ cup flour. Add 1 tablespoon vegetable oil, 1 egg, and 1 cup sour cream. Stir the mixture; do not use a beater. Fill muffin tins half full. Bake in preheated 350-degree oven for about 20 minutes. Makes 12 muffins.

Hints from the Winters: We adore these, spread with butter, and they've become a regular part of our own Sunday breakfasts. Unlike many muffins that are too sweet for our tastes, these are an excellent complement to eggs and breakfast meats. After 20 minutes' baking, either remove or test with a toothpick—don't wait for them to brown. They stay quite pale in color. Also, we found them to stick to muffin liners and prefer to bake them in well-buttered tins.

55
THE EMBERS
Mount Pleasant

The Embers is another of those *de rigeur* stops for vacationers traveling north or south on U.S. 27. And if you're not too far from Mount Pleasant, it's worth the extra drive to dine here any time. The dining room is large and the tables well placed and well spaced. It's an attractive contemporary room with lots of rusts and black, dark wood and brick, an open-hearth charcoal grill, and an interesting papered ceiling. We suggest that you reserve one of the appealing alcove dining areas, each opening onto the main room through brick archways and affording seclusion for parties of six or eight. We like the table settings, too: white cloths with pewter service plates. If you've been here before and some of this doesn't sound familiar, you should know that the Embers has recently been redecorated, and they've done an excellent job of it. And, yes, the quality has remained consistently good since 1958, when the restaurant first opened.

The menu suits most tastes. From the charcoal grill come such entrées as steaks, lobster tails, lamb chops, and shish kebab. "Gourmet" possibilities include chicken Mornay, trout Amandine, Lebanese-style lamb shanks, stuffed shrimp and flounder, Chinese shrimp, seafood *de Jongh*, and medallions of pork tenderloin Oscar. But the *pièce de résistance* is the Embers "Original One-Pound Pork Chop," created by the dedicated owner Clarence Tuma. Although some diners may not be charmed by large pork chops, we think this one would likely change their minds. Thankfully, Mr. Tuma has provided this recipe to his customers for years, and we think it so flavorful and so versatile an entrée that we include the recipe here so that you can try it at home if you're not adventurous enough to order it in Mount Pleasant. All dinners are served with a relish tray, bar cheese and garlic toast, Caesar or another salad of your choice, potatoes, homemade bread, sweet rolls, and coffee or tea. After dinner you might wish to choose something from the dessert cart—the Chocolate Angel Torte is exquisite.

The Embers also offers a few specials. On Sundays it is frequently duck with an orange glaze; and, mainly in the winter twice a month on Fridays, certain specialty nights are arranged. Call ahead about these. More than forty wines are offered. Many are satisfactory, but few are exceptional. We suggest that you examine the complete list because it contains a few errors in categorization—if you don't find what you want where you think it should be, it might appear elsewhere. Some California wines are also offered by the glass.

Glowing better than ever.

THE EMBERS, 1217 S. Mission Street, Mount Pleasant, Mi 48858. South of city center. Telephone (517) 773-5007. Hours: dinner 5-9 p.m. Monday-Thursday, 5-10 p.m. Fridays and Saturdays, Sunday brunch 10 a.m.-2 p.m., Sunday dinner noon-8 p.m. Closed Labor Day, Memorial Day, July 4, December 24 and 25, New Years Day. Full bar service. Children's menu. Background music. Free parking. Credit cards: AE, MC, V. Reservations taken Mondays through Thursdays only.

THE EMBERS ORIGINAL
ONE-POUND PORK CHOP

Mix together ingredients for the marinade in a large saucepan: 2 cups soy sauce, 1 cup water, ½ cup brown sugar, 1 tablespoon dark molasses, and 1 teaspoon salt. Bring to a boil. Let cool. Place six 1-pound pork chops vertically in a deep pan with the bone side up. Pour over the marinade. Let stand overnight in refrigerator. The next day, remove the chops from the marinade, place in a baking pan, and cover tightly with foil. Bake in a 375-degree oven until tender, about 2 hours.

While chops are baking, combine red sauce ingredients in a heavy saucepan: 1 tablespoon dry mustard, ½ cup brown sugar, ⅓ cup water (mix these first, leaving no lumps), one 14-ounce bottle Heinz catsup, and one 12-ounce bottle Heinz chili sauce. Bring to a slight boil, and remove from heat. When the chops are tender, remove from oven, dip each into the red sauce, and return them to the baking pan. Bake 30 minutes at 350 degrees or until slightly glazed. For additional flavor, place finished chops on a hot charcoal grill, as high as possible from the coals. Let cook slowly, not more than 15 minutes. Serves 6. Chef's note: both marinade and red sauce can be reused if brought to a boil and then refrigerated or frozen.

Hints from the Winters: This is a most versatile recipe for pork chops. We've cooked them both with and without the final charcoal grilling and have at times broiled them briefly in the oven before serving if we wished a darker crust. The chops work well with a barbeque theme and also make a marvelous Chinese entrée, accompanied by stir-fried vegetables and rice. We find that a 350-degree oven is sufficient for the initial baking, and we usually check the chops for tenderness after about 1½ hours. Smaller sizes of chops can also be cooked successfully by this method.

If you like our recommendations, tell the proprietor. If you don't, tell us. Write Beech Tree Press, 2673 Ramparte Path, Holt, Michigan 48842.

56
THE DOHERTY HOTEL
Clare

"The North begins with lunch at the Doherty in Clare"—
this was one definition that appeared in a 1979 column by
George Cantor in the *Detroit News*. That's what we always
thought, too (but the definitions are legion). For years a stop
at the Doherty either going to or coming from points north
in Michigan has been traditional. Depending on our travel
schedule, we've stopped for breakfast, lunch, and dinner
innumerable times and have always enjoyed it. The Doherty is
a short and convenient side trip off the freeway; it's open daily
all year; it's reliable and consistent; and its Bloody Marys (see
the recipe below) are among the best in the state. The prices
are moderate, and for a restaurant of this quality there are
even some bargains.

At breakfast the smoked pork chops, bacon, and toast from
homemade bread are favorites of ours. The luncheon menu
changes daily and offers something to please most tastes.
The specialties and most popular dinner entrées are prime rib
and broiled whitefish, but the evening menu is much more
reassuring than this suggests. Try, for instance, the broiled
pork tenderloin on rice, Chinese pepper steak, turkey with
Poulette sauce, veal Parmesan, or marinated steak kebab
with curried rice. Steaks, seafood, ham, baby beef liver, pork
chops, Chateaubriand for two, fried chicken, Spanish omelette, spaghetti, and some hearty sandwiches and salads
round out the versatile and appealing menu. Dinners include
soup (the Canadian cheese is a treat), potatoes or wild rice or
vegetable, rolls, beverage, and a generous salad table. A daily
dinner special is also offered, on the order of freshly caught
trout or a chef's favorite. Wines can be had at very attractive
prices. No great chateaux are offered, but the Doherty has a
fine selection, practically all under $20. (The 1966 Siglo from
Spain is worth considering.) The cellar is open to the public,
too. Why not take a look before deciding?

The Doherty Hotel was opened in 1924 by the first A. J.
Doherty, the grandfather of the present owner, A. J. Doherty
the third. It has always been successful—even in the Depres-

sion years, since oil was struck in the area. It has even been touched by notoriety: in 1938 a member of Detroit's Purple Gang was shot here. But the notorious has now become the nostalgic—A. J. Doherty guesses that at least 500 people, including the infamous Art Flint, have claimed to have been in the bar on the Saturday night that Isaiah Leebove was shot and killed.

It's fun reading the *Clare Sentinel* of May 20,1938; on the same day as the shooting, the paper felt it was worth printing that "120 air mail letters have been sent out from Clare in observance of National Air Mail Week," that "according to state bug men the farmers of the west side of Isabella County can expect to be troubled by grasshoppers," and that the weekend special at Chaffee's Grocery was pecans at 21¢ a pound. The special edition of the *Sentinel* came out in 1979, and two other items caught our interest: on April 10, 1919, "Michigan did well...burying the Wine and Beer amendment abomination by a majority of more than 100,000. It may just as well be understood now that this state is done with the saloon and will have no more of it," and on November 14, 1918, under the headline "Woman Suffrage Carries in Michigan by Fair Majority" are the lines "We predict that this result will end the attempt of the liquor interests to again revive the saloons in Michigan." If the prophecies had been accurate, there might have been no Purple Gang shooting, and there certainly would have been no famous Doherty Bloody Marys. So much for history.

The hotel has four dining rooms, though most customers see only the two open regularly to the public. The main dining area has minimal and unobtrusive decor but is pleasant enough. We prefer the bar because it's cozier and we like the comfortable banquettes. The best tables here are numbers 2, 3, and 5 for parties of two to four and number 4 for groups of six. On Wednesday through Saturday here a pianist plays in in the evenings. In the winter the Doherty features special ethnic nights and offers an occasional dinner stage show. For New Years Eve it arranges a package of hotel room for two, prime rib and champagne dinner, two Bloody Marys in the morning, and a gourmet breakfast. (When we visited on Labor Day, the New Years Eve overnight packages were already sold out.) There is nothing elegant about the Doherty (yes, come as you are), but it has the appeal of a solidly established, perennially popular hostelry. And we hope it will continue that way—there *is* an A. J. Doherty the fourth.

One of the last of the good downtown hotel restaurants.
THE DOHERTY MOTOR HOTEL, 604 McEwan Street, Clare, MI 48617. On Business U.S. 27 in the city center. Telephone (517) 386-3441. Hours: 7 a.m.-10:30 p.m. (on Friday and Saturday till 11 p.m., on Sunday till 9 p.m.). Open year round. Free parking. Children's menu. Full bar service. All major credit cards. Reservations recommended, but *not* taken for Easter or Mothers Day.

THE FAMOUS DOHERTY BLOODY MARY

Interestingly, according to James Beard, from 1929 until about 1945 the Bloody Mary was made with gin instead of vodka (and was a creation attributed to the comedian George Jessel). As Mr. Beard writes, "The vodka Bloody Mary swept the country and still remains the eternally popular morning and hangover drink." It generally incorporates one constant, a dash or two of Worcestershire sauce. This one is an exception, but an extraordinary one. For each drink, fill a 14-ounce glass with ice cubes. Add 1½ ounces vodka, a good pinch of celery salt, and about 1/9 ounce or 1 teaspoon (or less to suit your taste) of Smither's Beef Tea. Fill to the top with V-8 juice, and add a lime wedge and celery stalk.

Hints from the Winters: We like this very much but prefer ours a bit hotter. Try adding a drop or two of Tabasco, or use the new Spicy-Hot V-8. We also like the lime *squeezed* into the drink for a bit more tartness. For those in the Lansing area, Goodrich's Shop-Rite, our favorite store, carries the Beef Tea.

57
THE OLD MILL
Rockford

The restoration of a feed mill, ravaged by fire in the late 1960s and renovated in 1970 as a restaurant, was the first step in a proliferation of shops and studios known as Squires Street in the century-old village of Rockford. The Old Mill, a bakery and coffee shop, has a country kitchen atmosphere with a wooden floor, early American furniture, and a full measure of bric-a-brac on the walls. It's generally bustling—patrons have come here from every state in the Union and from 37 foreign countries (check the guestbook). Even the host John Kvieck admits it becomes overcrowded at times. But that's part of the fun: sociability is thrust upon you. There are two dining areas downstairs, one adjoining the bakery and the other in the porch, as well as tables upstairs where you can escape the crowds if you wish. We prefer to stay downstairs with the tourists, watch the cooks at work, and smell the baking bread.

The Old Mill has a very limited menu, printed on a baker's bag. There are five options for breakfast, and at lunchtime until closing you have a choice of a few sandwiches, salads, or a quiche Lorraine, followed by dessert, notably seasonal fresh fruit pie or the Old Mill's specialty, mile-high lemon pie. Or have an old-fashioned malted shake instead. The French dip roast beef sandwich is most popular, and we also like the Old Mill special: sliced ham or turkey with a choice of cheese and garnishes on toasted white or black Kimmel bread. It's good, flavorful bread, made of unbleached flour and honey. Sandwiches may be ordered in two sizes, worth considering if the pie tempts you. The soups vary; try the chicken corn chowder. On a warm, pleasant day you might prefer to buy carryout sandwiches from the Old Mill and picnic beside the picturesque Rogue River dam.

We like the Old Mill for its easy charm and as a resting place while browsing in the interesting little shops on Squires Street, many of them antique or crafts oriented—a toy train museum, clocksmith, apple and cider shop, rug hooking studio, hand-blown glass emporium, toymaker's shop, and others. While in Rockford, you might also stop in at the Little Red Shoe House, a factory outlet of Wolverine World Wide, manufacturers of Hush Puppies shoes. It's located only two blocks to the north and offers some real bargains. Two yearly events in the village are a start-of-summer celebration in June and the October cider festival.

Historic Michigan recaptured.

THE OLD MILL, 31 Squires Street, Rockford, MI 49341. About 10 miles north of Grand Rapids; 1 block west of Main Street, near the railroad. Telephone (616) 866-4306. Hours: breakfast 8-10:45 a.m., luncheon 11 a.m.-8 p.m. Closed Sundays and holidays. From the end of October to June 1, closed at 4:30 p.m. No alcoholic beverages. Children's menu. Background music. Free parking. No credit cards or reservations accepted.

LEMON MERINGUE PIE

Bake one 9-inch pie shell, and cool. (See Kenville's for an excellent pie pastry.) Mix together 1½ cups sugar, 4 tablespoons cornstarch, 4 tablespoons flour, and ¼ teaspoon salt. In a large saucepan heat 1¾ cups water to a boil. Lower the heat to medium, and slowly add the sugar mixture, stirring all the while. Cook, stirring, for 5 to 7 minutes till the mixture holds a line when cut through with a spoon. (Don't let it boil.) Remove from the heat. Beat 4 egg yolks slightly, and slowly stir in one-half of the hot mixture. Return this mixture to the pan. Cook, stirring, for 3 to 5 minutes until it thickens and mounds (remove some with a spoon and place it on the surface; it should remain mounded). Remove from the heat. Stir in 1 tablespoon grated lemon rind, ⅓ to ½ cup fresh lemon juice (to taste), and 2 tablespoons butter. Cool.

Pour filling into the cooled pie shell. Beat 4 egg whites and ½ teaspoon cream of tartar till foamy. Sprinkle in ½ cup sugar, 1 tablespoon at a time, and beat until mixture holds stiff peaks. Pile onto the pie filling. Bake in a preheated 350 to 375-degree oven till browned, about 10-12 minutes. For a "mile-high" lemon pie, use 6 or more egg whites and increase the sugar—use 2 tablespoons to each egg white.

58
THE THORNAPPLE VILLAGE INN
Ada

An especially tasteful blend of old and new in both interior design and cuisine, the Thornapple Village Inn is a welcome newcomer to the dining scene in Michigan. There's an easy sophistication here in the apple green, white, and light oak of the walls and furnishings, in the superb use of space and subtlety of structural patterns, in the classical background music, and in the creative Continental and American cooking. Featured in the April 1979 issue of the prestigious *Interior Design* magazine, this is certainly one of the most aesthetically appealing restaurants in the state. The exterior of the building conforms to the rather pedestrian style of the shopping center in which it's located and gives no hint of the three charming dining rooms on the ground level or the extremely well-executed wine cellar with its adjoining dining area.

If the Thornapple isn't busy, we suggest that you first look at all the rooms and then make a choice. For lunch we like the airy, brick-floored Solarium, with trailing greenery that evokes the sunny outdoors, even in cloudy Michigan weather. Our favorite room for dinner is the Harvest Room, a solid, warmer, and more formal setting with a cozy fireplace and an understated and effective use of stained glass. For semi-private dining for four persons, try table 12 in the corner; two other somewhat secluded corner tables (numbers 4 and 7) that seat five or fewer are especially comfortable, with upholstered, sofa-like seating. Large parties (up to eight people) should ask for Harvest 8 in the center of the room. The River Room is, however, the most popular dining room, with a view of lawn and the Thornapple River both day and night since the lovely grounds are lighted after sunset. It's tempting to be seated here at the chic green velvet banquette, accentuated by antique-framed mirrors overhead, but we still prefer the tables for four near the windows in the River Room.

On warm days lunch and cocktails are also served on the deck. And, off the wine cellar on the lower level—which shouldn't be missed no matter where you dine—is the Vintage Room, with its wood-burning fireplace and latticed windows affording a look at the cellar itself, the most dramatic we've seen in a Michigan restaurant. Hundreds of well-organized bottles are kept at a constant temperature in a room specifically designed for both storage and observation. You might want to select your wine in the cellar before dinner. The list is impressive and growing larger (about 300 to choose from).

Bottles are also displayed outside the River Room, but we opt for a browse through that remarkable cellar.

The menu at the Thornapple Village Inn is a pleasure—and a dilemma. For both luncheon and dinner there are specialties on the basic menu (in itself more than adequate) as well as "selections from the inn repertoire," which vary each day. About every three months the basic menu, too, is changed, making the temptation to return irresistible. Let's look at just a few of the extraordinary dinner entrées: baked fillet of whitefish with Norwegian lobster sauce, mousse of scallops with sauce Duglere, veal scallops à la Berrichone (with mushrooms, shallots, and cheese), lamb chops en croute with mint butter, navarin of lobster Paul Bocuse, veal sweetbreads Piccata, brace of Pharoah quail Derby (see the recipe following), roast duckling Amaretto, steak au poivre verte (with green peppercorns, flamed with brandy), and breast of capon au vinaigre. Specialties for luncheon, though less extensive, include quiche Niçoise, whitefish meunière, baked eggs Thornapple, and croque monsieur as well as a few of those unbeatable "selections from the inn repertoire."

At least two exemplary soups are regularly offered, a classic French onion and a soup of the day. The appetizers are mouth-puckering: among others likely to be on the menu are Westphalian ham with seasonal fruit, escargots Bourguignonne encased in pastry, potted mushrooms with artichoke hearts, and smoked rainbow trout with horseradish cream. As for desserts, there are sweets to satisfy the most demanding palate: frozen chocolate soufflé with rum, profiteroles with caramel, fresh pastry varié du chef, and fruit with crème fraîche, among other possibilities.

The restaurant is under the able management of the two co-owners, D. J. Sulisufaj, who came to Michigan from Albania in 1965 and has worked at, among places, the Four Seasons in New York, and Robert Shafer, the chef and a graduate of the Culinary Institute of America (our favorite CIA). It's unlikely that you'll meet Mr. Shafer (and we'd just as soon keep him in the kitchen), but probably you'll be greeted by Mr. Sulisufaj, whose charming manner combines a refreshingly tasteful humility and sincere professionalism.

Distinctive dining and design—one of the best.

THE THORNAPPLE VILLAGE INN, 445 Thornaple Village Drive, S.E., Ada, MI 49301. Just east of Grand Rapids; take the Ada exit from I-96. Telephone (616) 676-1233. Hours: luncheon 11:30 a.m.-2:30 p.m., dinner 5:30-10 p.m. Closed Sundays and holidays. Full bar service. Background music. Free parking. Credit cards: AE, MC, V. Reservations strongly recommended. We suggest reserving a day in advance for a weeknight and four or five days ahead for Friday and Saturday evenings. You might dress up a bit.

THE THORNAPPLE VILLAGE INN'S
BRACE OF PHAROAH QUAIL DERBY

Preheat oven to 450 degrees. Mix 2 cups cooked rice pilaf with 5 tablespoons *foie gras* with truffles. Season to taste. Stuff 4 quail with this mixture. Secure cavities closed with toothpicks. Wrap each bird with a strip of bacon. Heat 1½ cups brown stock with 1½ tablespoons butter to a simmer. Mix ½ cup Madeira wine, 1½ tablespoons arrowroot; add to brown stock mixture. Return to a simmer. Stir until it starts to thicken. Season to taste, and set aside. season the stuffed quail. Place in an ovenproof glass pie plate. Bake 20 minutes or till the juice runs clear when breast or thigh is pricked. Transfer quail to a suitable platter, and coat with the Madeira sauce, reserving some to be served at the table. Garnish with fresh watercress and dilled baby carrots. Serves 2.

Hints to the Winters: Don't use a purchased pilaf mix unless you know it's very mild in flavor; the spices might overwhelm or disagree with the *foie gras*. We include a recipe for pilaf below. Purchase a good French *pâté de foie gras* (with or without truffles); a favorite brand of ours is Louis Henry. You can find a recipe for brown stock in any good cookbook if you don't regularly keep it on hand. Julia Child's first volume of *Mastering the Art of French Cooking* includes a classic version and a shortcut based on canned bouillon.

For the pilaf, heat 1½ tablespoons butter in a skillet. Add 2 tablespoons finely minced onion, and cook till transparent but not browned. Add ½ cup long-grain rice (better yet, Indian Basmati rice), and cook till rice begins to turn opaque. Sprinkle lightly with salt and garlic powder (you can sauté a small clove of minced garlic with the onion, but the powder works surprisingly well here). Pour in 1 cup chicken stock (or canned   chicken broth or 1 teaspoon instant bouillon dissolved in 1 cup hot water). Bring to a boil. Cover skillet, and turn heat down to simmer. Steam for about 14 minutes. Check rice; if liquid is not absorbed, cover and steam a few more minutes. (Timing depends on what kind of rice you're using. We find that Basmati is done in 12-14 minutes, but long-grain Carolina rice takes about 18 minutes.) Fluff rice with a fork. Season to taste with salt and more garlic powder. This should be sufficient for the quail stuffing. If you were serving the pilaf as a side course (it's excellent with lamb), this quantity will serve 2. For more servings, the recipe can be successfully doubled or tripled. For better flavor as a side dish, you might want to mix in 1-1½ tablespoons butter after cooking.

59
THE CASTLE
Grand Rapids

It's difficult to choose the most appropriate superlative for the Castle. Built in the late 1880s as a private residence, the stone, castle-like building in the Heritage Hill district of Grand Rapids was converted in 1978 into an unusually appealing restaurant. Dwight Dodge, the chef and one of the owners, tells us that he doesn't know of another restaurant like his—and we certainly agree. The Castle is elegant, an overused and misused word that for once can be applied accurately. There's not a trace of tinsel or plastic here. There's not a hint of the Disneyland for adults that prevails in so many self-proclaimed "sophisticated" and "distinctive" restaurants.

The building itself has been designated a local, state, and national historic site. We believe that the restaurant deserves an equally impressive designation for what it's attempting to do. The cooking is clearly gourmet, the service—by waiters in formal, turn-of-the-century attire—meticulous, the background music soft and restful and just that—background, the decor splendid, the linens immaculate, the furnishings antique, the crystal Portuguese or Fostoria, the service plates and flatware silver, the China Bavarian. The original natural wood has been preserved in the foyer, hall, and staircase. Each of the five Edwardian-style dining rooms has its own special appeal. We think (but still keep debating it) that we like the Emerald and Garnet Rooms best. But each room is small enough for really gracious dining; all have antique gas or electric wall sconces, fireplaces, and interesting chandeliers, also often gaslit. In case you have a favorite gem color, the other rooms are labeled Onyx, Amethyst, and Sapphire.

The seven-course dinner is price fixed, and the menu is fixed, too—but designed to please and enabling the kitchen to bestow loving care on each item. Included for what was last year about $23 are appetizer, soup, fish, main course with two side dishes, salad, dessert, and coffee or tea. The menu changes at least every four days and is planned four to six weeks in advance, so you may call well ahead for information. Since it does vary, we can give you only an idea of the cuisine served here. The soup might be cream of onion, chilled cream of tomato, or chilled canteloupe. Appetizers range from hot mussel crepes to curried ham to chicken Jezebel to frog legs with herbed butter. The fish course? Possibly baked swordfish or chilled salmon with mayonnaise *verte*. *Tournedos Rossini*, veal Orloff, veal cutlets Vêndome, and chicken breast stuffed with cheese and topped with Paprikash sauce have been popular entrées. The chicken is especially well prepared at the Castle—always boneless, skinned breast and often poached to preserve its juiciness and tenderness. Frequently seasonal fresh fruits Chantilly are offered for dessert, and the delicate crepes are exquisite. The wine list has an exceptional selection and a commendable price range (there are many more than 100 to choose from). It leans towards the French reds, although the favorites of Mr. Dodge are white Burgundies. You might ask his advice when you're selecting since he's quite knowledgeable in this matter, too.

There are two seatings and three arrival times in the evening (7, 7:45, and 8:30), and for the last two the table is yours for the entire evening. Occasionally there's entertainment in keeping with the tone of the restaurant—for example, a harpist or cellist. Luncheon is available only on Thursdays and in two seatings, at 11:30 a.m. and 1 p.m. Two courses are served, an entrée and salad or soup, with bread and coffee or tea, at a fixed price. Crepes, *ragouts*, and other entrées are lighter than those on the dinner menu; dessert is extra.

We give the highest marks to this most elegant and stylish place. The polished charm of that self-contained, aristocratic world of the Edwardians has been beautifully simulated by Dwight Dodge and John Wittmann. And the culinary imagination and expertise more than match the surroundings. Wear jackets; dress up for the Castle.

Without a doubt, beautiful and one of the best.

THE CASTLE, 455 Cherry Street, S.E., Grand Rapids, MI 49503. In city center. Telephone (616) 459-8000. Hours: luncheon 11:30 a.m. and 1 p.m. Thursdays only, dinner Wednesday through Saturday at 7, 7:45, and 8:30 p.m., Sunday brunch (table service). Closed Sunday evenings, Mondays, Tuesdays, and holidays. Full bar service. Background music. Valet parking is mandatory from the management's point of view. All major credit cards. Reservations necessary (call well ahead, especially for Saturdays).

AMBER CHICKEN
WITH TARRAGON SAUCE

This isn't a Castle recipe, but one of our own of which we think Mr. Dodge would approve. Use 4 whole chicken breasts for four persons. Halve the breasts, bone and skin them, and pound them very thin between sheets of waxed paper. Salt and pepper. Dip each piece first into flour, then into a mixture of 2 beaten eggs with 1 tablespoon milk added, and last into dry bread crumbs (a little nutmeg or Parmesan cheese mixed into the crumbs is a good variation). Set the chicken in the refrigerator while making the sauce,

For the tarragon sauce, heat 2 tablespoons butter. Add 2 tablespoons flour and mix. Cook very slowly for 2 minutes, without browning. Gradually add ¾ cup chicken broth and ¼ cup dry white wine or Vermouth. Cook until thickened. Add

¼ teaspoon crumbled dry tarragon leaves, salt and white pepper to taste. Remove from heat. Stir in a mixture of 1 egg yolk beaten with 3 tablespoons heavy cream. Return to heat and cook till just hot. Sauté the chicken in a mixture of 2 tablespoons butter and 2 tablespoons oil, about 5 minutes until cooked through and golden brown. Turn only once. Place on a heated platter or in individual ramekins, and spoon a little sauce on each piece of chicken. Sprinkle with chopped parsley if you wish. Serves 4.

This dish can be varied in many ways with additions of garnishes and the use of other sauces. The *escallopes* can be placed on hot ham slices (or over ham and cheese and then set in a hot oven a few minutes to melt the cheese). The sauce can be converted into a citron sauce by omitting the tarragon and substituting lemon juice to taste for some of the wine or broth. In this case a lemon slice and sprig of parsley would be an attractive garnish.

60
THE SCHNITZELBANK
Grand Rapids

There's a lot of variation in German restaurants. They are generally appealing to the hungry because portions are often large and the cooking style is hearty. One thinks of mounds of noodles and potatoes and dumplings; of thick slabs of dark bread, plump sausages, and rich meaty gravies; of pungent scents emanating from the kitchens of *hausfrauen*. And they can occasionally offer "gourmet" cuisine, as has Karl Ratsche's in Milwaukee. But what we find appealing about the Schnitzelbank is the tasteful Bavarian decor (no *schmaltz* here) and the changing luncheon and dinner menus. The prices are most satisfactory, and everything is included—even dessert and coffee. The popular house specialties are wiener schnitzel, roast leg of lamb, baked spareribs, pot roast with potato pancakes, braised lamb shanks, and sauerbraten. Some German entrées include a choice of sauerkraut or red cabbage. Other dishes worth considering, if offered during your visit, are the German pepper steak, beef rouladen, boiled pig hocks or smoked Mettwurst with sauerkraut, and Viennese roast chicken. In addition, well-prepared steaks and chops are always available.

The restaurant was started in the building next door in 1932 by the grandfather and father of the present owner, Karl Siebert. It moved from its location within a drugstore to its current site in 1938 and was further expanded in 1954. Today the Schnitzelbank holds more than 350 people; and, we warn you, it generally *does* hold that many at serving hours. We believe that credit for its popularity must go to the highly professional management of Mr. Siebert and the fine cooking of the chef, Karl Staeglich, who has been with the restaurant for 24 years. Mr. Staeglich, originally from Hamburg, Germany, was fortunately discovered in 1955 cooking on a cruise ship, the *S.S. Italia*. Ever since, he's been turning out some of the best German food in Michigan.

A minor disappointment is the rather limited wine list, with the best selection white dinner wines, especially and understandably the German varieties. The house wine is a California red and New York white.

Wunderbar!

THE SCHNITZELBANK, 342 Jefferson Avenue, S.E., Grand Rapids, MI 49502. In city center, ½ block north of Wealthy Street. Telephone (616) 459-9527. Hours: luncheon 11 a.m.-2:30 p.m., *à la carte* and afternoon suggestions 2:30-5 p.m., dinner 5-8 p.m. Closed Sundays, major holidays. Full bar service. Children's portions. Background music. Free parking. Credit cards: AE. Reservations recommended on weekends.

THE SCHNITZELBANK'S SAUERBRATEN

We are pleased to present this recipe for a house specialty at the Schnitzelbank. We received one other recipe for Sauerbraten (see Weathervane Inn); why not try them both?

Combine ½ cup dry red wine, ½ cup red wine vinegar, 2 cups cold water, 1 medium sliced onion, 8 peppercorns, and 3 bay leaves in a 3-quart saucepan. Bring the marinade to a boil, remove from heat, and let cool to room temperature. Put a 4-pound bottom beef round roast, trimmed, into a deep

crock, and pour marinade over it. The marinade should come
halfway up the sides of the roast. Cover the crock, and refrigerate for 3 days, turning each day. After removing the roast
from the marinade, pat dry with paper towels. Strain the
marinade, and retain the liquid. Discard spices and onions.

Melt 3 tablespoons lard in a 5-quart roasting pan. Add the
meat and brown it on all sides over high heat. Transfer the
meat to a platter. Save 2 tablespoons of the fat in the roasting pan. Add ½ cup chopped onions, ½ cup chopped carrots,
and ¼ cup chopped celery to the fat. Cook 5 minutes over
moderate heat until light brown. Add 2 tablespoons flour, and
cook 5 minutes longer. Add 2 cups of the retained marinade
and ½ cup water. Bring to a boil. Place roast in pan, cover,
and put in a preheated 350-degree oven for about 2 hours.
Remove meat to the platter; cover with foil to retain heat.
Pour liquid from roasting pan into a saucepan, and skim off
the surface fat. Add ½ cup crumbled ginger snap cookies,
and cook for 10 minutes, stirring often. Strain and return to
saucepan, and let simmer till ready to serve. Slice the roast
into moderately thick slices, and arrange on the platter.
Sauerbraten may be served with boiled potatoes, dumplings,
noodles, and red cabbage. Serves 6-8.

61
THE BELTLINE BAR
Grand Rapids

For north-of-the-border Mexican cooking with south-of-
the-border prices and geniality, the Beltline can't be beat.
One of the most popular gathering places in Grand Rapids,
it hums with activity day and evening. Ask almost anyone
on the streets of Grand Rapids what's the best restaurant
bargain in town, and the name "Beltline Bar" comes up with
astounding frequency—that's how we first discovered it a
couple of years ago. It has an American roadhouse/tavern
exterior and decor, which is about the same as saying it
has no decor at all. There are two eating areas, a small
paneled dining room and a spirited bar with jukebox and
pool table (MSU students rate it as a "best bar").

At noontime here it's a swarming mass of people, mostly employees on their lunch hour; when it gets close to 1 p.m., there's a simultaneous rush for the door. Still, there's something to be said for a place that can get you in and out within an hour or less. Which brings us to service—this may be the fastest in the Midwest. On our last visit, in the midst of the midday crush, we received our food from a nimble-footed, jeans-clad waitress only four minutes after putting in our order. (If you want to linger over a cocktail, make it clearly known or order from the menu later.)

Ask almost anyone in Grand Rapids about Mexican food, and the answer (in affectionate tones) is usually "the wet burrito at the Beltline Bar." The Famous Wet Burrito is an assemblage of beef, refried beans, lettuce, and tomatoes, wrapped in a tender flour tortilla and covered with a red sauce and melted cheese. One variation of it here is the all-meat burrito, and we've heard what seems to be a running argument among Grand Rapiders as to which is best. The dish has acquired a local fame, we think as much for its size as for its flavor. Portions are huge; you might consider sharing (after all, if you want another, you can get it in minutes). We're not sure if the dish originated at the Beltline, but we first tasted it here years ago. Since then we've noticed more and more "Famous Wet Burritos" showing up on menus throughout the state.

Our own preference, though, is for the "Natchos"—also enormous and we think more interesting. There's a pleasing contrast in flavors and textures, and it's most appetizing to look at. (see our version in the recipe below.) Other Mexican dishes include acceptable cheese and meat enchiladas, tostadas, tacos, guacamole salad, and a combination plate. The recipes originated with a one-time Mexican chef, but now some good, fast American cooks dish up the food. And they start dishing up Mexican food at 8 in the morning! The specialty drinks are tequila-based cocktails, Mexican root beer, and a Sangria described as "lemonade with Spanish Burgundy, brandy, and fresh fruits." The house dessert is all-American: hot apple pie with ice cream and whipped cream.

The Beltline should appeal to families and the budget-minded, too. There's nothing on the menu that costs more than $5, including a bargain 8-ounce sizzler steak for $4.25

(last summer), served with garlic toast. "Gringo" sandwiches run from $1 to $1.65, and most other items are in the $2-3 range.

An American setting with a Mexican flavor, a bargain.
THE BELTLINE BAR, Division at 28th Street, Grand Rapids, MI 49508. Take the 28th Street exit off I-96; about 6 miles west on 28th Street. Telephone (616) 245-0494. Hours: 7 a.m.-2:30 a.m. (breakfast service starts at 7 a.m., Mexican food served 8 a.m.-1 a.m.). Closed Sundays and holidays. Full bar service. No children's portions (ask for extra plates, and share). Free parking. Credit cards and reservations not accepted.

NACHOS

This is our re-creation of the Beltline dish (we spell it the Mexican way). We think you'll like to try this at home, though you might miss the lively atmosphere that goes with it at the tavern. First, make a quick Mexican red sauce by combining 1 can Gebhardt's enchilada sauce, one 6-ounce can tomato sauce, and one 6-ounce canful water. Add salt, pepper, and Tabasco sauce to taste. Stir or whisk to blend, and simmer this while preparing the Nachos.

If you have ovenproof plates or individual platters, cook and serve the Nachos in these to save doing extra dishes and to help keep the food warm while eating. Put a layer of crisp taco chips or tostada shells on each plate. Top with layers, in order, of canned refried beans (about 12-16-ounce can for 4 servings), taco meat (use for 4 servings 1 pound ground beef and 1 package dry taco seasoning mix, prepared according to package directions—or omit meat; it's still good), about 2 cups in all of shredded Mozzarella cheese, and about 2 cups in all of shredded medium Colby cheese (or medium or sharp Cheddar). Sprinkle over the top 2 cups (in all) sliced black, ripe olives. Pour some of the sauce around the outer edge of the dish, and sprinkle a little over the cheese. Bake 10-15 minutes at 350 degrees till the cheese is melted and the dish is hot. Serve with side dishes of chopped tomatoes, chopped onions, quacamole, sour cream, and extra sauce. Serves 4 generously. Beer is best with this.

62
LAKOS THE OTHER PLACE
Grand Rapids

"Old Grand Rapids" is the theme of Lakos The Other Place, and considerable thought and effort have gone into the re-creation within a single restaurant of various periods in the history of the city. The exterior of this new tavern, with its hammered metal roof, stained-glass windows, and weathered wooden boardwalk, might be more imposing if the building weren't located on one of Grand Rapids' busiest commercial strips. Unless you know about Lakos, you might confuse it with one of the dozens of fast-food chains that appear at regular and too close intervals along this highway. But once inside, we think you'll enjoy the imaginative approach to decor, the variety of ambience in the five dining rooms and bar, and some fine menu offerings.

Each room represents a special period of local history. The bar, off the Gay Nineties Room, is topped with cherry-wood and faced with carved, hand-painted decorations, and the room features attractive white pine tables and blue plush Victorian chairs. In the Factory Room are tables built to represent cabinetmakers' benches with tools laminated into the surface. The Lumber Room displays heavy solid pine beams and booths, and the fireplace here also serves the adjacent Log Cabin Room in the center of the tavern, with chairs hewn from single pine log sections and split log tables grouped around the rough fieldstone fireplace. Finally there's the Agricultural Room, especially appealing to children and with some more private booths. Throughout the tavern the lighting reflects each period—pewter candle-type sconces, plain industrial lights, and "gaslights." Dimmer switches are built into each booth so that guests can create their own mood lighting. You might find some of this a bit gimmicky, but the intentions are so good that we find it quite acceptable.

The luncheon menu offers assorted sandwiches, seafood, small steaks, salads, and three varieties of crepes. But the most popular item by far is the Blackboard Special, which varies daily and might, if you're lucky, turn out to be one of the fine preparations of the Greek cook: braised lamb shanks, lemon chicken, or beer-battered shrimp, for example. These are often sold out, so arrive early.

The dinner menu offers the usual steak and seafood assortment, barbequed ribs (our students' favorite), plus several more creative dishes: sautéed frog legs Provençale, turbot Veronique, veal Cordon Bleu, pork scallops Esterhazy, duckling flambéed in Grand Marnier, and a surprising veal Piccata—blending veal, cheese, bacon, and mushrooms. The wine list, like the dessert list, is limited but adequate (at times even a 1972 and 1973 Lafite is available). There are four house wines available by the glass or liter. On Fridays and Saturdays a pianist offers some light music in the Gay Nineties Room.

Imaginative restoration of old Grand Rapids.

LAKOS THE OTHER PLACE, 2500 28th Street, Grand Rapids, MI 49508. Take the 28th Street exit off I-96 and drive west about 2 miles. Telephone (616) 942-4740. Hours: luncheon 11 a.m.-4 p.m., dinner 5 p.m.-midnight. Closed Sundays and holidays. Full bar service. Entertainment 9 p.m.-midnight (till 1 p.m. on Fridays and Saturdays). No blue jeans. Free parking. Credit cards: MC, V. Reservations recommended, especially for groups larger than 4 persons.

BRAISED LAMB SHANKS

These are economical and delicious. Heat 1 tablespoon oil and 2 tablespoons butter or margarine in a pressure cooker pan. Over high heat, brown 2 lamb shanks, each weighing from ¾ to 1 pound. When meat is browned all over, pour off the fat, and salt and pepper to taste. Add 1½ cups beef broth, ¼ cup dry white wine or dry Vermouth, 1 medium whole peeled onion, 1 teaspoon pressed or finely minced garlic and ⅛ teaspoon dry thyme leaves, crumbled. Stir well, place on high heat, and put the lid on the pressure cooker with the pressure regulator in place. When the regulator begins to rock gently, turn down heat and maintain a gentle rocking of the regulator for 50 minutes. Let pressure go down of its own accord.

Remove cover when pressure is reduced. Discard onion. Place lamb shanks on a platter and keep warm. To the pan liquids add ⅛ teaspoon Kitchen Bouquet or Brown Quik (for an appealing color), 1 tablespoon dry red wine, and salt and pepper to taste. Mix 2 tablespoons cornstarch with 2 table-spoons cold water or beef broth. Add gradually to the simmer-ing gravy till desired thickness is reached. To serve, pour some gravy over each shank, and sprinkle with about 2 tablespoons chopped parsley. Serve remaining gravy in a separate bowl. Serves 2.

Some notes: Accompaniments might include buttered wide egg noodles or potatoes. Vegetables we like with lamb are green beans, zucchini, and roast carrots and onions. This dish, as well as all other lamb dishes we prepare, is best cooked in a pressure cooker (though, of course, it can be oven-braised or simmered on the range for several hours). The pressure cooker separates out the fat nicely and leaves the lamb exceptionally tender. We think the results are so good that, if you like lamb, it's worth buying a pressure cooker, even if you don't use it for anything else.

63
GUTHERIES
Wyoming

Nestled in a small grove of trees in the Ramblewood shopping center, Gutheries is sleek, chic, expensively decor-ator designed, and ultracontemporary. At first glance a more subtle rendition of one of the prefabricated and plastic high-priced chains, it is in fact related to the Great Lakes Steak Co. but is much more imaginative and interesting than what you might expect. The interior is a sophisticated blend of angles, planes, and patterns in wood, showcasing hand-made pottery, green plants, and effectively illuminated pen-and-ink drawings by Allen Reid of Ann Arbor—Tolkien-like, amusing, and meriting your scrutiny. The sunken lower level serves as a lounge and waiting area, and the three dining rooms are intimate without being in any sense confining. We especially recommend Gutheries to those who enjoy an in-crowd experience where atmosphere is almost as impor-tant as food.

The luncheon menu offers several creditable choices: pork tenderloin Cordon Bleu, chicken Divan, beef tenderloin medallions with Bernaise, beef Stroganoff, and more traditional American dishes such as a hefty four-egg omelette with a choice of fillings. There's a "chef's turn" that varies daily: a meat entrée (possibly stuffed pork chop with baked apple), a fish dish such as pan-fried walleyed pike, and a sandwich.

Evening customers here tend to choose the prime rib and steak. But some other options worth considering are scrod Darné (a broiled fillet topped with crabmeat, broccoli, and Hollandaise), veal da Vinci (breaded medallions sautéed in seasoned tomato, onion, and Vermouth), steak *au poivre*, beef Wellington, chicken Kiev, stuffed trout with Choron sauce, baked shrimp and scallops in sauce Mornay, scampi, and an excellent veal Cordon Bleu, stuffed with Yorkshire ham and Havarti cheese. Our own preference for dinner, however, runs to the chef's weekly preparation: on the order of *tournedos Rossini*, roast duckling, or steak and crabmeat sauced with Bernaise. A few additional offerings are labeled "lighter choice" for the less hungry—a nice touch.

Soup and salad are included; but vegetables, even potatoes, are à *la carte*, so be prepared to add two or three dollars to the price of the main course. There's a choice of two salads: tossed mixed greens and the trendy spinach with hot bacon dressing. An offbeat variation on the serve-yourself theme is the soup bar at Gutheries—with three soups, always seafood chowder and the other two changing daily. The wine offerings are somewhat sketchy, and years aren't listed. The restaurant imports its own wines and revises the list twice a year. But we'd like to see Gutheries provide a selection more in keeping with the style of the place.

A voguish setting and menu.

GUTHERIES, 2759 W. 44th Street, Wyoming, MI 49509. Just southwest of Grand Rapids; 4 miles west of U.S. 131. Telephone (616) 538-0450. Hours: luncheon 11:30 a.m.-2 p.m., dinner 5:30-11 p.m. (Fridays and Saturdays till midnight). Closed Sundays and holidays. Full bar service. Background music. Free parking. Credit cards: AE, MC, V. Reservations not taken on Saturdays.

SAUTEED SHRIMP
WITH SHALLOT-WINE SAUCE

This is the sort of dish we can imagine having at Gutheries, though we haven't had it there. The style, however, is all Gutheries—lovely to look at, delightful to eat.

Heat 3 tablespoons butter. Add 2 large cloves garlic, put through a press or chopped finely, and 4 large finely chopped shallots. Cook a minute or so on medium heat until golden and translucent. Add ¾ pound jumbo shrimp (peeled and deveined), 1 pinch each of tarragon and marjoram. When the shrimp begin to curl and turn pink, add ⅓ cup American sauterne wine (or Chenin Blanc, Rhine, Reisling), 2 to 3 tablespoons dry sherry, and 1 tablespoon lemon juice. Salt to taste and generously grind on black pepper. When the shrimp are opaque (in all, about 5-6 minutes), they are done. Serve with rice. 2 large servings. With this dish we like to mix melted butter, sautéed mushrooms, and chopped scallions into hot boiled rice.

64
THE OLD SCHOOL HOUSE
Borculo

A combination of good American home-style cooking, a nostalgic background, and one of the best bargains in the state, the Old School House is fast becoming a major attraction in the little Dutch community of Borculo. The wood-framed building, surrounded by massive oak trees and once a four-room country schoolhouse, now houses three dining rooms, thanks to the vision of Shirley and Hersch Weaver.

The school, dating to 1908 and first built at a cost of $250, was closed down when the school system was annexed to nearby Zeeland. The Weavers had never operated a restaurant before and, except for the charming old building with its towering belfry, started absolutely from scratch in 1977. Fortunately, they retained the old chalk boards as originally installed (they now display the luncheon and dinner menus), the maple flooring, and the high, pressed-tin ceilings.

The three classroom-*cum*-dining rooms, still visited by former students and teachers, are now called the Lunch Box, the Kindergarten Room (with a collection of the school's class and graduation pictures from 1908 to 1970), and the Dutch Room. But the menus are the same in each. Marian Boetsma does most of the cooking, and it's really well done. For breakfast there are blueberry pancakes and muffins in addition to the predictable fare. When we visited, the lunch menu featured cabbage rolls, stuffed green peppers, lasagne, and liver and onions, each for $2.50, as well as sandwiches, salads, and soups—including the Dutch "buttermilk pop."

The menus change daily, although chicken is regularly served in the evening. Popular dinner entrées ($3.50 last summer) are those listed above in addition to barbequed beef short ribs (see the recipe following), rolled beef roast, ham, Swiss steak, pork and veal cutlets, quiche Lorraine, baked cod, and other seafood. Lemon pie, cream and fruit pies, hot fudge cake, and a full line of soda fountain treats are the dessert offerings. For parties of twelve or more, the Weavers will, with advance notice, arrange a family-style dinner.

In a way we envy those in the local community who attended this school many, many years ago and can now return to their old classrooms for something more pleasurable than lessons. And we commend the Weavers for preserving so well this dimension of Michigan history.

Nostalgic Americana at bargain prices.

THE OLD SCHOOL HOUSE, 9354 Port Sheldon Road, Borculo, MI 49464. Six miles east of U.S. 31; 9 miles northeast of Holland. Telephone (616) 875-7200. Hours: summer 8 a.m.-9 p.m. Tuesday through Saturday; winter 8 a.m.-8 p.m. Monday through Wednesday, till 9 p.m. Friday and Saturday. Closed Sundays, holidays, and the month of January. No alcoholic beverages. Background music. Free parking. No credit cards. Reservations recommended.

THE OLD SCHOOL HOUSE'S
BARBEQUED BEEF SHORT RIBS

Mix together 1 cup catsup, ¼ cup brown sugar, ¼ cup vinegar, ¼ cup Worcestershire sauce, 2 teaspoons salt, and

1 teaspoon celery salt. Bake 3 pounds of beef short ribs for 2½ hours in a moderate oven. When ribs are browned, baste with above mixture, then drain, and baste the other side. Bake till glazed.

Hints from the Winters: Once again, this is a recipe that proves that simplicity and good eating go hand in hand. You won't taste catsup in the sauce. All you'll see and savor is a beautifully glazed, tender, meaty dish that will please the beef-and-potato fancier as well as the discriminating *bon vivant.* The working wife can shorten the cooking time by browning the ribs and then cooking (with about 1 cup beef broth or water and a clove-studded onion) in a pressure cooker for about 30 to 40 minutes. Finish by basting the ribs and baking in a 400-degree oven, turning once, for 30 minutes or so.

65
POINT WEST
Macatawa

No restaurant in southwest Michigan has a lovelier setting than Point West. The low, modern structure of brick, flagstone, and dark wood lies at the extreme west end of Lake Macatawa, close to the water and overlooking a large yacht basin. The main dining room faces the lake and features beamed ceilings, red chandeliers and carpeting, and floor-to-ceiling windows interrupted in the center by a handsome, massive fireplace. The decor is a mix—nautical, Victorian, and contemporary that somehow work very well together. There are two levels to enhance the exceptional view. We prefer the lower, nearer the windows (ask for one of the lower-level booths—actually velvet banquettes on the north and south walls of the room). The dining room is partitioned so that one part of it may be used for private gatherings, but on busy evenings it might be expanded to its full length, accommodating up to 300 diners.

The luncheon menu is fairly conventional and includes a daily special as well as a quiche of the day, crepes Monaco, Spanish omelette, and an unusual hamburger served with asparagus and Swiss cheese. Breakfast is also available, and an early morning view of Lake "Mac" is a pleasure. Sunday brunches are popular and vary each week. One recent menu, for example, included chicken à la king, broiled turbot, scalloped potatoes, Italian-style zucchini, poached eggs Florentine, bacon, sausage, and roast pork.

The most popular items on the dinner menu are prime rib, tenderloin Stroganoff, chicken Kiev, and sautéed Dover sole (when available). Other tempting entrées are the *tournedos Rossini*, baked Boston scrod, breast of chicken Oscar, and various well-prepared seafood and beef dishes.

There are some good, classic appetizers and a fine clam chowder. For dessert you might order a parfait, fresh warm pie, cheesecake, or the luscious French chocolate pie (see the recipe below). Another possibility is the house after-dinner drink, the Nauti-Mac, a foamy concoction of rum, Kahlua, and cream (take home the glass with its Point West emblem). The wine list is only fair, and vintages aren't on it. House wines are available by the carafe.

On warm evenings we suggest that you arrive early and enjoy a cocktail on the shaded waterfront patio, as nice as any we've seen in Michigan. Or, if it's cool, settle down near the round fireplace in the lounge. There's a band and dancing nightly in summer, and after Labor Day through the winter months entertainment on Wednesday, Friday, and Saturday. The dress code is "no blue jeans," but we'd go beyond that and recommend that men wear jackets to feel comfortable here. It's a rather formal place, though certainly far from stuffy. Prepare yourself, too for crowds and congestion in the summer months, especially on weekends. We highly recommend making a reservation or calling ahead.

A striking waterfront setting, inside and out.

POINT WEST, Macatawa, MI 49434. Seven miles west of Holland; follow Southshore Drive to the end. Telephone (616) 335-5894. Hours: breakfast 7-11 a.m., luncheon 11:30 a.m.-2:30 p.m. (in summer lunch is served all afternoon), dinner 5:30-10:30 p.m., Sunday brunch 10 a.m.-2 p.m. Closed Christmas Day. Full bar service. Children's menu. Background music, dancing, entertainment. Free parking. Credit cards: AE, MC, V. Reservations recommended.

POINT WEST'S FRENCH CHOCOLATE PIE

Bake four 9-inch pie shells. Combine 1½ pounds whipped butter and 2 pounds confectioners sugar; whip for 2 minutes with an electric mixer on low speed. Scrape the bowl; whip again for 2 minutes on medium speed. Scrape bowl, and whip once more for 2 minutes on high speed. Scrape down bowl. Add 8 ounces melted Bakers Chocolate, and whip on medium speed for 5 minutes. Scrape down bowl and whip on high speed for 4 minutes. Turn mixer speed to high and add 14 whole eggs, one by one, while beating. When all eggs are incorporated, stop mixer, scrape down bowl, add 2 tablespoons vanilla extract, and whip in. Spoon into pie shells.

Hints from the Winters: For one pie beat together 6 ounces, or about ⅔ cup, of whipped butter and ½ pound of confectioners sugar. Beat about 5 minutes, starting on low speed and ending on high. Add 2 ounces melted chocolate and 1½ teaspoons vanilla, and beat another 5 minutes. Add 3 whole eggs and 1 egg yolk, one at a time, while beating. Fill a baked and cooled pie shell. This is terribly (and marvelously) rich—plan on at least 8 servings.

66
THE BIL-MAR INN
Grand Haven

The Bil-Mar advertises itself as "~~Directly On~~ (*sic*) Darn Near In Lake Michigan." The corrected version is more accurate, as you'll see if you visit this popular restaurant built right on the beach of Lake Michigan. The only view is of lake and sand, and the water is only fifty feet from the windows. In fact, the Bil-Mar Inn is one of the very few places where beautiful sunsets and major storms on the lake can be enjoyed without any distractions. The menu is typically American, focusing on steak and seafood. The decor is semi-utilitarian, a bit plastic, and with a slightly dated look. There are two levels, but the lower is best; it has the windows and that wonderful view. (In fact, any table near the window on the lower level is fine. But avoid numbers 22, 23, and 29, by the bar entrance, and the six tables on the upper level near the main entrance.)

The separate bar and lounge, the Pirate's Den, has a more nautical decor and also one of the more colorful bartenders in the area: Bob sports a black beard, shaves his head every summer, and whips up some unusual specialties in 17-ounce fishbowl champagne glasses. (Ask him for the 101 or the Tidal Wave.) The atmosphere is casual, and the Bil-Mar is very busy in the summer months and on weekends. Do call for a reservation if you want to enjoy the view to its fullest.

The most popular items for lunch are fried lake perch and Melon Extraordinaire (a half melon filled with tuna salad). There are also a cold seafood platter, sandwiches, and salads. For dinner the Bil-Mar sells more prime rib, broiled whitefish, and fried perch than anything else, but the choice is certainly adequate: steaks, seafood, frog legs, pork chops, barbequed beef ribs, chicken livers, and Cornish hen among others. Entrées include salad and rolls. The house specialty is deep-fried cauliflower in an enticing, seasoned batter; this is available *à la carte* in two portion sizes. Desserts include lemon crunch pie (our own preference), key lime pie, and parfaits. The wine selection is weak (no chateaux, ubiquitous German whites, and too many of the sweet and soft).

Expect some traffic congestion, especially on Sundays; the Bil-Mar Inn is on a two-lane road just a short distance from a state park. The dress code: no swim wear or bare feet. **On the beach.**

THE BIL-MAR INN, 1223 S. Harbor Avenue, Grand Haven, MI 49417. One mile south of town on Lake Michigan. Telephone (616) 842-5920. Hours: luncheon 11:30 a.m.-2:30 p.m., dinner 5-9:30 p.m. (till 10:30 on Fridays and Saturdays). Service expanded during the summer. Closed Sundays, Thanksgiving, Christmas, and New Years Day. Full bar service. Children's portions. Background music, jukebox in bar. Free parking. Credit cards: MC, V. Reservations recommended.

67
THE HEARTHSTONE
Muskegon

We are only two among the throngs who are glad that Gina and Frank Lister turned from careers in psychotherapy to the culinary. There's a world of difference between shrinking heads and distending tummies. As a result, Muskegon can boast one of the very best soup and sandwich restaurants in the country. It's easy to drive past the place, since the Hearthstone is hidden in a motel on a busy intersection. But don't miss it, even if you need to do a bit of hunting. And don't let the plain exterior mislead you; it doesn't reflect the intimate, charming, and convivial atmosphere inside— somewhere between British pub and the upper East Side of New York.

The lighting is subdued, and the place is cozy and warm with flocked Victorian wallpaper, a small bar, a number of black booths, and a few less comfortable center-room tables. Larger groups should reserve the circular seating area referred to as the Fireplace—it is indeed built around a gas fireplace and accommodates up to twelve diners. Background music is a tasteful combination of chamber music and easy-listening jazz. One welcome feature is that the Hearthstone serves during most of the day and night, so you can eat well at any hour if you have a timing problem.

The appropriately small menu (beautifully hand lettered by Gina Lister) offers nine substantial sandwiches (plus frankfurters), five excellent salads, an innovative "sandwich of the week," and an extraordinary soup of the day. The breads are specially made for the restaurant in Grand Rapids. Of the sandwiches, we recommend the Hearthstone (corned beef, ham, sliced onion, and melted Swiss cheese) or the sandwich of the week, alternating between various "exotic and unlikely combinations of smoked ham, roast beef, turkey breast, salami, relishes, fresh vegetables, and garnishes." All sandwiches are gratifyingly available in half portions or partnered with the soup, a combination well worth ordering.

But the soup of the day is what fills us with admiration.

It's always freshly and carefully made and ranges from the conventional to the remarkable—for example, beef barley, Brazilian chicken and rice, Italian rice and cabbage, lentil, comsommé with crepes, gazpacho, Mulligatawny, American cheese and beer, seashell chicken, and many, many more. All receive the meticulous attention and TLC of the Listers, and many are enhanced by fresh vegetables that seemingly have been searched out on a daily basis. No one should leave the Hearthstone without trying the soup. If you're not sure you'll like it, the Listers will, because it's their special custom, provide you with a small free sample to help you decide.

Five refreshing renditions of traditional salads are also offered: tossed, chef's, antipasto, spinach with a hot sweet-sour bacon dressing, and *Salade Niçoise* with a classic *vinaigrette*. Soups and salads are served with warm egg-and-butter bread. California wine is available by the liter and half-liter. Prices are fair.

The best for soups and sandwiches.

THE HEARTHSTONE, 3350 Glade Street, Muskegon, MI 49444. In the Cornerhouse Motor Inn, 3 miles east of town on Business Route 96, across from Meijer Thrifty Acres store. Telephone (616) 733-1056. Hours: 11 a.m.-2 a.m., Sundays 5 p.m.-midnight. Closed holidays. Full bar service. Background music. Free parking in motel lot. All major credit cards. Reservations required for lunch, recommended any time.

THE HEARTHSTONE'S
CREAM OF CAULIFLOWER SOUP

In an enameled saucepan bring 1½ cups water and 1½ cups chicken stock to a boil. Add approximately 4 heaping cups fresh or frozen cauliflower (in flowerets), turn down heat, cover, and simmer until tender. When tender, remove about 2 cups of the cauliflower (without water), cover, and set aside. The remaining cauliflower may continue to simmer. In a second heavy-bottomed enamel saucepan (3½ to 4 quart size), cook ¾ cup minced celery and ¾ cup minced onion in 3 tablespoons butter for 8-10 minutes, until tender but not browned. When almost done, add 1 tablespoon sesame seed and stir together a minute or two . Add 3 tablespoons flour, and stir over moderate heat for a few minutes without browning. Remove from heat, cover, and set aside.

To the simmering cauliflower add 1 cup heavy cream, 1 cup milk, 1 teaspoon salt, and 1 teaspoon white pepper. Bring soup close to the boiling point, but don't let it boil. Pour the soup into the flour mixture. Simmer a few minutes over medium-low heat, stirring constantly with a wire whip or wooden spoon, until it thickens slightly. Purée the soup in an electric blender. Add the reserved cauliflower (cut up into small flowerets, if desired), and adjust the seasoning to taste. To serve, pour soup into tureen or soup cups. Garnish with either shredded Cheddar cheese, steamed broccoli flowerets, or buttered browned crumbs. Any one or a combination of these garnishes may be used; one of the Listers' favorites is the addition of steamed broccoli into the soup itself and a topping of browned and buttered crumbs. Serves 6 to 8.

Notes from the Listers on making soup: (1) Don't be afraid to experiment or substitute ingredients. Some of our finest soups have evolved from the addition of substitutions. (2) Garnishes should not be just an afterthought. They can be whimsical like the popcorn on our Cheddar cheese soup or can affect the flavor of the soup itself like the grated Swiss cheese in our potato and onion soup. (3) Cream soups may be made in advance of serving, making them more practical for presenting to guests. However, they should never be reheated over direct heat. We suggest using a *bain-marie* (double boiler) or microwave oven.

Hints from the Winters: This is a lovely soup, and the broccoli and crumb garnish makes it most attractive. For convenience, you can use canned chicken broth or mix some instant bouillon (though your own stock is much preferable). To save some time, the onions and celery can be sautéed in the microwave oven. In puréeing the soup, it's best to add only about 1 to 1½ cups soup at a time to the blender unless you want to decorate your kitchen walls with cauliflower soup. And be sure to hold down the lid on the blender when you start the machine. If you're using the crumb garnish, do use fresh bread crumbs rather than purchased dry ones. We find it convenient to crumble all our leftover bread into plastic bags and keep them in the freezer for making crumbs or bread stuffings. Then simply brown them in a little melted butter and set aside for garnishing.

68
THE CROSSWINDS
Whitehall

The Crosswinds is so new that we can't guarantee consistency on the culinary aspects of the restaurant, but we can tell you that for leisurely dining at the water's edge the appeal of its waterfront setting on White Lake is considerable. Sailing boats and launches from many Great Lakes harbors tie up on the 100 yards of dock that flank the building on three sides. The interior combines a nautical decor with an old logging theme, both appropriate for this area. The bar and the dining tables are handmade, and the management is collecting some interesting antiques for display. Of course, the best tables are by the windows. In the summer you can dine on the porch amid the pilings and have an unobstructed view of the water and vessels. The Crosswinds is also one of the few restaurants in Michigan where boaters can reserve a dock berth along with a table for dinner. And for the occasional boater and chinook fisherman, charter fishing boats are available here all summer.

The restaurant, in keeping with its decor and location on the waterfront site of the old White Lake Marina Club, stresses seafood, although assorted sandwiches are offered for lunch and prime rib, steaks, and beef kebab for dinner. The local favorite at the Crosswinds is the platter of steamed or broiled Alaskan King crab legs. The dinner menu also features Oriental-style fantail shrimp, broiled lobster tail, French-fried and boiled shrimp, and fresh lake perch. On weekends the Crosswinds is open at 8 in the morning for breakfast, and it offers an excellent menu, including smoked kippers, assorted omelettes, fresh fruits, corned beef hash, hot cakes, and eggs Benedict. Prices throughout the day are reasonable.

The special buffets, however, are what really draw the customers. A luncheon buffet is offered daily. On Sunday there is an all-day buffet, including two meat entrées, two soups (the clam chowder and potato soup are especially notable), a full salad bar. And for a treat on Friday there is a seafood buffet, featuring crab legs, shrimp, frog legs, turtle soup, oyster stew, and other delicacies. But wine drinkers should expect to be disappointed. On our visit last summer there was no wine list, and apparently one could only choose from California carafe wines and Blue Nun. Nevertheless, we like the setting of this relatively new restaurant, and if it provides food as good as the view, you'll enjoy the place. But be sure to check with the locals when you get to Whitehall because the Crosswinds was just getting underway when we first sighted her.

Nautically nice when last visited.

THE CROSSWINDS, 302 Lake Street, Whitehall, MI 49461. North of Muskegon, west of U.S. 31. Telephone (616) 893-4655. Hours: breakfast on weekends only 8 a.m., luncheon daily 11 a.m.-2 p.m., dinner 5-9 p.m. (till 10 p.m. on weekends and Wednesdays). Full bar service. Children's portions. Background music. Entertainment on weekends. Free parking. Credit cards: MC, V. Reservations recommended on weekends.

CROSSWINDS DEEP-FRIED FISH

The Crosswinds uses a dry coating on damp fish, which results in a thinner breading than one finds in many restaurants. The chef suggests that the clean and wet fish be held on ice to keep them firm before rolling in the breading and frying. For a finer batter, you can dip the fish in beaten egg first, if you wish. We suggest that you try it both ways and compare. The coating is a mixture of 1 part flour, 2 parts dry commercial pancake mix (for example, Aunt Jemima brand), and 2 parts dry bread crumbs (or a commercial breading mix). Season this as you wish—you might try white pepper, paprika, or nutmeg.

69
McGUIRE'S
Cadillac

There's not much that's Irish about McGuire's except the name and the recently redecorated, cozy Irish Pub, serving as a cocktail lounge and providing evening entertainment. The attractive, contemporary lodge is the center of a resort complex that offers year-round sporting packages (its own eighteen-hole golf course, tennis courts, heated indoor pool, Finnish sauna, snowmobile warmup trails, cross-country skiing) and is only minutes away from the famous Caberfae ski area. Set high on a glacial moraine amid 230 acres of pine trees and well-maintained landscaped grounds, McGuire's is also fast becoming a major convention center. It's hard to believe that it started in 1948 as a hamburger stand with only four stools. As for dining now, we found it to be certainly the best choice in the Cadillac area.

Three meals a day are served here, and the breakfast and luncheon menus are strictly all-American. But dinner can be a treat, and McGuire's is especially popular for its fine, fairly priced Friday and Saturday evening buffets, the first featuring seafood and prime rib and the second a smorgasbord with four meat courses. On Sundays brunch is served from 11:30 a.m. to 3:30 p.m. and offers several elaborate desserts on the buffet. Sunday through Thursday evening, McGuire's provides rather predictable fare (prime rib's the specialty) but with a few nice additions: chicken Kiev, baked cod, frog legs, trout amandine, and Savory Chicken (baked, stuffed, and succulent). There's an all-you-can-eat salad bar and some excellent homemade cakes and pies. The wine list is modest.

The main dining room, the Viking Room—wood paneled and in soft blues and greens—overlooks the golf course and the city of Cadillac. The view doesn't equal that of Shanty Creek, but at night the flickering candlelight indoors and the twinkling city lights in the distance are especially pleaant. There is also a smaller, appealing Patio for those who prefer a different setting. After dinner, you might drop into the Irish Pub for dancing or listening: Wednesday through Saturday a disc jockey takes requests for your favorites. Dress at dinner varies from quite casual to semiformal; jackets are common. **A sporting center, best in the area for fun and food.** McGUIRE'S MOTOR LODGE AND RESORT, 7880 Mackinaw Trail, Cadillac, MI 49610. One and a half miles south of the city; ½ mile south of M-131. Telephone (616) 775-9947. Hours: 7 a.m.-10 p.m. (off season till 9 p.m.). Closed Thanksgiving, December 24 and 25. Full bar service. Children's menu. Background music. Credit cards: AE, MC, V. Reservations recommended, especially for larger groups on Saturday evenings.

McGUIRE'S OLD-FASHIONED CABBAGE SOUP

Saute 12 ounces finely diced onions and 8 ounces finely diced celery in 10 ounces butter until tender. Add 10 ounces four to make a *roux*, Cook a few minutes, and set aside. Cook 5 pounds shredded cabbage in 9 quarts chicken stock until cabbage is cooked through. Add the *roux*, and simmer ½ hour. Add 1½ pounds sliced frankfurters, 1½ cups diced mushrooms, 2½ pounds frozen, unthawed green peas, 2 teaspoons salt, and ½ teaspoon pepper. 50 servings.

Hints from the Winters: For 8-10 servings, use the following measurements—½ medium onion, ¾ medium celery stalk, ¼ cup butter, ½ cup flour, 7 cups chicken stock, 1 pound cabbage, 3 or 4 frankfurters, ⅓ cup diced mushrooms, 10-ounce package of frozen peas, ½ teaspoon salt, and ⅛ teaspoon pepper.

70
CHIMNEY CORNERS
Frankfort

Set amidst hundreds of acres of forest, fields, and orchards, with a beach on Crystal Lake and distant views of Lake Michigan and the Sleeping Bear dunes, Chimney Corners is one of the most impressive rural hostelries in Michigan. The resort has been in business for 45 years and has an affectionate, devoted clientele who extol both its hospitality and its excellent American/Continental cooking. It's the sort of place we'd prefer to keep to ourselves, but in the interests of honesty, it *is* one of the hundred or so most special eating places in the state.

The dark rustic lodge is nestled among large evergreens, and inside are two attractive dining areas: the main dining room, appropriately decorated in greens and with traditional furnishings and lots of good antiques, and the more casual beach dining room, with sturdy modern furniture, where breakfasts, snack-bar lunches, and informal dinners are served. In pleasant weather you might prefer to eat on the deck off the beach room.

There is one menu daily and one seating for each meal. All dishes are carefully chosen with consideration for the guests' pleasure, and all are completely home cooked. Mollie Rogers, who with her husband James owns and manages the resort, even has had her own cookbook published. First-rate roasts, a matchless lasagne, good fresh vegetables, an outstanding brioche (see the recipe for it below), and desserts and breads beyond praise—you name it, Mollie can cook it.

Vacationers staying at Chimney Corners, of course, have the best opportunity of all to sample Mollie's specialties. But it is possible to eat at the resort without being a guest by calling a day or two in advance (though we always think it's worthwhile trying at the last minute—you could be calling right after a cancellation). Ideally, however, you might think about staying in a room at the resort, even if for one night. For a longer period you can reserve a cottage (either rustic or modern) on the shore of beautiful Crystal Lake or the bluff overlooking it. Each unit has a fireplace and screened porch or deck. And a variety of boats are available for rent: rowboats, small sailboats, and even a 26-foot sloop, the Arcturus III. Lawn games, tennis, and a nearby golf course offer even more leisure-time activity. Nature lovers, incidentally, will be interested in seeing the American chestnut grove on the property—the largest remaining in this part of the country.

Charming countryside dining.

CHIMNEY CORNERS, 1602 Crystal Drive, Frankfort, MI 49635. About 35 miles southwest of Traverse City; 7 miles north of Frankfort on M-22, on Crystal Lake. Telephone (616) 352-7522. One seating only for meals (call). No alcoholic beverages. Free parking. No credit cards. Reserve a day or two in advance.

CHIMNEY CORNERS' BRIOCHE

Dissolve in ½ cup warm water, 2 packages active dry yeast, 2 tablespoons flour, and 1 teaspoon sugar. Allow to rise in warm place until it is very light; this won't take long. Beat 8 eggs till lemon colored and light; add ¼ cup sugar and 1 teaspoon salt, blending well. Add, a little at a time, beating steadily, 4 cups flour and ¾ cup melted butter or margarine. When all is combined, add another ½ cup flour and beat thoroughly. Add yeast mixture, and beat again. Allow dough to rise in a warm place until doubled, about 1½ hours. Punch the dough down, cover with plastic wrap, and refrigerate overnight.

The dough will keep for several days, covered, in the refrigerator. Or you can bake the brioches ahead and freeze them. When you are ready to bake, turn out the dough onto a lightly floured board. Reserve ¼ of the dough. Roll the rest into cylinders 2½ inches in diameter. Cut these into pieces 1½ inches long. You'll get 12 from each cylinder. These will half-fill the traditional brioche molds or will do equally well in large muffin tins—which is what Chimney Corners uses. Make a cut through the center of each and shape small bits of dough from the reserved portion into the shape of a cone. Insert the small end of the cone into the cut. Allow the brioches to rest for about 20 minutes. Paint the tops with a mixture of 1 egg yolk and a little water. Bake at 450 degrees for 15 minutes. Serve hot. Makes 24.

CHIMNEY CORNERS' REFRIGERATOR ROLLS AND BREADSTICKS

To 1 cup scalded milk in a bowl, add 6 tablespoons melted shortening or salad oil, 2 tablespoons sugar, and 2 teaspoons salt. Measure 1 cup warm water, and use part of it to soften 2 envelopes dry yeast or 2 yeast cakes. Add the remaining water to the milk mixture. When this liquid is lukewarm, add the softened yeast and 5 cups flour. Beat as well as you can, and then turn out onto a well-floured board. Knead just 1 minutes, to get the dough smooth. Cut off pieces about the size of walnuts. Put three pieces in each cup of well-greased muffin tins, greasing the tops and tucking all rough edges under. For breadsticks, cut off longer pieces and roll between your oiled hands; then put into breadstick pans.

Let the rolls rise about an hour, more or less depending on room temperature. Or make the rolls in the morning, and place in the refrigerator; they'll rise slowly until you're ready to bake them. Remove from refrigerator, and let rise in a warm place about ½ hour. Bake at 425 degrees for about 20 minutes.

71
JOE'S FRIENDLY TAVERN
Empire

The name says it all. For more than thirty years Joe Wiesen's Friendly Tavern has been the social center of the small village of Empire an a recreational mecca for campers at the Sleeping Bear National Lake Shore and the D. H. Day campground, only seven miles away. It's an ideal spot for kids, for large familes eating out on a small budget, for enthusiasts of local color, and for hamburger lovers. It's friendly, clean, very informal, and a bargain. Dress down for Joe's, or you'll feel out of place. And don't expect "atmosphere" in the usual sense—the decor here might be labeled "fun and games." The large open dining room and connecting bar are stocked with pool tables, shuffleboard, television games, and pinball machines as well as a piano, jukebox, and popcorn machine. Some of the tables are bare, and some sport bandanna cloths. Seating for groups is unlimited—just push the tables together.

The Friendly Tavern has a small bar-type menu, and food is served all day and much of the night. Basically, the choices are the famous Friendly Burger, one of the best hamburgers in Michigan (Joe serves up 11 tons of meat a year, all in the form of hamburgers!); a jumbo beef frankfurter; five dinner ba ⸱⸱s (shrimp, smelt, fish, clams, chicken); and unusually good homemade soup and chili. There's wine by the glass and a large variety of beer offered, and both beer and soft drinks may be ordered by the pitcher. In the summer the Friendly Tavern also serves breakfast, and we highly recommend the spicy homemade pork sausage. A takeout service, including beer and wine, is also available.

That carryout service is something to consider, depending on your mood and how busy the tavern is. In the evening especially, the bar is often crowded with a wide variety of age groups and occasionally breaks the sound barrier. If this isn't your idea of fun, we suggest that you plan a picnic instead. Pack your car with Friendly Burgers, French fries, and beverages and drive west on Lake Street, following the signs to Lake Michigan. In a few hundred yards (you can walk if you prefer) is a very pleasant city park with beaches and picnic tables. Drive to the north end and enjoy a fine beach and a marvelous view of the bluffs of Sleeping Bear to the north.

Some say, the best hamburger in Michigan.

JOE'S FRIENDLY TAVERN, Empire, MI 49630. Two blocks west of the blinker light at the intersection of M-72 and M-22, in the center of town; 22 miles west of Traverse City. Telephone (616) 326-5506. Hours: summer 7 a.m.-2 a.m., winter 11 a.m.-2 a.m. Closed Christmas, Easter. Full bar service. Entertain yourself.

THE FRIENDLY TAVERN'S CHILI

Brown 8 large chopped onions in ½ pound butter. Add 6 pounds of ground beef and brown. Stir in 1 cup flour. Add 4 tablespoons salt, ½ tablespoon pepper, 4 tablespoons chili powder. Mix well, then add four 46-ounce cans of tomato juice and two 10-pound cans of kidney beans. Simmer for 1 hour. 72 servings.

Hints from the Winters: Craig Claiborne once went so far as to say that chili con carne is conceivably America's greatest contribution to world cuisine. Not a Mexican dish despite its name and once a regional dish in the United States, it's now found throughout the country and varies considerably in degree of spiciness, in ingredients used, and especially in beans or lack of them. This is a mild version with beans and a good recipe for serving a crowd.

For a smaller amount, 8 to 12 servings, we suggest the following measurements: 1 pound of ground beef, 1½ medium large onion (chopped), 3 pounds of canned dark red kidney beans, 3 tablespoons flour, 2 teaspoons salt, ¼ teaspoon pepper, 3 teaspoons or more chili powder (we use lots more, to taste), 24 to 30 ounces tomato juice. The entire dish can be made easily and quickly in the microwave oven, and leftovers freeze well. Serve with saltines and side dishes of grated Cheddar cheese and chopped green chili peppers.

72
THE HOMESTEAD
Glen Arbor

The Homestead is reached by way of a long, not especially well-marked drive, after which visitors park in a large lot and complete their journey by van. If you expect the exclusivity suggested by this rather complicated entry, you may be disappointed by the, nice as it is, less than elegant "country porch" decor of the dining room. Still, the Homestead is an ideal place for those wishing a quiet, somewhat reserved lakeside dining experience in pleasant, candlelit surroundings. The food is well prepared and efficiently served by professional young waiters and waitresses in formal attire. But the menu is somewhat limited. Even so, the overall atmosphere rises above the ordinary, and you'll have the feeling of being in a special place.

Furthermore, there's special promise for the future: as this goes to press, we understand that a major renovation will be taking place, along with interesting additions to the menu. We look forward to seeing what improvements have been made. (We also hope to see a change in the background music; on our visit we heard everything from Bob James jazz to John Philip Sousa to the Warsaw Concerto, even more disconcerting when the same tape was repeated throughout the evening.)

None of this is meant to suggest that we don't highly

recommend the Homestead. It's a relaxing place in attractive environs (we suggest a stroll before or after your meal along the waterway and on the well-kept grounds). Most tables are good; the kitchen is off a hallway so that none of them are in a major traffic lane—a problem we find too common in restaurants. But those by the windows overlooking Lake Michigan and the spacious, verdant lawn shaded by mature trees offer the best seating.

The luncheon menu offers a few somewhat trendy but laudable items: gazpacho, smoked whitefish, the Avocado Delight (stuffed with crabmeat), shrimp salad Polynesian, marinated fresh mushroom salad, an avocado club sandwich, and seafood and chicken crepes. At dinner, the possibilities are few but flavorsome, with the most popular entrées the Chateaubriand for two, the steak Oscar, and the baked whitefish (reportedly fresh from Leland, only a few miles away). An inspired introduction to a Homestead meal is the fresh, hot popovers. We could gorge ourselves on these. They seem to keep coming and require enormous self-restraint if you want to save your appetite for the following dishes (see the recipe for them below). What followed for us on our last visit was an admirable Caesar salad, efficiently tossed by our friendly and courteous waiter, Jim. The flambéed duck was tender and juicy (order it crisp, and unless you're wild for orange sauce—and it's a good one—ask for it in a side dish). We also understand that more pyrotechnic presentations are in the offing, including an old favorite, steak Diane.

The wine list is adequate but to our tastes too limited in the French—only three reds, none distinguished. Wine may be ordered by the glass or carafe. Three desserts are offered, and they're winners: cheesecake, baked custard flan, and flaming cherries Jubilee. Or, if you prefer, order the bar specialty, the Sunken Treasure, a scrumptious, frothy concoction of strawberries, Amaretto, and ice cream.

In the bar from 11:30 to closing time (11 p.m.or till midnight on Fridays and Saturdays) fresh oysters and clams are served. In the summer you can eat on the terrace, which features the same menu as in the dining room. On weekends a combo plays in the lounge or outdoors by the pool.

A lakefront hideaway.

THE HOMESTEAD, Glen Arbor, MI 49636. About 30 miles

northwest of Traverse City' 2 miles northeast of Glen Arbor on M-22. Telephone (616) 334-3041. Hours: breakfast 8-11 a.m., luncheon 11:30 a.m.-2 p.m., dinner 6-10 p.m. (till 11 p.m. on Fridays and Saturdays), Sunday brunch and dinner buffet 10 a.m.-2:30 p.m. Open June 1-Labor Day weekend. Full bar service. Children's menu. Background music, entertainment. No blue jeans or shorts (dress up a bit for the Homestead). Free parking. Credit cards: AE, MC, V. Reservations usually necessary.

THE HOMESTEAD'S POPOVERS

Mix together 12 cups all-purpose flour, ½ cup sugar, and 1 tablespoon salt. In a separate bowl mix together 24 eggs, 3 quarts milk, and ¾ cup salad oil. Blend the two mixtures together, using a wire whip. Preheat muffins pans in a 350-degree oven for 15 minutes. Oil pans, and add popover batter. Each individual cup should be completely filled. (A spray shortening works well for oiling the pans.) Bake popovers 45 minutes at 350 degrees. Serve hot with honey butter.

Hints from the Winters: We want you to see this recipe for a large number of popovers, because you might find it useful for entertaining at a brunch. For fewer servings, 12 popovers (serving 4 to 6 at most—we guarantee you can't eat just *one*), use these measurements: 3 cups flour, 2 tablespoons sugar, ¾ teaspoon salt, 6 eggs, 3 cups milk, and 3 tablespoons oil. You can save time by mixing everything in the blender. Plain butter and honey or jam are good with these. For honey butter, blend about 2½ tablespoons honey into ½ cup softened butter.

73
A PICNIC IN LELAND

What is special about eating out in Leland, Michigan, is the town and its setting, not just its restaurants. Considered by many to be the most charming and picturesque fishing village on Lake Michigan's shores, Leland is worth going out of your way for—or, better yet, planning for. We suggest, to enjoy it fully, that you try something different here. First, stop at the Manitou Farm Market (open May-October), a mile south of the intersection of M-204 and M-22 (three miles south of Leland) for the makings of a picnic. Here you'll find, under one roof, a fine bakery, delicatessen, farm market, and grocery store with a small wine "cellar" offering a surprising selection in terms of type (Michigan wines included) and price (you can buy—though, heavens, not for a picnic—a $60 Chateau Lafite-Rothschild). Also available are homemade fudges and jams, chutneys, and dessert toppings. Select the foods and beverages of your choice, and then drive to Leland's dock area parking lot and walk over to Carlson's Fishery on the river for an additional treat of smoked fish or a delicious smoked fish sausage.

You can enjoy your lunch in the Harbor Park, and there's even a small playground for the kids. Be sure to walk both the boardwalk river frontage and the pier. Along the river are weathered buildings and pilings of the restored village, and you can watch the daily catch being cleaned at Carlson's and look into the various shops and fish-smoking establishments. On the pier are boats and launches from many Great Lakes ports. Cruises also leave here for the Manitou Islands in the summer, and yachts and fishing boats may be chartered. Leland is an artists' colony, and you'll find a number of interesting small shops for browsing along the main street.

In inclement weather or if you prefer not to picnic, we recommend the Blue Bird, Fisherman's Cove, or the Leland Lodge. For a lighter lunch or informal evening entertainment, you might want to try Fischer's Happy Hour, a popular roadhouse known for good sandwiches and soup, located about eight miles north of town on route 22. Eating out (that is, in) in Leland can be very pleasant, but in good weather eating out (out of doors) is better—the surroundings here seem to cry out for a picnic.

A picturesque port.

74
SLEDER'S FAMILY TAVERN
Traverse City

Bob Classens, who has owned Sleder's since 1974, was once a barber and antique dealer. He gave up barbering (fortunately for diners in Traverse City) but still retains a lively and active interest in antiques, as the tavern well illustrates. In only four years he restored the interior of an old building to what it was some 70 to 80 years ago. It is now a veritable mecca for the antique enthusiast. Look at the authentic, ornate old embossed metal ceiling; the ceiling fans (it's not air conditioned, but it's cool) and chandeliers; the cash register with its nonfunctioning clock; the old jukebox; the ice-cream-parlor chairs; wooden booths; window shutters; game trophies (including a stuffed eagle over the peanut roaster); and the great old beer signs. You might not notice it at first amid all this fascinating clutter, but even the floor is an antique—with marks from the hobnailed boots of loggers, made years ago when the "Slabtown" mill was nearby.

We love the history of this place. It was started in 1882 by a Czech, Vincel Sleder (note the old Columbia Hall sign on the side of the building) and was in the hands of the Sleder family for 90 years. Originally there was a theater and dance hall upstairs. Since the building was constructed, there has *always* been a tavern here—even during Prohibition years, when the chief of police was known to come in for a drink. When you visit, you might catch sight of former owner Louie Sleder, a third-generation family member who lives a block away and still comes in to make sure the place is being run correctly. Most of the stuffed animals and birds on the walls were raised and/or shot at some time or another by the Sleders; today they're authentic collectors' items. By the way, Bob Classens has official permission to keep the stuffed eagle and display the antique liquor sign, because both were there before the prohibitive laws were passed.

There are three dining rooms now. We prefer the large one that houses the long old oak and ash bar and that offers more things and people to gawk at. But if Sleder's is busy (and it generally is), you may have to sit in the back room (once called the Indian Room and later the College Room—we'll let Bob tell you about that) or in the dining room once known as the Ladies' Room. Those were discriminating days. But wherever you sit, it's noisy and bustling. There's no background music to distract from the talk. The joviality and cheerful service here make Sleders the closest thing we've seen to an Americanized version of a friendly English pub. Children seem as much at home as adults. And, perhaps most important, it's a perfect place for a lunch or snack in Traverse City—you can still get a great sandwich for less than a dollar.

The menu is simple and American: mostly steaks, sandwiches, "baskets" with assorted side dishes. There's a daily luncheon special from Labor Day to Memorial Day, at a bargain price—on Mondays goulash, Tuesdays hot turkey sandwich, Wednesdays cabbage rolls, Thursdays meatloaf, Fridays fish, Saturdays beef stew. The most popular items are the bean soup, chili, and the Westsider, a 1-pound ground chuck hamburger with fried onions. The head cheese is homemade, and Bob chose to feature here (suffocate your qualms, and give it a try; it's good). And certainly we can't neglect to mention a special treat at Sleder's: the freshly roasted unsalted peanuts. About 300 pounds are dished out each week, and they're kept warm in an old-fashioned popcorn machine.

We give the highest marks to Sleder's and Bob Classens for creating a nostalgic turn-of-the-century charm, on the one hand, and for keeping quality high and prices reasonable, on the other. Everyone should see the tavern—if possible, for lunch or a snack. Or, if you've eaten elsewhere, at least stop by for a Coke, beer (six brands on draft, including dark), or cocktail.

Charming, festive, a bargain—don't miss it.

SLEDER'S FAMILY TAVERN, 717 Randolph Street, Traverse City, MI 49684. One block west of Division Street (U.S. 31 at M-37). Telephone (616) 947-9213. Hours: 9 a.m. to midnight, 2-10 p.m. on Sundays. Closed holidays. Full bar service. Free parking across the street from the side entrance. No credit cards or reservations accepted.

SLEDER'S HEAD CHEESE

Boil 2 well-cleaned pig's heads until the meat comes easily off the bones. Cook 2 Spanish onions (each the size of a softball). Grind meat and onions together. Add salt, pepper, and sage to taste. Pack into bread loaf pans, and bake in a 350-degree oven for 30 minutes. When grease rises to the top, skim off. Remove from oven and cool. This can be frozen but not for too long. Makes about 11 pounds of head cheese.

Hints from the Winters: This is one recipe we haven't yet tested, but when we do, we'll probably refer to one of our most reliable cookbooks, Rombauer and Becker's *Joy of Cooking*, for directions on cleaning the heads (the authors include good information on a head cheese made of a calf's head that would be useful here).

75
THE TOP OF THE PARK
Traverse City

This is the easiest restaurant to find in Traverse City—on the tenth floor of the Park Place Motor Inn, the tallest building in the area, topped by a red and white striped cupola. The hotel has been a landmark for years, and from the vantage of the Top of the Park is a marvelous panoramic view of Grand Traverse Bay, the Leleenau Peninsula, and the Old Mission Peninsula. It's lovely during all four seasons—spring, when the cherry blossoms are on display; fall, with the changes of color; winter, with ice in the bay; and summer, with the blues and greens of water and forest and the brightly colored spinnakers on the horizon.

There are two dining rooms: the East Room, with a view of the Boardman River and the bay, and the North Room, directly overlooking the bay—the two areas separated by a small bar. The decor is attractive and traditional, with a red, black, and gold color scheme; brick walls; beamed ceilings; Austrian draperies; and a collection of historical pictures of Traverse City. We prefer the North Room; all the tables here are good, especially for smaller groups. There are four tables for two and two tables for four in front of the windows. But if you do eat in the East Room, try to avoid tables 14 and 23. In pleasant weather you might consider arriving early and having cocktails in the adjacent Crow's Nest.

Luncheon here is particularly enjoyable. Entrées include *tournedos à la Traverse* (served with steamed artichoke hearts and Madeira sauce), hot prime rib sandwich *au jus*, shrimp and crabmeat crepes, quiche Lorraine, cold marinated beef slices, the ever popular broiled whitefish, and several other interesting choices. Gazpacho and a soup *du jour* are regularly offered, and the desserts are most appealing—brandy snaps with hot blueberry sauce (an almond candy filled with ice cream), fresh cherry pie, Black Forest torte, to name a few. At dinner, tableside service is a specialty, and the most popular entrées, as we would expect, are the prime rib, steak Diane, Chateaubriand, and whitefish. Also on the menu are *scampi pescatora*, steak *au poivre*, veal steak Walevska, rack of lamb *bouquetiere*, roast duck *à l'orange*, and other exceptional steak, veal, and seafood dishes. Dinners come with salad, potatoes or buttered snow peas, and French sourdough bread. Two other salads may be ordered separately: the Caesar and the Salade Speciale (both for two persons).

Soups include French onion, gazpacho, and consommé Celestine. The appetizers are classic: *coquilles St. Jacques*, *escargots à la Earle* (sautéed in garlic Chablis butter), melon and ham, Sevruga caviar on ice, shrimp de Jongh, and hot smoked rainbow trout. Some additional desserts other than those mentioned above are several crepes flambéed at the table, imported cheeses with fresh fruit, and assorted French pastries. Or, if you prefer, the Top of the Park offers a variety of dessert cocktails, each prepared with French vanilla ice cream, and Spanish or Irish coffee.

We are impressed with the room, the view, the handsome table settings, and the food. But we're most impressed with the wine list. It is certainly the finest we've seen in the the northern part of the state and will interest anyone who appreciates fine wine. Even the internationally known connoisseur Harm de Blij of Coral Gables, Florida, would like this list. The choices range from the modest to the exquisite—for example, there are a 1937 Haut Brion, a 1945 Margaux, a 1947 Latour, and a 1961 Lafite, among many, many more. The selections are largely French, followed by Californian, then German whites, and a sprinkling of Italian, Portuguese, and even Michigan wines. You may instead order wine by the glass: a German white or a California Burgundy. And if you wish to visit the cellar, see Larry Williams, the knowledgable food and beverage manager.

A place for all seasons.

THE TOP OF THE PARK, Park Place Motor Inn, 300 E. State Street, Traverse City, MI 49684. At the corner of State and Park Streets, downtown. Telephone (616) 946-5410. Hours: daily in summer, luncheon 11:30 a.m.-2 p.m., dinner 5:30-11 p.m. (Friday and Saturday till midnight); off season, closing days and dates subject to change. Full bar service. Background music. Dancing and entertainment. Free parking. Credit cards: AE, MC, V. Reservations recommended. Policy is to take reservations for 5:30 to 7 p.m. period, but after 7 requests for tables are accommodated as other guests finish dining and depart. No dress code, but we suggest jackets, dressing up a bit.

PARK PLACE CHERRY-NUT PIE

Traverse City is known as the site of the Michigan Cherry Festival each year, and the recipe from Klaus Baecchle for Cherry-Nut Pie is most appropriate. Prepare pastry for two 9-inch pie shells and enough additional pastry for a lattice top on each. Chop 3 cups pitted fresh cherries. Mix with 1 cup pecan pieces, 1½ cups sugar, 2 tablespoons flour, ¼ teaspoon salt, 3 tablespoons water, and 1 tablespoon melted butter. Spoon into the pie shells. Cover with a lattice top. Brush pastry with beaten egg yolk. Bake at 350 degrees for 30 minutes.

Hints from the Winters: This recipe can be halved very nicely for one pie. And we like a bit more filling—say, half again as much (or else, use 8-inch tins). We usually have Traverse City cherries in our freezer, but when trying this recipe, we had to resort to canned tart cherries. They were fine; just drain them first. And they're as good whole as chopped. To avoid a soggy bottom crust, brush the pastry before filling with beaten egg white. The timing in the Park Place recipe is obviously suitable only for those hot restaurant ovens. We find that 10 minutes at 450 degrees, followed by 45 minutes at 350 degrees, is much more reasonable for the home oven. Serve the pie slightly warm and with ice cream, if you like.

76
BOWERS HARBOR INN
Traverse City

On Old Mission Peninsula overlooking Bowers Harbor and the West Arm of Grand Traverse Bay, the blue and white, two-story frame inn nestled in tall pines has been a landmark for a century. It was built as a private home by a Grand Rapids family and in 1960 converted into a restaurant by the Bryants, who had already been successful in business elsewhere on the peninsula. In 1974 it was purchased by a Grand Rapids company; and still later a new dining area, the Bowery, was added. But the nostalgic need not fear drastic changes. Bowers Harbor Inn remains much the same in food and quality. And tradition and community spirit linger—Frank Lyon is the night cook, and five of the ten Lyons, children of the cherry farmer about two miles down the road, work at the restaurant.

The decor is charming. The old, original curving stairway still greets visitors at the front entrance. In the bayside dining area there are four rooms on one level and another upstairs. The Harbor Dining Room, decorated in black, gold, and neutrals, has a marvelous table for eight by the bay window (reserve Harbor 3; but reserve well ahead; it's usually booked a month or more in advance). The only tables to avoid here are 10, 11, and 12 near the exit to the kitchen; all the others are fine. Adjoining this room is the Patio, done in shades of red, pink, and orange and primarily used for larger groups of 6 to 22 persons. The Bay Dining Room overlooks the patio and bay, and its cheerful yellows and golds are enhanced by plants and latticework. Bay 5 and 6 at the windows are the choice tables here.

The Alcove, off the Bay Room, carries the same decor and is especially appealing for those wishing privacy—only four tables for four (our favorite is Bay 11, under a Tiffany lamp). The fifth dining room, on the upper floor, is labeled the Study. Tables here are for two, and the room has its own bar. But we much prefer the downstairs rooms and suggest that, if at all possible, you wait for a table there—or at least be sure to get one near the wall in the Study. During the summer season cocktails are served on the patio outside in the evening, and a seafood bar is set up. A buffet brunch is also served outdoors on Sundays.

The menu at first sight appears limited—primarily steak, prime rib, and seafood. But there's more here than meets the eye. Chef Greg Niccolau, a graduate of the Culinary Institute of America, offers a creative specialty each evening, on the order of beef Wellington or trout *en croute* (see the recipe for it below). And on the regular menu are some appealing dishes: fillet of sole stuffed with crabmeat and served with a delicate cheese sauce, duckling (the favorite of Ernie Hall, the young and talented senior manager), lobster Newburgh, Cantonese-style shrimp, and what everyone here seems to end up with, the highly recommended "Fish in a Bag," a specialty of the restaurant since its beginnings and featured in *Bon Appetit* magazine. Dinners include appetizer (your choice of chowder or onion-cheese bake—delicious) and salad. Vegetables may be ordered *à la carte*. Only one dessert is offered, and it's noteworthy: French-fried ice cream with hot fudge-Kahlua sauce and whipped cream.

The wine list, printed up like a shipping manifesto, is limited in number, quality, and information. For example, under the heading of "French Red" is "Classified Red Bordeaux $35"—no mention of chateau, district, or year. Even so, you can probably find something adequate, and three of the California offerings are available at fair prices by the glass and liter.

The Bowery, which opened in June 1978, looks much older, with its weathered barn siding and beams, antiques, and stained glass. There are two levels, the main room, with a large fireplace, and a balcony that overlooks it. The newly added dining area serves a good purpose. It's more informal; it has its own, less elaborate menu with some prices lower than those in the front dining rooms; and it offers entertainment and dancing nightly from June to September. The Bowery attracts the locals, too—when the bayside up front is busy with tourists, this is an alternative and a good meeting place. And, unlike the rest of the establishment, it's open four days a week out of season for cross-country skiers. **The west bay's best.**

BOWERS HARBOR INN, 13512 Peninsula Drive, Traverse City, MI 49684. Three-quarters of a mile north of Traverse City on M-37, then 8 miles northwest on Peninsula Drive (about 12 miles from the downtown area). Telephone (616) 223-4222. Hours: 5-9:30 p.m. April through November (bayside closes November 1); in winter closed Mondays and Tuesdays. Full bar service. Children's menu. Background music. Entertainment and dancing in the Bowery. Free parking. Credit cards: MC, V. Reservations recommended for the bayside inn, not taken in the Bowery.

BOWERS HARBOR TROUT EN CROUTE

Remove head, tails, and fins from four 10-ounce boneless rainbow trout. Wash and dry the fish. Soften 8 ounces butter and blend in 1 tablespoon dill weed, 4 dashes Tabasco sauce, and a dash of white pepper. Place 2 ounces of the seasoned butter in the body cavity of each fish. Mix 2 pounds of flaky pie dough, and roll it out ¼-inch thick. Wrap each fish in the dough, being careful to seal all the edges and trim off the excess dough. Bake in a 400-degree oven about 25 minutes or until golden brown.

While the fish are baking, make Hollandaise sauce: In a double boiler over simmering water, put 4 egg yolks and whip them constantly till they thicken and their color lightens to a lemony yellow. Remove from heat, and slowly add 1½ cups warm, not hot, clarified butter, whipping constantly while adding. Whip in the juice of 1 lemon, a dash of cayenne pepper, and a dash of salt. Serve over the baked fish. Serves 4.

Hints from the Winters: Use 1-1½ pounds (4-6 cups) flour in making your favorite pie pastry. Purchased pastry sticks or mix can be used successfully, too. To clarify the butter, melt it over very low heat. When completely melted, remove from heat and let stand a few minutes so that the solids settle at the bottom. Skim or pour the clear butter fat off carefully, and store the curds for use later in flavoring vegetables and other dishes. We find even smaller trout quite ample. If you don't have fresh trout, you can buy two 10-ounce packages of boned frozen trout (2 in a package). The simplest way to remove the heads and fins from the fish is to use sharp shears. For a golden crust, brush the pastry with beaten egg yolk just before baking the fish.

77
HILTON SHANTY CREEK
Bellaire

This is one of the few eating places we chose to include primarily for factors other than gastronomic. Structurally, the Shanty Creek lodge is perhaps the most dramatic building for its purpose outside of Detroit. Few places in Michigan can boast such overall attractiveness of entrance grounds, architecture, and interior design in the dining room and lounge. These rooms are beautiful—large, open, contemporary, even with full-grown trees—and the view is outstanding. Lunchtime or daylight is best, but the evening view to the west from high on the Port Huron moraine can be spectacular.

Shanty Creek was built as a private club and has been in business since 1962. Over the years it's had problems and changed hands several times, the last change of owners in 1973. The Hilton franchise went into effect in March 1978, and the lodge appears to be doing a successful convention business and attracting its deserved share of customers now. This is the only nationally franchised establishment we've included, and we think you'll see why. It's one of the very few ski lodges located on top rather than at the bottom of the slope, affording an exceptional view unlike most lodges in Michigan's ski areas.

As for cuisine, Hilton Shanty Creek is admittedly eclectic and features dishes that have proved their popularity in other restaurants throughout the country. It aims at giving its customers what they want—and if this means flourishes and fanfare, so be it. There is a feeling here that management creativity surpasses chef creativity. But the food is well prepared and the setting so delightful that we don't think you'll be at all disappointed.

The menus are imaginative and appeal to a variety of tastes. At breakfast, for example, you might consider the crab Benedict, quiche Lorraine, crepes Riccota with fruit sauce, or Eggsparagus (sliced eggs, asparagus, and Hollandaise). The luncheon fare comprises salads and sandwiches as well as the Odyssey, a winsome Greek dish of *filo* pastry, broccoli, and cheese; a shrimp salad sandwich on English muffins topped with melted cheese; breaded "steak fingers," served with sweet and sour sauce; and Idaho pie, a cheese, potato, and ham casserole baked in a crust (see the recipe below). The prices are not bad. Even those on a budget can enjoy lunch here, but in the evening things get a bit more pricey.

The dinner menu is *table d'hôte* and offers steaks, seafood, three "twosomes" (Chateaubriand, rack of lamb, or shellfish for two), and several house specialties, among them sirloin and shrimp kebab, Teriyaki chicken, and crepes Stroganoff with a sour cream sauce. Entrées come with relishes, choice of salad (Caesar, wilted spinach, or tossed), wild rice or potato, and bread. The desserts are seductive: parfaits, strawberry Bavarian, chocolate mousse, Viennese apple pie, cheesecake, and three tableside preparations—flaming coffee, fruit flambé, and baked Alaska. Twice a year the menu changes to suit customer tastes.

About 30 wines are available, and most are undistinguished at reasonable to low prices. These include three from a nearby Michigan vineyard. Three fine wines can also be purchased—a Latour, a Clos de Vougeot, and a Taittinger *brut* Champagne—but you'll need to inquire as to their years, because they're not on the list. House wines (from Michigan and Italy) are available by the glass or carafe.

You might dress up a bit for this restaurant, especially in the evening. But don't feel intimidated at all. At Shanty Creek, when we last visited, one of the large double entrance doors was locked, a nuisance we generally associate with more mundane establishments.

A best view from a beautiful building.
HILTON SHANTY CREEK, Bellaire, MI 49615. Between Tra-

verse City and Charlevoix; two miles southeast of Bellaire, 1 mile east of M-88. Telephone (616) 533-8621. Hours: breakfast 7:30-11 a.m., luncheon noon-2:30 p.m., dinner 6-9 p.m. (till 10 on Fridays and Saturdays); Sundays, breakfast 7:30-10:30 a.m., buffet brunch noon-3 p.m., dinner 5-9 p.m. Open year round. Full bar service. Children's menus at breakfast and lunch. Background music. Entertainment 6 nights a week in season, 5 p.m.-2 a.m.; piano at 5 p.m., band and dancing 9 p.m.; off season, 3 nights a week. No blue jeans. Free parking. All major credit cards. Reservations recommended.

SHANTY CREEK'S IDAHO PIE

Fit pie pastry into a 5 by 10-inch casserole dish (or other 1-quart baking dish). Mix together gently 2 cups cooked cubed potatoes (about 2 large Idahos), 1 cup cubed smoked ham, 1 cup small-curd cottage cheese, 1 cup sour cream, ½ cup (or more) grated Cheddar cheese, 2-4 tablespoons grated Parmesan cheese (to taste), and 2-4 tablespoons chopped fresh parsley. Fill the pastry-lined casserole. Sprinkle with paprika. Bake about 1½ hours at 350 degrees, till brown and bubbling. Garnish with Parmesan tomatoes. 4-6 servings.

Hints from the Winters: This works well as a side dish with unsauced meat entrées or as a main course (in which case you might want to add more ham). It's an excellent recipe for leftovers,too; the amounts of cheese, ham, and potato can be varied according to taste. You might also wish to use other cheeses, alone or in combination: Swiss, Romano, Muenster, Edam, Wisconsin brick, Havarti will all do. And for a more pungent ham flavor, try Prosciutto instead (½ cup is sufficient). For a simple Parmesan tomato garnish, spread a mixture of dry crumbs, grated Parmesan, garlic, and oil on tomato slices and broil till golden brown.

78
THE BROWNWOOD FARM HOUSE
Central Lake

Brownwood Acres has been the Brown family's farm since 1939. In 1947 the family built a roadside stand to sell honey and home-grown vegetables, and from that modest beginning has evolved a complex of commercial enterprises, including the Honey House (a five-room gift shop), the Schoolhouse (Antrim County's oldest log school, now an ice cream shop), the Country Store (a rebuilt stagecoach inn), the Barn Boutique and Brownwood Squire (clothing establishments), and of special interest to diners, the Farm House and Farm House Barn, a large and lively restaurant and entertainment center seating 240 people and amiably decorated in rural early American with wagon-wheel chandeliers and red-checked tablecloths.

There are three seating areas under high, open-beamed ceilings: the Farm House, the Harvest Room, and the Barn—in which a four- or five-piece band plays dinner and show music Tuesday through Sunday (dancers might prefer to be seated here). In warm weather one wall opens, and there's dancing outside, too. This is a cheerful, informal place for crowd-lovers and the gregarious. You won't find any secluded, quiet little spots, but you can have a good time, especially if you're with a group or the family. The prices range from moderate to moderately expensive, but the portions are large, and the Friday and Sunday specials are quite reasonable. Those of you who are familiar with Brownwood should know that the all-you-can-eat seafood (and the bargain that went with it) has changed. But the restaurant's still worth visiting.

The menu is American, dominated by steaks, prime rib, barbequed ribs, fried chicken, fish, and seafood. The most popular items are the steak and seafood combinations, the small steak (10-ounce strip), specially priced on Friday, and the Sunday special—family-style chicken, all you can eat. Dinners include homemade soup (see the recipes below), biscuits with Brownwood's special cherry butter or honey, baked potatoes or French fries, and a personal salad bar at your table. The wines are uninteresting and modest. But they are also sold by the glass; and the house offering (a Michigan wine with Brownwood's label), by the liter and half-liter. The house cocktail is the Torch Lake Special, made with gin and blue Curacao.

One doubtless unique feature of Brownwood is that, as far as we know, it's the only place in Michigan where you can have cocktails while riding on a stagecoach! If you're with a group, it's easy to arrange, it's fun, and it's reasonably priced. The Central Lake-Brownwood Overland Stage, drawn by a team of four black horses, is available to charter for the cocktail hour at 6 p.m. any evening. Bring your own drinks, and Brownwood will supply the ice and mixes. The stage returns at 7 p.m. in time for dinner. It costs only $2 per person for a group of ten. But you must call ahead to reserve the coach and dinner table. By the way, if you're with the family or a smaller group, you still might want to take a ride: the stagecoach travels from Brownwood Acres to Central Lake four times a day.

Lively doings down on the farm.

BROWNWOOD FARM HOUSE, East Torch Lake Drive, Central Lake, MI 49622. Three miles south of Eastport. Telephone (616) 544-5811. Hours: luncheon noon-3 p.m., dinner 5-10 p.m. (till 11 p.m. Fridays and Saturdays). Call to confirm hours off season. Full bar service. Children's menu. Entertainment, dancing. Casual dress. All major credit cards. Reservations recommended if you want seats near entertainment area while dining.

BROWNWOOD'S CREAM OF BROCCOLI SOUP

Combine 3 bunches chopped broccoli with 1 gallon chicken stock, and boil till tender. In saucepan sauté 2 pounds chopped ham with 2 medium chopped onions till onions are transparent. Add the ham and onions to the soup. In a second saucepan heat 1 cup oil and add 1 cup flour, whipping constantly, until a medium paste is prepared (*roux*). Add 1 quart cream. Add *roux* to soup, stirring continuously, until the desired thickness is reached. While stirring, add ½ cup Parmesan cheese. Add salt and white pepper to taste, and garnish with ½ cup chopped parsley. Serves 12.

Hints from the Winters: We've also cut this recipe to a third very successfully. The quantities to use for 4 servings would be 1 bunch broccoli, ½ pound ham, ½ onion, 1 cup cream, 4 cups chicken broth, ¼ cup oil, ¼ cup flour, 2 tablespoons Parmesan, and 2 tablespoons parsley. The soup is chunky and flavorful. If you'd like a creamier soup, put the broccoli through your blender after cooked. Since we often have broccoli flowerets for dinner, we find this recipe useful in that we can now use the hard stems from the bunch in this soup.

BROWNWOOD'S CREAM OF CHICKEN SOUP

Cook 5 pounds stewing chicken in 1 gallon (16 cups) water till tender, about 2½ hours. Remove chicken from stock, and take meat from from skin and bones and return to the stock. In a saucepan sauté ¼ cup corn, ¼ cup green peas, ¼ cup chopped onions, ¼ cup chopped carrots, and ¼ cup chopped celery until tender. Add the vegetables to the stock along with 1 quart (4 cups) cream. In saucepan, heat ½ cup oil and ½ cup butter until warm, and add 1 cup flour, whipping continuously until a medium paste is prepared (*roux*). Add *roux* to soup while stirring continuously until desired thickness is obtained. Add salt and pepper to taste. Garnish with chopped parsley.

79
THE JORDAN INN
East Jordan

On September 6, 1941, a young Polish soldier stationed in Scotland met and married a charming lassie—and we in Michigan, at least in this generation, are still celebrating that fortuitous union. In a homey old hotel that has its hundredth birthday this year, Christina and Tad Dobrowolski for the past four years have been astounding their grateful customers with a marvelous assemblage of dishes from some twenty different countries. These are most often classics that Tad has creatively modified and transmuted into the altogether new and rewarding. The Dobrowolskis are uncommonly cordial, and both are highly knowledgeable about some of the finest restaurants in the country. This awareness, with their combined Polish-Scottish heritage and enthusiasm for their work, results in some of the most successful and beguiling culinary products in Michigan.

The menu changes somewhat once or twice a week so that guests can always discover something new on it. A typical dinner, priced by the chosen entrée, includes a choice of soup, appetizer, and salad; desserts (and they're beautiful) are offered at a slight additional charge. During our visit the soups were a stimulating *sopa de pesce* and a rosy tomato Polonaise—both models of their kind. We had a croute Krystoff (a delicious crustless cheese quiche) and a lovely *pâté maison* (venison, rabbit, and pork), garnished with julienned beets laced with horseradish. Salad dressings included a *moutard douce* (sweet and sour mustard) and Polonaise (a piquant mixture of sour cream, dill, and spices). Six tantalizing entrées are offered each evening, changing according to what's available—for example, a pheasant dish might be substituted for the veal—or, we would guess, according to Tad's inspiration. On our visit, entrées included veal Sobieski (stuffed with spinach and Swiss cheese and served with lobster sauce), trout Navara (filled with mushrooms, tomatoes, and ham and sauced with tomato), curried lamb Sumatra, and a fascinating *makedonska brzola* (stuffed pork loin; one of Christina's favorites). One exceptional dish rarely seen on American menus is *couliabac*, which Tad fills with salmon and lobster, a skillful variation on the customary rice and salmon mixture. A lot of game is served at the Jordan Inn, and we were pleased to learn that the Dobrowolskis purchase it from our own valued purveyor, Czimers of Lockport, Illinois. Usually an *entrecôte* or other steak is available, and—American squeamishness be damned—we urge you to sample the sauce. Or, if you're quite sure you'll scrape it off, why not ask for it in a separate bowl and give it a whirl?

The soups are uniformly excellent, especially the borschts. The inn has served some 120 different soups in three years, including a heart-warming Polish mushroom and barley and more delicate varieties based on sorrel and fruit. The tortes and mousses are wickedly delicious, and when the pink gooseberries are in season, you must try Tad's ambrosial gooseberry fool. Prices are moderately high, but the value at the Jordan Inn is very high indeed. And wine prices are equitable. Any connoisseur would appreciate this list. The largest selection is French, and nearly all are under $20, including a most reasonably priced Langoa Barton and Beychevelle. The house wine is a nonvintage red and a white Reisling—much better than the usual house offerings in Michigan. This place just about has it all. By planning ahead, you can stay in rooms typical of a century-old inn, set within a landscape that is Michigan's equivalent to the glacially formed Finger Lakes of New York state, and eat in a dining room that ranks among the very best.

Incomparable innovations in cuisine—one of the best.
THE JORDAN INN, 228 Main Street, East Jordan, MI 49727. On Route 32 west of I-75; about 15 miles south of Charlevoix. Telephone (616) 536-2631. Hours: 6-10 p.m. in summer (till 9 p.m. in winter season). Closed Mondays, December 24 and 25, Thanksgiving. Full bar service. Credit cards: MC, V. Reservations essential.

STEAK CLASSICO

To repay the Dubrowolskis' hospitality, we offer two versions of a favorite dish of ours, one we devised after countless experiments with fond memories of its predecessor tasted in Beckley, West Virginia, many years ago. We think Christina will especially appreciate this—it's basically a beef *brzola*.

Purchase strip steaks or sirloin steak without any major muscle seams and, ideally, well marbled with fat. For each serving, buy ½ pound untrimmed steak (when trimmed, each will weigh 5-6 ounces). Trim off all fat. Pound steak very thin (⅛ inch or less), and cut so that when folded in half, both sides are symmetrical.

Make *pesto*: combine 2 tablespoons soft butter, 2 tablespoons olive oil, 2 large cloves of garlic put through a press, 1 teaspoon dry basil leaves, 3 tablespoons grated Parmesan cheese. This is enough for 4 servings.

Spread pesto on the steaks to within ¼ inch of the outside

edges. Lay a thin slice of a mild Provolone cheese or Mozzarella on half of the surface. Fold the other half over the cheese, tucking the ends inside. Grill 3 inches from a hot charcoal fire for 2½ minutes a side. (If you have any major flameups, you've used too much butter or cheese; reduce in the future.) We like this unsauced and served with spaghetti or linguine Carbonara.

Variation: Instead of *pesto*, spread the meat with a mixture of chopped shallots sautéed in butter for 3-5 minutes till golden. Instead of the cheese, spread half each steak with chopped sauteed mushrooms (½ cup sauteed in 2 teaspoons butter 6-7 minutes for 2 servings). In addition to the mushrooms, you can use a mild cheese like Havarti or Wisconsin Brick. If you want the meat to look more generous, place on *croutes* cut the same size as the folded steaks. (For the *croutes*, slowly sauté trimmed bread slices in a mixture of butter and oil till crisp and browned.)

80
THE ROWE INN
Ellsworth

The Rowe Inn reminds us of one of those marvelous little French restaurants trying to earn another star in the Michelin guide. For efficiency and cuisine, it can hardly be topped. The dining room is modest, unpretentious, and somewhat crowded; and the general atmosphere is convivial—the clientele are clearly among the most enthusiastic diners we've seen in Michigan. There are very few tables (only thirteen for standard seating), and the best are toward the west side of the room away from the doors. On our visit we were fortunate to be seated at the splendid table for two in front of the window and were able to enjoy a full moon along with a lovely five-course dinner. Our reservations were for 9, and we were led to our table at 9:05. And at 10:30 the Rowe was still going strong. The service was exceptional; the timing between courses nearly perfect. Our waitress, Ann, made us comfortable and appeared genuinely interested in pleasing us.

The decor in the small, L-shaped dining room is an improbable mix of French and north woods. The cuisine seems to be a combination of French and all other cooking styles of the world. And the menu, posted on a blackboard, gradually evolves so that within a week or two all items on the list are new. (Some 250 to 300 different entrées are served during a year's time.) There are four courses at dinner, priced according to the entrée; dessert is extra, and there may be a surcharge for more extravagant dishes.

We started with an excellent game *pâté* and a superb quiche. The scallop chowder was reminiscent in flavor and appearance of the fine *soupe de poisson* we enjoyed in Nice with our friends Jane and Georges Joyaux (but no *rouille*; knowing the Rowe, it will some day appear on the menu). We ordered the veal *rollatine* and shrimp Mosca as our main courses; it was a great contest between the two of them, but the veal won (mainly because neither of us like to peel shrimp). The green beans that came on the side tasted as fresh as if still on the vine. For dessert we had the *dacquoise au chocolat*—a dream of rich chocolate butter cream and nut-studded meringue.

The only lapse in an impeccable presentation was that the water in the fingerbowls was hotter than the soup; but we consider this a minor fault in a dinner so memorable (and we might similarly have complained at certain Michelin three-starred restaurants). We're eager to return and try some of the dishes we've heard are especially popular: the seafood *quenelles* with sauce Nantua, the veal creations, and the roast leg of lamb. Ann told us that her own favorite is the duck, served on various occasions with one of four or five different sauces. And if it were only possible (we may need to wait for retirement), we'd like to visit the Rowe Inn for its game dinner in the fall, on the first Thursday in November or the last Thursday in October. The inn has a fine wine list, too—not large in number but good in terms of variety of quality and type of offering. It's a bit heavy on the German for our tastes, but we realize these are popular.

The Rowe Inn was built as a hamburger and chicken spot in 1947, and in 1972 Wes and Arlene Westhoven turned it into one of the most appealing country inns in Michigan. Prices are high, but the value is even higher. Your chef will probably be Harlan "Pete" Peterson, who joined the Rowe Inn in 1976 after a previous career as a design engineer with the Ford Motor Company. No offense to Henry, but we like what Pete's designing now even better. This man is gifted! And if you get Ann as your waitress, ask her about the time the Russian delegation came to dinner for the beef Wellington.

Serious students of food and cooking might like to know that the Rowe Inn organizes several "Culinary Crafting" sessions, with each package including three participatory cooking demonstrations, lunches with wine, a wine tasting conducted by Wes Westhoven, two European five-course dinners, an appropriate seasonal field trip (for example, morel hunting in May, winery tours, cross-country skiing), and accommodations at the Jordan Inn in East Jordan (another superlative Continental restaurant in the area; see our description in this book). This must be the only notable culinary school in northern Michigan. Write for information.

Extraordinary country inn—one of the best in the country.

THE ROWE INN, Box 246, Ellsworth, MI 49729. On C-48, 12 miles south of Charlevoix; 6 miles east of M-31; on the outskirts of Ellsworth. Telephone (616) 588-7351. Hours: 6-10 p.m. daily in July and August. Closed Mondays in September, October, May, and June; closed Mondays through Wednesdays November through April; closed entirely for 2 weeks in December. Full bar service. Background music. Free roadside parking. Credit cards: MC, V. Accepts personal checks. Reservations necessary (but do call, and they may fit you in— they did for us).

THE ROWE INN'S SEAFOOD QUENELLES WITH SHERRIED SHRIMP SAUCE

Mix together thoroughly in a Cuisinart food processor ½ pound raw shrimp, ¼ pound scallops, 1 egg, 1 teaspoon salt, ¼ teaspoon freshly grated nutmeg, ¼ teaspoon white pepper, ¼ teaspoon chopped fresh tarragon, and ⅛ teaspoon cayenne pepper. Slowly add 1½ cups whipping cream until the mixture thickens. Add ½ cup bread crumbs and continue processing till the mixture forms a thick paste. Cover, and refrigerate about 2 hours.

Form each *quenelle* by dropping a large tablespoon of the

mixture onto a floured surface. Roll into a flattened egg shape and place in a large buttered skillet. Make enough *quenelles* to fill the pan without touching. Pour in enough simmering water to allow the *quenelles* to float. Place over medium heat, and simmer for 3 to 4 minutes. Remove and drain. Transfer to large or individual baking dishes, and spoon sauce over each. Bake 20 to 25 minutes or until the sauce is bubbly.

For the sherried shrimp sauce, combine ½ cup dry white wine and 2 tablespoons chopped shallots in a saucepan, and simmer 5 minutes. Add 2 cups clam juice and 1 tablespoon tomato paste, and bring to a boil. Boil till reduced to 1 cup, stirring occasionally. Add 1 cup whipping cream and 1 cup milk, and reduce to 2 cups or till slightly thickened. Season with salt and freshly ground pepper. Stir in 1 cup chopped shrimp that has been sautéed in butter (include cooking juices) and 2 tablespoons dry sherry or Cognac. Refrigerate until ready to use. Makes about 18 *quenelles*; 6 entrée servings or 1 *quenelle* per person as an appetizer.

81
THE WEATHERVANE INN
Charlevoix

It was converted from an old grist mill in 1953 and, if we date its origins, it goes back to 1887. Yet the impression is of a lovely modern building, very well maintained, architecturally interesting, and with furnishings worth a second look—if not close study. The fireplace at the entrance, for example, is a nine-ton marvel of masonry formed from huge glacial erratics; it reminds us of Stonehenge, but apparently the view from the inside reminds most people of the shape of the state of Michigan. (Look at it from the outside, too.)

The dominant wood in the main dining room is pecky cypress, and if you eat here, try to get table 9 or 10 or any table near the windows that overlook the Pine River—on a sunny day the color of that water is really something. We also like the Pine River Room to the back on the west; an especially nice table for six is Pine River 3. Call ahead (but not on Saturdays in the summer—reservations aren't taken then).

Cuisine at the Weathervane is basically American with some Continental touches. It's an appetizing luncheon menu: soups, salads, omelettes, a perch plate, the daily special, and some tempting sandwiches—the Swiss Connection (roast beef, melted cheese, and Thousand Island dressing on a sesame-seed bun), the Italian Submarine, and the especially creditable Devonshire (ham or turkey, broccoli, Cheddar cheese on an English muffin). The dinner menu, too, is extensive. You'll like the selections: steaks and seafood as well as barbequed short ribs, a seafood crepe, scallops *en brochette*, stuffed rainbow trout, chicken Leon (a boned and stuffed chicken thigh), and veal Piccata. But the favorites of customers here are the broiled planked Lake Michigan whitefish, the Chateaubriand for two, and the sauerbraten with braised red cabbage (see the following recipe). Daily specials are frequently available, on Friday a fisherman's platter, and often on Saturday prime rib or stuffed pork loin Bavarian-style. There's a welcome variety of prices and portion sizes (eight smaller plates on the menu for those who want a light dinner). You'll probably be pleased to find that the Weathervane Inn looks and behaves in an expensive fashion but that the prices are more reasonable than expensive.

Families on a budget or those with small appetites might prefer to eat in the downstairs Grist Mill Room, with its own menu and even closer to the water. Here you can watch the bascule (counterweighted) bridge over the Pine go up and down every hour and half-hour, and, if the time is right, you can literally touch the 600-foot freighters passing down the river. In front of the fireplace is a coffee table fashioned from a cross-section of an ancient redwood tree; the years are marked (1250 at the center), and brass plaques on the rings indicate historic events throughout the centuries. That tree had quite a lifetime. The downstairs dining room is open in the summer for lighter dinners, sandwiches, pizza, and such ethnic dishes as bratwurst and sauerkraut, potato pancakes, Greek souvlaki, Italian sausage sandwiches and subs, and quiche Lorraine.

Even if you don't frequent bars, do stop in to see the Shipwreck Lounge on the main floor of the Weathervane. The assorted shipwreck relics are fascinating, especially the enormous rudder that serves now as a piano bar. (It came from the wreck of King Ben's Rising Sun that went down off the Manitou Islands.) Here there's a dance floor, a jukebox, and a pianist at the bar nightly in season and three nights a week September to May. Bands and dancing are featured during the ski season.

Sunday brunch at the Weathervane, rather special as brunches go, offers more than 45 dishes, including eggs Benedict and fruit blintzes, at a reasonable price. A brief note on wine: the list is fairly small, and you can visit the cellar if you wish. The house carafe wine is Michigan's Chateau Grand Travers. We understand that recently there's been a change in management at the Weathervane. But if it continues in the future as it has in the past, you should be most satisfied. **Bon voyage, Weathervane.**

THE WEATHERVANE INN, 106 Pine River Lane, Charlevoix, MI 49720. In city center, near the bridge. Telephone (616) 547-9958. Hours: luncheon 11:30 a.m.-2:30 p.m., dinner 5:30-10:30 p.m. (till 11 p.m. Fridays and Saturdays), sandwiches served continually. Closed Christmas and for 2 weeks around Easter (you might call). Full bar service. Children's menu. Background music, entertainment, dancing. Credit cards: MC, V. Reservations suggested as a rule; not taken on Saturdays in the summer.

THE WEATHERVANE INN'S SAUERBRATEN

We received two recipes for sauerbraten (see the Schnitzelbank), and they're both very good. If you like this dish, try both versions. Place 1 fresh brisket or top round of beef into a container large enough so that the meat is about 2 inches from the top. Add 1 carrot, 1 onion, and 1 bunch of celery, all roughly cut up. Add ½ gallon cider vinegar, ½ gallon water, 1 tablespoon whole black peppercorns, 3 bay leaves, 1 clove garlic (cut in half), and 1 teaspoon coriander seeds. Let marinate for 96 hours. Then remove the brisket, and place in a hot pan with some oil. Make sure the pan is large enough so that the entire surface is touching the brisket. Brown the meat thoroughly on both sides. Place into a roasting pan.

Drain the vegetables from the marinade, and reserve the liquid. Brown the vegetables in the same pan you used to brown the meat. Add them to the roasting pan with the meat. Measure the reserved marinade liquid, and measure out an equal amount of beef stock. Add both liquids to the roasting pan so that meat is covered with liquid. Cover the pan with aluminum foil, and place into a 350-degree oven. Cook until tender. When fork-tender, remove from roasting pan and set aside for ½ hour before slicing.

Strain the cooking liquid from the meat into a saucepan. Skim off fat that rises to the top. Add 1½ cups claret wine (dry red wine) and 1 box of ginger snap cookies. Let simmer until the ginger snaps dissolve and the gravy thickens to the desired consistency. Strain gravy to serve.

Hints from the Winters: A brisket weighs about 3-4 pounds and will serve 6 to 8 people. Cooking time will be about 2 to 3 hours. Test the meat at the end of 2 hours; it should be fork-tender.

82
THE ARGONNE SUPPER CLUB
Charlevoix

There are few places these days where you can order for a single price all the jumbo shrimp and frog legs you can eat. This is the specialty at the Argonne, and though the price is not nearly as low as it once was, it's still a remarkable value for the shrimp lover. And they *are* jumbo. The only condition the restaurant makes is that shrimp "boats" (plates of six or ten shrimp) will not be served with the family-style dinner at the same table. The shrimp is cooked either by steaming or deep frying in a specially seasoned beer batter. And we're pleased with the choice of butter for the steamed shrimp— lemon, garlic, or drawn. The Argonne's method of steaming shrimp is a simple but surprisingly effective way to bring out the natural flavor—not the usual crab boil or pickling spices but the addition of celery seed, salt, and instant onion flakes to the steam bath. This is something we plan to try at home.

We can't imagine why anyone would even look at anything else on the menu, but there are some other agreeable offerings: fresh broiled whitefish, Alaskan King crab, surf (crab) and Turf (strip steak), steamed lobster tails, Land (strip again) and Sea (lobster), a 14-ounce char-broiled New York strip steak, and Southern-fried chicken. All dinners are served with either French fries or baked potato, cole slaw or tossed salad, and homemade bread (it may still be hot if you arrive before seven). The wine list is unimpressive; unless you want to splurge on champagne, probably your best bet is the California chablis by the carafe.

The Argonne, still family owned and operated, was built in 1929 and named for the original owner's brother who was killed in "that battle" of World War I. The large old building on spacious grounds houses a single dining room that can seat more than 150. With gold-colored carpeting and table-cloths, it's a pleasing, comfortable room; and of course again the best tables are those by the windows. The supper club is very popular, so it's wise to arrive early—especially on a hot summer evening. There's no air conditioning, and you'll really appreciate being close to the windows. Particularly inviting is the corner table for six at the window farthest from the entry. The service is competent and attentive: most likely you'll be served by Ann, Faye, one of the two Marys, or the excellent, experienced Bonnie Keie. The headwaiter, of course, in this tightly knit, family-run place is Bonnie's son Tom Keie.

For the shrimpomaniac.

THE ARGONNE SUPPER CLUB, Boyne City Road, Charlevoix, MI 49720. Just east of the city; turn right off U.S. 31 on Boyne City Road and drive about 2,000 feet. Hours: dinner only 5-10:30 p.m. daily. Closed November 1 to May 1. Full bar service. Children's (all you can eat) menu. Casual dress. Free parking. No credit cards; accepts personal checks. Reservations not accepted.

BEER BATTER

Sometimes the simplest is the best. Although we didn't receive a recipe from the Argonne, we want to offer this incredibly easy recipe for shrimp batter, one that we've used for years and one that reminds us of the supper club. Try it on fish, onion rings, chicken wings, and anything else you deep fry. We think you'll be pleasantly surprised. If you like to guard your cooking secrets, let your friends think this recipe is too elaborate to explain.

The recipe? Mix 1 cup of beer with 1 cup of flour. Whisk till smooth. That's it. Depending on your tastes and what you're cooking, you might add a bit more beer for a lighter batter. Dip your shrimp, fish, or other item into the batter, let the excess run off, and then deep fry in oil heated to about 375 degrees. Drain on paper toweling.

83
THE PIER
Harbor Springs

For those driving north or south on Route 31 through Petoskey, we suggest a short, picturesque seven-mile excursion to the exclusive coastal village of Harbor Springs for a visit to the Pier. The restaurant probably affords the finest view of Little Traverse Bay with the city of Petoskey visible on the other side. What we like about the Pier's Pointer Room is the combination of enjoyable food in various price ranges, a splendid view, and an assortment of things to do before and after a meal here. A veritable extension of the restaurant (hence its name) is the wide steel pier reaching out about 200 feet into the harbor and flanked by an incredible array of motor launches and sailing ships. Within walking distance is the small shopping district of Harbor Springs, catering to well-heeled tourists and boasting expensive little boutiques, art galleries, craft and gift shops.

Years ago, Tom Brooks, the well-known mushroom expert, introduced us to the Pointer Room during one of our annual expeditions for morels in May. The room was named after the "Pointer," which was once moored in this location and from 1930 to 1949 carried passengers across a small bay to Harbor Point, where automobiles were then prohibited. Harbor Point itself was founded as a resort area in 1878 and still retains some of the exclusive, turn-of-the-century flavor of its early days. All that is left now of the Pointer is its mooring place.

And it's still a welcome mooring place, especially for luncheon and even more if the water and sky are blue and the harbor filled with ships. The understated nautical decor, the sailing-blue table linens, and the historic photographs of the village on the walls contribute to a leisurely atmosphere (though sometimes the service is a bit too leisurely). The luncheon menu offers innovative sandwiches, standard salads, and a good number of entrees at tolerable prices. The liver and onions are good, as is the Pelican Hook (broiled crabmeat and cheese sandwich). The dinner menu includes fairly typical American restaurant fare. But there are some imaginative additions such as a chilled artichoke appetizer, either breast of chicken or veal *Jardiniere*, seafood Royale, baked pork loin San Francisco (sweet and sour), and some daily specials well worth considering. Denise Genoa, the helpful and friendly assistant manager, notes that the most popular items are lobster, whitefish, duckling, chicken, and veal—but her own favorite is the seafood Royale, a rich marriage of shellfish and white wine sauce with mushrooms and broccoli.

The wine list is limited but adequate, and carafes are available. Needless to say (but we'll say it), the best tables are by the windows. If you arrive for lunch before 12:30 or even earlier, you'll be most likely to get one. For dinner, call ahead and reserve a window table.

For the budget-minded and families, the Pier has another dining room downstairs, the Chart Room, offering family specials, sandwiches, light dinners, and—in the fall—seafood buffets, all at lower prices than in the Pointer Room, but lacking that excellent view. There's an attractive lounge, too, the Wheel House. Casual dress will do in the lounge and Chart Room, but we suggest something dressier for the Pointer Room.

A fashionable harborside gathering place.

THE PIER, 102 Bay Street, Harbor Springs, MI 49740. North of Petoskey, on the harbor. Telephone (616) 526-6201. Hours: in the Pointer Room, luncheon 11:30 a.m.-3 p.m., dinner 5-11 p.m.; in the Chart Room, luncheon 11:30 a.m.-5 p.m., dinner 5-11 p.m.; Sundays, luncheon and dinner in both rooms, noon-10 p.m. Closed Christmas Day. Full bar service. Children's portions. Background music. Free Parking. Credit cards: MC, V. Reservations recommended for the Pointer Room, not accepted in the Chart Room.

THE PIER'S PEANUT BUTTER PIE

This one's easy, can be prepared in advance, and is a guaranteed hit with children of all ages. Blend together till well mixed ⅔ cup peanut butter, ¼ cup Karo Syrup, ¼ cup water, and 1 quart vanilla ice cream. Pour into a 9-inch prepared graham cracker pie shell. Freeze. To serve, top with a mixture of ⅔ cup peanut butter and ¼ cup Karo Syrup. Sprinkle liberally with Spanish peanuts. Serves 6-8.

84
THE LEGS INN
Cross Village

One word for the Legs Inn, and normally we'd hesitate to use it, is "unique"—and if it were correct, we might even say "extremely unique." Our aim in this book is to describe, but how do you describe the indescribable? This is a place that must be seen to be believed. The building is extraordinary—both the exterior and interior are unlike those of any other restaurant we've seen. Stanley Smolak, the uncle of the present owner, made the Legs Inn a lifetime project, starting in 1932, and he was still working on it twelve years ago before he died at the age of 81. He laid all the field stones by hand and constructed and carved nearly everything within the large masonry building, from the chairs and doors to the bars and window carvings. His sculptures are contortions in wood, protean, imaginative, grotesque, wonderful. A colorful local figure in his day, Mr. Smolak was even made Honorary Chief White Cloud by the Ottawa in this Native American village (see the museum across the street). The "legs," by the way, refer to the line of stove legs that are perched atop the front of the building, giving it the appearance of a fort as seen by, say, Salvador Dali.

But what is most important about the Legs Inn is that the eastern European food here is as good as any you'll find in the state, and on top of that, it's a bargain. Eating out in Michigan has certainly been enhanced since Helen Smolak, the attractive owner's wife, assistant manager, sometime bartender, and chef, came here from Poland in 1974. She's already built up quite a following. Customers sometimes call ahead to see if she's baked one of her superb tortes that day and, if not, might change their minds about coming. The breads, the tortes, the soups are always freshly made; and Helen is in charge of the marvelous European specialties: homemade Kielbasa with sauerkraut, *golombki* (stuffed cabbage rolls) with a choice of sauces, and *pierogi* (Polish-style dumplings stuffed with potato and cheese or meat and sauerkraut; seven to a plate). If you're fortunate, you might be able to try some of Helen's red borscht or sauerkraut soup before your main course. On Fridays and Saturdays the Legs Inn features a 12-ounce pan-fried whitefish fillet, at a lower price than in any restaurant we've found in Michigan. Do, when you visit, ask what's special that day or evening.

The Legs is open for breakfast and lunch, but we prefer the dinner menu. Still, if you can, visit at any time and see this remarkable place. There's a small gift store adjacent, and the inn smokes and sells its own fish daily. Takeouts are also available. On Fridays and Saturdays a band plays from music from the 50s and 60s (no acid or hard rock), and there's a dance floor in the large bar and lounge area.

Either go due west from U.S. 31 at Levering or take one of Michigan's most pleasant drives by going north from Harbor Springs on M-131. You might even catch a glimpse of a maneuvering B 52 bomber traveling hundreds of miles per hour only a few hundred feet above the lake. But, however you get to the Legs Inn, get there. There's nothing like it in Michigan. It's one of our favorites.

Bohemian, bizarre, beguiling—a bargain.

THE LEGS INN, Lake Shore Drive, Cross Village, MI 49723. In village center, across from the museum. Telephone (616) 526-5087. Hours: 10 a.m.-10 p.m. from May 1 to November 15; rest of the year open only on Fridays, Saturdays, and Sundays. Full bar service. Children's menu. Casual dress. No credit cards. Reservations recommended.

SUE KOVACIK'S LISTY

When it comes to Southern hospitality and eastern European cooking (or maybe any other kind), Sue Kovacik of

Columbia, South Carolina, is unexcelled. This is her recipe for an ethereal Czech pastry. You probably won't get these at the Legs Inn, but ask—we're sure Helen Smolak knows how to make them.

Measure and then sift 1½ cups flour. Mix together in a bowl ½ cup heavy cream or sour cream, 3 slightly beaten egg yolks, 1 tablespoon whiskey, and 1 pinch salt. Add the flour slowly until a soft dough similar to pie pastry is obtained. (Use more flour if necessary.) Knead the dough on a floured board until it no longer sticks to the board or your hands. Place in a bowl, cover, and let stand 15 minutes. Cut dough into 3 balls, and cover again for 15 minutes. Roll out very thinly (like strudel dough). Cut in any shape and slash with a knife in the center of each piece. Deep fry in ½ pound lard or vegetable oil. Sprinkle with confectioners sugar.

85
THE DAM SITE INN
Pellston

From the entryway, furnished with handmade cherrywood tables and hutches, to any one of the five dining rooms, decorated attractively in modern but not avant-garde style with a few country touches, the Dam Site Inn is very well maintained and pleasing to the eye. We especially like the Coral Room (try to get table C6); unfortunately reservations aren't taken, so only early and late comers are likely to have much choice. But the restaurant seats about 240, and many of the tables have views—of the surrounding countryside or the dammed Maple River, giving the illusion of a small lake. If it's necessary to wait, you'll enjoy the lounge with its white Saarinen chairs and roomy bar. The country restaurant has been in business for more than a quarter of a century and is now under the new management of Betty and Joe Church—but with the continuing advice of the original owners, Kathy and Ken McLaughlin. And if the new owners do as well as the old, it should remain popular for at least another 25 years.

The specialty of the house (and by far the most frequently ordered item) is the exemplary pan-fried chicken dinner, family style, all you can eat, served with excellent homemade noodles cooked in broth, gravy, potatoes, peas, and beverage. You may call ahead if you prefer your chicken stewed. (Call ahead, too, if you want the Churches to save the livers and gizzards for you.) The steaks and seafoods are also well received, particularly the butter-broiled scallops. Dinners are served with a generous relish plate, salad, vegetable, potatoes, and hot buttermilk biscuits. There are a few additional side orders such as soup (a special chowder on Friday only) and onion rings; and desserts are à *la carte*. If you can make room for it, try the chocolate angel food cake—with a chocolate mousse center and topped with whipped cream and fudge sauce.

The Dam Site Inn has a better than average wine list with a few exceptional offerings (such as the 1959 Lafite, Mouton, and Haut Brion and the 1961 Latour)—at substantial prices, however. You may visit the cellar if you wish, but the setup isn't especially impressive. The kitchen, too, is always open for your inspection, and we found it extremely well kept. **Comfortable country dining.**

THE DAM SITE INN, Woodland Road, Pellston, MI 49769. About 7 miles west of I-75, 1½ miles south of Pellston off U.S. 31; about 18 miles northeast of Petoskey. Telephone (616) 539-8851. Hours: 5-10 p.m., Sundays 3-9 p.m. Closed about six months of the year, from the end of trout season (the third Saturday in October) to the end of April; opens on the last Friday of April. Full bar service. Soft background music. Free parking. Credit cards: MC, V. Reservations not taken (large groups should call ahead).

86
VIVIO'S
Indian River

Vivio's is a special favorite of ours, a perfect spot to visit after a long day of morel hunting in May. You can expect efficient service, good food, fair prices, and, if you order the right thing, it's also a bargain. And it's unquestionably unpretentious and a delightful place for families—there are seven high chairs, but it seems that these are never enough. Northern Italian cooking has been the specialty here since the restaurant opened in 1938. The pasta is homemade and *al dente*, and the sauce is superb—we've seen and been duly impressed by the enormous vat in the kitchen, where it simmers constantly and, we like to think, ages beautifully like vintage port.

The loyal clientele, understandably devoted to the place, generally order the pizza, veal Parmigiana, spaghetti, and ravioli. Our own first choice is the splendid combination pasta plate, half spaghetti and half ravioli. Dinners include individual antipasto salads, soup or juice, potatoes or spaghetti, bread, ice cream, and beverage. Or you may order any of the various pastas in a full or half portion, served with salad and bread. Three enticing new additions to the dinner menu that old visitors to Vivio's may be interested in trying are the cannelloni crepe, chicken Milano crepe, and the spaghetti and fresh shrimp Sicilian. Beguiling crepe desserts, too, are now on the menu. Assorted steaks, chicken, sandwiches, and seafoods are also available at reasonable prices. But we think that once you breathe in the pervasive and mouth-watering aromas emanating from that bubbling sauce in the kitchen, you'll stick with the Italian specialties.

Vivio's now has two dining rooms (an addition was recently completed off the bar area), but we still prefer the large original room with the huge stone fireplace and open-beamed ceiling. The building, an authentic log cabin, is decorated in northwoods rustic with checked tablecloths and with stuffed birds and game on the walls and overhead. It's very cozy and warm, as is the bar—you might ask Jim O'Hara, who's tended bar here for eighteen years, to make you his popular Bloody Mary or, for the kids, some Big Lukes, Vivio's special kiddie cocktails. On pleasant evenings you can also have your before-dinner drinks outdoors under the red and white canopy in front.

If you're on your way north or south, it's worth an extra few miles' side trip to stop at Vivio's for dinner. And if you're still around in the morning, we suggest you have breakfast at nearby Christopher's in town: the feature is the seldom seen "eggs in a nest," cooked here as well as anyplace.

Italian, inexpensive—both the best and a bargain.

VIVIO'S NORTHWOOD INN, U.S. 27 and M-68, Indian River, MI 49749. Between Petoskey and Cheboygan; take the Indian River exit from I-75; 1 mile southwest of town on M-68. Hours: 5 p.m.-midnight (till 1 a.m. Fridays and Saturdays), 4-II p.m. on Sundays. Open daily May 23-November 25; closed Mondays and Tuesdays in winter and December 1-25. Full bar service. Jukebox. Free parking. No credit cards. Reservations not taken except for large groups by request.

VIVIO'S CANNELLONI CREPES

First, mix the crepe batter: combine 4 eggs, a pinch salt, 2 cups flour, 2¼ cups milk, and ¼ cup melted margarine. Beat till smooth, and refrigerate 1 hour. Cook crepes in a lightly buttered or oiled crepe pan or small skillet and set aside.

For the filling, mix together by hand 2 cups small-curd cottage cheese, one 8-ounce package Philadelphia cream cheese, and 4 tablespoons butter. Add 4 tablespoons of chopped parsley, 2 eggs, 2 chopped scallions, and a dash of salt. Spoon 3 tablespoons of filling onto each crepe. Roll up, and place in a baking dish, seam sides down. Cover filled crepes lightly with your favorite spaghetti sauce. Sprinkle grated Romano cheese on top. Bake till hot in a 350-degree oven, about 20 minutes.

87
THE HACK-MA-TACK INN
Cheboygan

Located on the east bank of the fast-flowing Cheboygan River that drains Mullet Lake and in a wooded country setting, the Hack-Ma-Tack Inn is clearly the best restaurant in the Cheboygan area. The site, at one of the northern openings into the Southern Peninsula's largest wilderness areas, drained by the Black and Pigeon Rivers, encourages the imaginative to recall the Ojibwa, the French trappers, and Michigan's spectacular era of river logging. Today, however, you'll find a rambling, well-worn building with a large, airy dining room decorated in early American. The tables are spruce and cheerful with vibrant blue tablecloths and glistening glassware. The open-hearth grill adds to the interest of the place, but most attention is drawn to the pleasing view of the woods and river through a sparkling facade of windows. Adjacent to the dining room is a small bar and lounge with glass doors opening to within a few feet of a 400-foot docking area along the river bank. On nice days some guests arrive by boat, and many prefer to enjoy their refreshments outdoors rather than in the lounge.

The menu appeals to basic American tastes for charcoal-grilled steaks, prime rib, lobster tails, and whitefish. Numerous other offerings are in the same vein. The menu is not particularly innovative, but what this restaurant has is fine quality and adequate servings. These are enhanced by several appetizers, yet another salad bar, and a decent, though not distinguished, dessert selection. According to our information, the baking is done on the premises, which always seems an advantage. This combination of food and setting makes the Hack-Ma-Tack rather special for this part of the state, and if you're heading southeast on Route 23 toward Alpena, it's a long, long way before you'll find anything as good.

Down by the riverside, a serene setting.

THE HACK-MA-TACK INN, Beebe Road (Rural Route 4), Cheboygan, MI 49721. Five miles south, 2 miles southeast of the junction of M-27 and 33. Telephone (616) 625-2919. Hours: mid-June to Labor Day, luncheon noon-3 p.m., dinner 5:30-10:30 p.m., Sunday luncheon noon-3 p.m., dinner 4-10 p.m.; after Labor Day to mid-October, dinner 5:30-10 p.m., Sunday 4-10 p.m. Closed mid-October to late March, also on Mondays and Tuesdays after Labor Day. Full bar service. Children's plates. Background music. Free parking. Credit cards: MC, V. Reservations recommended.

If you like our recommendations, tell the proprietor. If you don't, tell us. Write Beech Tree Press, 2673 Rampart Path, Holt, Michigan 48842.

88
KENVILLE'S
Mackinaw City

This is a cheerful, bustling, plain, family-style restaurant across from the docks in downtown Mackinaw City. Kenville's is strictly traditional American cooking with an attempt at a few fancy extras, and it caters to those who prefer not to have beer, wine, or cocktails with dinner. We like it for several reasons: the efficiency and cleanliness, the large servings, the flavorful and hearty fare at low prices, and the convenience to the docks if you're waiting for or returning from a ferry to Mackinac Island. The best seats are in the booths by the windows, but avoid the first two or any of the tables near the entry. There's no waiting room, and the place is packed daily with what appears to be half the population of Mackinaw City. In fact, we've been told that people stand in line outdoors, even in the rain, at Kenville's.

The restaurant offers plate dinners (including potatoes and rolls) at very reasonable prices. Dinners may be ordered *table d'hôte* or *à la carte*, another boon for the budgeter. Full dinners are accompanied by soup or juice, potatoes, choice of salad, rolls, and dessert. Entrées include roast beef, steaks, shrimp, meatloaf, beef stew, fish, fried chicken, liver with onions or bacon, pork chops, and the favorite item—baked chicken and biscuits. Each day a special is also available, again by the dinner or the plate.

But the homemade pies are what bring many customers to Kenville's—it may be the best restaurant pie in Michigan. Hunt Sweitzer of Lansing's City Fish Co., a Kenville admirer, tells us that the first time he sat down to eat there, the waitress—before even providing him with a menu—set a piece of lemon pie in front of him and said, "This is the last piece; I thought I'd better bring it now." We think its reputation is well deserved. The lemon filling is superb, but the crust takes the cake. It's the best we've tasted, and we'll be forever grateful to Jack Kenville for letting us pass it on to you (see recipe below).

If such home-style food in a Midwestern café setting does not at first appeal to your adventurous instincts, we urge you to give it a second thought. It's surprising how many times in gastronomic conversations hundreds of miles from Mackinaw City we've listened to the words "You've probably never heard of it, but there's a terrific little place called Kenville's..." The American cooking here is not prosaic or prototypical. The recipes used here have been passed down through three generations of the Kenville family, You won't find them in a cookbook; they're not even written down for the Kenville cooks. Any family member who wishes to be part of the restaurant must commit them to memory and learn every phase of the business as well. These people are dedicated. That's what gastronomy is all about.

Family fare at its best, a bargain.

KENVILLE'S CAFE, 112 S. Huron Avenue, Mackinaw City, MI 49701. Across from the docks, at the railroad tracks. Telephone (616) 436-7131. Hours: 8 a.m.-10 p.m. daily. Open April 1 to October 20. No alcoholic beverages. Background music. Reservations not accepted.

GRANDMA'S PIE CRUST

This is a sought-after recipe we're very pleased to be able to publish. We think you'll like the combination of shortening, which makes for an exceptionally rich, tender, and flaky crust. Plan on making this a day ahead. Mix until smooth and creamy 5 pounds of pure lard, 6 pounds Crisco vegetable shortening, 3 pounds butter, and ¼ cup salt. Add 35 cups of flour, and mix to a paste. Mix in 5 quarts of water. Cover and refrigerate dough for 24 hours before using.

Hints from the Winters: Unless you're baking for the Swiss army, you probably won't be using the quantities listed above. We suggest the following amounts for a double-crusted 9-inch pie: 5 ounces lard (or ½ cup plus 2 tablespoons), 6 ounces Crisco (¾ cup), 3 ounces butter (6 tablespoons or ¾ stick), ¾ teaspoon salt, 2¼ cups flour, and 1¼ cup water. When rolling out this dough, be gentle and use lots of flour. It's unlike most pie pastry you may have tried—but the results are worth the extra care. After putting your pie together, use your lightest pastry brush (one of those feathers is perfect) and brush the top crust with beaten egg yolk. (Brushing the bottom crust with beaten egg white before filling will also prevent seepage and keep the crust dry.)

89
THE GRAND HOTEL
Mackinac Island

Graciousness, serenity, nostalgia, the Good Life—no one word or phrase can capture the personality of the aging but still lovely queen of Michigan's resort hotels. More tourists from throughout the country have seen photographs of it or pointed it out from across the water than have set foot on its long colonnaded walkway or huge white veranda overlooking the Straits of Mackinac. Certainly the best-known structure on Mackinac Island, the Grand Hotel has an honorable history, dating from 1887, as the summer stopping place of presidents, ambassadors, generals, and kings. Once the social scene of the elite—Mrs. Potter Palmer, the Cudahys, and other tycoons of the Chicago business world—it now hosts a steady stream of conventions, booked at least two years in advance, and visitors from all walks of life who want to luxuriate in the unhurried quality and niceties of a bygone era.

The Grand Hotel, an imposing Classical Georgian building set on 500 acres, advertises itself as the "world's largest summer hotel" and has long been known as the "showplace of the North." (The island itself has been called the "Bermuda of the North," but we think that's pushing it.) The surroundings are geared to leisure, like a cruise ship on the Caribbean; a stay at the hotel lends itself to lazy and self-indulgent pleasures: walks through the beautiful sunken gardens, carriage tours, riding instruction, tennis and golf, bicycling through the 2,000-acre state park nearby, or just sitting on the veranda and looking back on the rest of Michigan. And, of course, savoring some of the state's finest meals.

There's but one dining room in the Grand Hotel: the spacious Salle à Manger, seating 600 to l,000 people. Appropriately the decor is 1930s "summer style" and the colors— green, white, yellow—fresh and summery, too. There is something reassuring and uncomplicated in both decor andmenu.

The food, by design, is traditionally American. Meals are price fixed, *table d'hôte*, and somewhat, though not surprisingly, expensive (as of our last nformation, breakfast $8, luncheon $12.50, and dinner $25). The menus change daily. Dinner includes your choice of a number of appetizers, soups, salads, entrées, vegetables, desserts, and beverages. Prime rib and broiled trout or whitefish are regularly served (and regularly ordered), but the other entrées vary: shrimp Creole, roast loin of pork, steamed finnan haddie with scrambled eggs, smoked ox tongue, lamb curry, broiled sweetbreads, omelettes, tenderloin of beef *à la Deutsch*, baked ham.

On any one menu, the choices are generally roasts, chops, and broiled fish plus one or two "gourmet" offerings. Usually three soups are available, on the order of gazpacho, Indian corn chowder, bisque of crab, or cream of chicken Delmar. First-course options might include such dishes as smoked Nova Scotia salmon, marinated mushrooms, assorted canapes, fruit, and a seafood appetizer. There are generally two potato choices and two or three other vegetable offerings. In the sugar and spice category are pies, ice creams (sometimes unusual ones, like coffee cognac), cakes, fruit compote, almost always baked custard, and always cheese. Available wines include Dom Perignon, Le Montrachet (1973), and a 1964 Lafite with prices appropriate to their distinction. Most of the remaining 23 offerings are less than $20, and many of these cost less than $10. The breakdown is expectable: three rosés, six sparkling, nine whites, and eight reds.

Another meal of which staunch Anglophiles (and inveterate snackers) will approve is the high tea served each day in the main parlor of the Grand Hotel. When we traveled to England, we regularly took tea and found it a delightful transition between a busy afternoon and the evening's activities. Somehow, back home, we're still busy at 4 p.m. and are never able or willing to make time for the inconsequentiality of tea. But at the Grand Hotel it's one of our favorite meals: the leisurely tempo, the very fact that it *is* inconsequential, and the array of delicacies served by attentive waiters all contribute to one of life's most sedate and soothing experiences.

Mackinac Island—originally called the "Great Turtle" by Native Americans—is formed of 350,000,000-year-old Devonian rock. The topography, however, evolved late in earth's history, and wave-eroded notches from higher levels of Lake Huron thousands of years ago are apparent in many places—in fact, the Grand Hotel is nestled into one of these. With European settlement, the island and its nearby areas became commercially and strategically important for the French, then the British, and finally the Americans. Remember, St. Ignace, the closest mainland village, was established more than 300 years ago! Now, of course, the island's main function is recreation. And the combination of history; setting; scenery; transportation only by foot, bicycle, or horse and carriage; and this grand old hotel makes a visit to Mackinac Island one of the most adventurous experiences in Michigan.

Grand in every respect.

THE GRAND HOTEL, Mackinac Island, MI 49757. Telephone (906) 847-3331. Hours: breakfast 8-9:45 a.m. (Continental breakfast till noon), luncheon noon-2 p.m., high tea 4 p.m., dinner 7-8:45 p.m. Open mid-May to late October. Full bar service. Entertainment and dancing. Gentlemen, coats and ties requested after 6 p.m.; ladies, wear dresses or your better pantsuits. No credit cards or reservations for meals.

MACKINAC MORELS

Northern Michigan is noted for its delicious morel mushrooms, and here is a recipe for a dish we've made from morels we've found in the Mackinac area. If you have morels, you're fortunate. But if you haven't, you may substitute commercial mushroom caps.

This is simple and versatile and, we think, in the high American style of the Grand Hotel. Clean 2 pounds of fresh mushrooms. Leave whole if small to medium in size; halve them if they're very large. Sauté the mushrooms in butter (4-6 tablespoons) till browned and just cooked through. Make 1 cup of medium thick cream sauce: melt 2 tablespoons butter, and add 2 tablespoons flour. Cook, stirring, on very low heat for 2 minutes. Gradually add 1 cup milk, and cook until thickened. Season to taste with salt and white pepper. Add 1 cup sour cream, and mix well. Add the sautéed mushrooms and 6 to 8 thinly sliced scallions. Season to taste. Place in a buttered casserole, and bake 20-30 minutes at 350 degrees. Serves 6-8.

90
THE HUNGARIAN KITCHEN
St. Ignace

Half-hidden in Lake Michigan's shoreline dunes, the Hungarian Kitchen is one of the most agreeably evocative eating places in the Upper Peninsula. Once a beach house, it now contains a small dining room with latticed windows, knotty pine walls, and just eight tables, each seating up to six people. Robert Du Chai (the name is French but the nationality Hungarian) is obviously devoted to quality and is planning an addition to his restaurant—to hold three more tables. Much of the charm here is that small, intimate, homespun setting and an elusive eastern European aura that affords a wistful glimpse into an all-but-forgotten past.

As for the food, we give it top billing—but only if you order the authentic Hungarian dishes. The dedicated chef from Budapest regularly offers two soups, *bab leves* (bean) and *csirke leves* (chicken)—both virtuoso performances. Entrées include genuine food: a marvelous chicken *paprikash*—large pieces of meltingly tender chicken and tiny, succulent Hungarian dumplings in gravy; stuffed cabbage rolls with a pungent, genuine sauerkraut; and an exceptionally savory goulash, made with braised sirloin tips (a hearty Magyar dish, this goulash, and no kin to that travesty of hamburger and macaroni that resembles it in name only). Each of these is served with a small loaf of homemade bread, fresh vegetables, and your choice of potatoes or dumplings (we definitely prefer the superb fingertip-sized *nokedli* dumplings). Three desserts are offered on the standard menu: a wonderful torte with either an apple or cherry filling and *modarte*, an unalloyed delight of creamy custard with a fluffy meringue topping. There's no wine list, but you might call about bringing your own beverages.

There are several other small, similar restaurants in the area, but if you want to sample some of those Kovacikian, Transylvanian treasures, be certain to stop at the Hungarian Kitchen, located on the north side of the highway across the road from Lake Michigan. And be prepared for parking in the sand dunes. If the restaurant is full, you may need to walk

a short distance and end up with sand in your shoes—but this is a small price to pay when you think of what awaits you.
The best of Budapest—and a bargain.
THE HUNGARIAN KITCHEN, Route 2, St. Ignace, MI 49781. Twelve miles west of St. Ignace on Rte. 2; 8 miles south of Brevort. Telephone (906) 643-7693. Hours: after Labor Day until September 15, open daily noon-10 p.m.; closed September 16-June 15; open daily June 16-30 noon-10 p.m.; open daily July 1-Labor Day 8 a.m.-10 p.m. No alcoholic beverages. Children's portions. Casual dress. Free parking. No credit cards. Reservations recommended.

MARIAN'S HUNGARIAN TORTE

This is a family recipe that we're sure Monsieur Du Chai would appreciate and that we feel is appropriate to the Hungarian Kitchen. It's a beautiful thing—luscious, rich, and calorie-ridden.

Beat 8 egg yolks until light and fluffy. Add 2 cups sugar, ½ cup water, 2 cups flour (sifted 3 times), 2 teaspoons baking powder, and a pinch salt. Fold in 8 egg whites, beaten stiff until they hold peaks. Add 2 teaspoons vanilla. Bake in 3 round layer-cake pans in a preheated 350-degree oven for 40 minutes. (Note: the batter will be *very* thin.) Remove from pans and split to make 6 layers.

For the icing, cream 1 pound sweet unsalted butter with 1 pound confectioners sugar. Add 8 egg yolks (beaten thick) and 1 ounce melted baking chocolate. Into this fold 8 stiffly beaten egg whites. Spread this mixture thickly between the cake layers and on the outside of the torte. Refrigerate. Serves 8-12.

91
THE ANTLER'S
Sault Ste. Marie

The Antler's bills itself as "a little bit o' Ireland," but the atmosphere and food is a lot more American than Erin. The history of the place dates back more than four generations and three family ownerships to the era when it was known as the Bucket of Blood and Ice Cream Parlour (the latter providing a "front" during Prohibition). It was closed down, however, when internal revenue agents found that it sold only one quart of ice cream a month and yet took in a profit of $900. It has been said that since that time the Bucket of Blood became the first lemonade stand in history that refused to serve minors.

The decor is probably best described as "a chaotic assemblage of artifacts" (junk?), primarily hung from the ceiling and attached to the walls—including bear traps, farm equipment, old flags, golf clubs, mounted fauna and fish, swords, hardhats, a stuffed black bear and assorted other animals, street signs, and an erormous collection of bells (do ask the bar man to "ring the bells"). None of this is apparent from the unimposing exterior, done in American roadhouse style.

Sit anywhere at the Antler's. There is no "best" table—no matter where you are, you're surrounded by noisy, happy eaters and the clanging of bells or the sizzling of steaks. If you happen to find yourself at the table by the window near the bar, don't be too surprised to look up and see a stuffed python peering down at you. And don't look for intimacy; small parties may find themselves sitting at long tables with other groups. Obviously this is not the place for those wishing stylish elegance—but it's certainly fun.

The menu at the Antler's should be registered with the Library of Congress (in the humor section) and possibly used as an "example" by a diligent English teacher (read every word, and try to count the number of misspellings). As for what is offered on that menu, there's something for everyone, from grilled cheese sandwiches to a 28-ounce porterhouse steak. There's an Irish onion soup, fresh lake trout, barbequed ribs, assorted steaks, seafood platter, fried chicken, crab legs, shrimp, and scallops. Dinners include "choice of potatoe (sic), salad, tea or coffee, placemat, napkin, knife, fork, plate, and table-n-chair." If you're in the mood for something simpler, say, a hamburger, you can order the Family Burger—5 pounds of ground beef on a 16-inch bun (we defy you to find a bigger burger in Michigan). You can even get a peanut butter sandwich (for $5.95; jelly is extra).

Specials of the week include on Monday deep-fried pop-corn shrimp, on Tuesday clams, on Wednesday and Friday fish, and on Thursday "leftovers from Monday, Tuesday, and Wednesday ground up into 1-pound servings for $14.95 (Alka Seltzer extra)." Only two desserts are featured: strawberry shortcake and baked Alaska (the latter available only at the Antler's "Juneau, Fairbanks, Anchorage, and Key West franchises"). Only a few of the items here are priced above $5, and the budget-minded can find something suitable without much difficulty.

Wines are served by the glass, half-liter, and liter; and a very small selection of other undistinguished wines are also available. Beer seems to be the popular beverage. "Fancy drinks" may be ordered, too, including a half-liter of Martinis or Manhattans.

The Antler's is a fine place for the whole family from Grandma to the babies. Furthermore, the food is good and the prices low. But be sure to dress down for the place unless you want to be conspicuous. Noise and all, as far as we're concerned, when we're in Sault Ste. Marie, it's our favorite place. In fact, we like it better than the locks.

If you're staying overnight at Sault Ste. Marie (and you probably are), we suggest heading for the Ramada Inn when you wake up. Here you can enjoy the best French toast in Michigan, made of thick French bread in a vanilla-flavored egg batter. Good morning!

A boisterous, bell-ringing bargain.

THE ANTLER'S, Portage Avenue, Sault Ste. Marie, MI 49783. At the east end of Portage Avenue, paralleling the east approach to the "Soo" locks. Telephone (906) 632-3571. Hours: 10:30 a.m.-midnight. Closed Christmas. Full bar service. Free parking. All major credit cards. Reservations not accepted.

THE ANTLERS' VEGETABLE BEEF SOUP

Cut up one 900-pound steer into very small pieces (1-inch cubes). Finely chop one truckload of mixed carrot, corn, and potatoes, and combine with the contents of one tanker of crushed tomatoes. Place all ingredients into a very large vat; then, with the vat, get into one very old birch bark canoe, preferably one that has been hanging from the rafters for quite some time (this adds to the taste), and paddle rapidly to make sure everything is well mixed. Finally, simmer for 3 weeks, or until the soup is just ready to boil. Shut off heat and let cool. (If this is done around February, it cools much faster.) After the mixture has cooled, pour into 47,000 soup bowls and hope for the busiest winter you've ever had!

Hints from the Winters: A tanker and a half of tomatoes may be more reasonable. Or you might want to use several gallons of beef stock until the proper consistency is reached. We like a bit more seasoning—say, 600 crushed bay leaves and about 100 pounds of salt (to taste). The birch bark canoe is essential for an authentic flavor, but an aluminum canoe, if paddled at top speed, will almost do the trick.

92
THE DOGPATCH
Munising

T-shirts emblazoned with "Dogpatch" have been seen from Detroit to Disneyland, but until recently we'd never paid much attention to the source—Munising, Michigan. Munising, for us, always meant a boat tour to the Pictured Rocks—a 37-mile and 3-hour trip that shouldn't be missed if you're in the area. But the Dogpatch was something new to us—and, at certain times of the evening, as colorful as Pictured Rocks. It's an ultra-casual, American-style restaurant and bar with some exceptional bargains in food. We think families will appreciate the portions and prices, and groups can have a good time here. Near the sidewalk in the front of the Dogpatch is a Model A Ford—take a good look, feel it, and marvel at the kind of metal from which fenders were once made.

The frame building was erected by the owner in 1966, and over the years there have been additions to the place and its surroundings. It's heated 70 percent by a wood-burning furnace in the rear. The decor is, of course, rustic, and the walls are profusely decorated with country-humorous signs and colorfully painted figures from Al Capp's famous cartoon, "Li'l Abner." The retaurant is cooled by a ceiling fan and for entertainment offers pool, skittles, and a jukebox. For dining we like the upper level, constructed of old power line poles. Larger groups and families desiring some privacy can call ahead for tables in the alcove off the bar.

But back to those bargains. Two steak dinners, the "dinner of distinction" and Earthquake McGoon's Rib-Eye, include at very reasonable prices soup or juice, choice of potato, salad, onion rings, and rolls. The steaks are all U.S. Choice and beautiful! The Lake Superior trout dinner, too, can be had for a lower price than any we've seen in this area and is the most popular menu item along with the Li'l Abner, a large char-broiled ground round burger on a toasted bun. On our visit a bar treat of 21 shrimp in a basket was priced at only $2.50. Colonel Bullmoose Backyard Golden Fried Chicken may be ordered in varying portions of 8 to 16 pieces. Soups are homemade (the Russian cabbage is a winner). The Dogpatch specializes in ice cream dessert drinks, among them the popular Blue-Tail Fly. Sundaes and malts are also offered, "cuz they luv ya." A daily luncheon and dinner special is often available, especially in the winter. (If you happen to visit then, you might catch sight of the Shoveler. Don't be surprised if he lets on that he owns the place; however, if you'd like to meet the real managers, see Karin and Bill Ramsey, who, in addition to being youthful and friendly, are obviously tol-erant.)

Whimsical and lively, a bargain.

THE DOGPATCH (Tap Beer 'n Vittles), 325 E. Superior Street, Munising, MI 49862. In city center. Telephone (906) 387-9948. Hours: 11 a.m.-midnight, Sundays noon-midnight. Closed Christmas, New Years Day, Easter, and Thanksgiving. Full bar service. Children's portions. Free parking nearby. No credit cards. Reservations recommended.

DOGPATCH LAKE TROUT

Trout should be filleted and cut into 1-inch pieces. Beat together 12 eggs with salt (it should taste very salty). Mix together 3 cups flour and 2 cups finely ground cracker meal. Dip the trout pieces in the egg mixture for a few minutes, long enough to absorb the salt seasoning. Then coat with the flour mixture. Deep fry until the fish floats and is a nice golden color. Enough batter for 8 to 10 trout.

93
THE CROW'S NEST
Marquette

On the sixth floor of the Old Marquette Inn, anchored on Precambrian bedrock and overlooking Lake Superior, the Crow's Nest may be the closest thing Michigan can offer in the setting and tradition of an Atlantic coast seafood restauant, complete with a raw bar in the lounge. (Ignore the "Heritage" sign on top of the building—the hotel has reverted to its original name.) The room is furnished in nautical and rustic early American with a few antiques, a cork ceiling, and varied woods (pine, hemlock, oak, and cedar) used throughout. There's a splendid view, probably the best in the city, and since the dining room is on two levels, customers at most tables can enjoy it. (Tables 6 through 11 are nearest the windows, with 4 to 7 the best for parties of four and 6 and 11 best for larger groups.)

Appropriately the accent at the Crow's Nest is on seafood, but the cooking is even more inventive than this suggests. For luncheon there's a choice of smelt, flounder, scallops, shrimp, scrod, clams, squid, mussels, oysters, lobster, and a "catch of the day," most of them cooked in traditional styles. In addition, you can order a Lobster Bake (including a whole lobster, clams, mussels, corn, redskins, slaw, bread), a Greek poached fish salad, assorted sandwiches served on rolls or in Lebanese pocket bread, Polish cabbage rolls, Irish stew, Cornish pasty, and barbequed beef ribs. This is an elaborate luncheon menu and varies from the dinner menu mainly in that the latter offers prime rib in three portion sizes, prime rib and seafood combinations, several chicken entrées, and steaks. Our own preferences are for the flounder (Florentine-style—see the recipe following) and the garlicky Portuguese style scrod.

The salads, side orders, and desserts on both menus are

much the same—and quite intriguing. The Crow's Nest mixes some unexpected and refreshing salad dressings (among them Louie, yoghurt, lemon-honey, cucumber and egg), and you have the option of adding shrimp or tuna to your salad. Five large full-meal salads, too, are available. Most entrées come with salad or slaw and are fairly priced. We like the choice of side orders at an additional charge—corn on the cob, *ratatouille*, sautéed mushrooms, wild and long-grain rice, and Chinese-style vegetables. We also like the oysters and clams, served in several ways and priced individually; Why not mix and match? Or try the raw bar in the lounge with cocktails before dinner. Aside from oysters, clams, and shrimp, there are fried squid and mushrooms and occasional other delicacies.

When we were last there, the wines listed included nine reds, ten whites, three rosés, six sparkling wines, and three house wines that may be purchased by the glass or carafe. The mix of offerings and the prices are reasonable, but there is little of distinction, and those, like us, who prefer a French white Burgundy with fish won't find it, even though the Mouton Cadet is incorrectly listed as coming from that area.

In the lounge the Crow's Nest regularly has entertainment, low keyed and conducive to dining. On our last visit Harvey Griffin, the well-known Bay City harpist, was performing. Raw seafood, deli, and baked goods are for takeout sale and on display near the cashier's desk.

Great setting, great seafood.

THE CROW'S NEST, 214 N. Front Street, Marquette, MI 49855. In city center. Telephone (906) 228-7993. Hours: luncheon 11 a.m.-2:30 p.m., dinner 5-11 p.m. (till 11 p.m. on Saturdays). Closed Sundays. Full bar service. Live background music. Free parking. Credit cards: AE, MC, V. Reservations not accepted.

THE CROW'S NEST
FLOUNDER FLORENTINE

Prepare the sauce. Cook ½ large chopped onion in 2½ tablespoons butter until golden. Add 8 ounces finely chopped raw flounder, and cook for 4 minutes. Add 1½ cups dry white wine and ¼ cup lemon juice. Bring to a boil, and then simmer slowly 5 minutes. In a large saucepan, melt 3¾ tablespoons butter. Stir in 5 tablespoons flour, 1¼ teaspoon chicken soup base (or instant bouillon), and 1¼ teaspoon Dijon mustard.

Prepare the fish. For each serving, you'll need two 4-ounce pieces of flounder fillet and a handful of clean raw spinach. Place spinach in an oval *au gratin* dish. Fold fillets in half. Lay one overlapping the other on top of the spinach. Pour over one ladleful of Florentine sauce. Bake at 450 degrees for 12 to 15 minutes. Five minutes before serving, add 1½ tablespoons dry white wine and 2 thin slices Monterey Jack cheese and then brown. If necessary, set under broiler to brown lightly.

94
THE VILLA CAPRI
Marquette

David Goldsmith, the extraordinary Sturgeon River guide, has the following comments on this Upper Peninsula favorite:

"The Villa Capri is by far Marquette's most popular restaurant. Located at the west end of the city, smack on U.S. 41, it has a large clientele of loyal Marquette diners plus a good-sized tourist trade, especially in the summer months. The attraction? Good food, sensibly priced. The restaurant offers a butt steak dinner, called the Capri Sizzler, for under $5, and you would be hard put to find a tastier piece of beef in town at twice the price. The Sizzler is served with a better-than-average salad and excellent garlic bread. It's the *pièce de résistance* of the Villa.

"The Italian menu is not extensive, the dishes tasty and well prepared, however. No surprises here. The lasagne, while more American than Italian, is nevertheless delicious. Pizzas, quickly prepared, are the best in town, with a thick crust and plenty of cheese. There is no seafood on the menu.

"Cocktails are avoided by many of the regular customers in favor of the reasonably priced Chiantis or Lambruscos. You may need to ask to insure that your red wine is served at room temperature.

"Service is friendly, if uninformed. The turnover in waitresses must be great, and the similarity in age and appearance makes them seem stamped out of a mold. If you want to linger, you'll have to impress this fact upon the waitress, perhaps several times. Otherwise, you'll be in and out in a half hour.

"On weekends (and even some weeknights) the Villa is extremely crowded. No reservations are taken, so you'll have to get a number from the *maitre d'*. Your wait could run to two hours on a peak night, but fortunately there's a cocktail lounge adjoining the restaurant (entrance outside) where you can watch your number coming up on closed circuit television. The decor of the lounge is similar to the restaurant's, pleasant if typical. Waitresses won't hustle you here; you may dawdle as long as you like over a drink. They know you're waiting for a dinner table.

"You'll get your money's worth at the Villa, especially if you order the Sizzler. Alfredo's, next door, takes the overflow. Don't let it take you."

David's right. This is the Upper Peninsula's counterpart to Lansing's Casa Nova—very popular, bargains on the menu, the number system in effect with the resultant long waits, but still for most customers worth the hassle. The Italian specialties include veal Scallopine, chicken Cacciatore and Tetrazzini, lasagne, ravioli, four spaghetti variations, and three portion sizes of antipasto salad.

May be the U.P.'s most popular—a bargain.

BARBIERE'S VILLA CAPRI, West U.S. 41, Marquette, MI 49855. Two miles west of the city center. Telephone (906) 225-1153. Hours: 5 p.m.-midnight (till 1 a.m. on Fridays and Saturdays). Closed Mondays. Full bar service. Background music. Free parking. Credit cards and reservations not taken.

95
THE NORTHWOODS
Marquette

Our own memories of the Northwoods go back some twelve years ago to one of the best lake trout dinners we've had in

Michigan. And though the place has had its ups and downs over the years, its many regular customers and continued popularity attest to its efforts to please. Established in the middle 1930s and still family owned and operated, it first became known for its chicken dinners; and later, as in many of the restaurants in this part of the state, the whitefish and lake trout became specialties. The luncheon menu lists the usual sandwiches, a flavorful shrimp salad, smoked pork chop with German potato salad, and that excellent trout. The Northwoods has a standard American dinner menu with the additions of daily specials and a few "gourmet" offerings— among them, *tournedos à la Bernaise*, veal Parmigiana, glazed medallions of sirloin, and chicken Kiev. For starters, the cream soups and baked French onion soup are fine, as is the whitefish caviar. It's a good, varied menu with a wide range of prices.

The most popular entrée is (you guessed it) prime rib, with the lake trout running a close second—and even a bargain on Friday evenings. We also recommend, on Friday, the "catch of the day," at a reasonable price. On Tuesday evenings the Northwoods sets up a smorgasbord with a versatile assortment of meats and vegetables, a salad bar, and a dessert table. The Sunday brunch is equally elaborate. The wine list here is small but adequate, with a number of offerings less than $10 and several wines by the glass and carafe.

The baked goods at the restaurant are irresistible—we hope you'll be lucky enough to arrive when the sweet rolls are still warm. Shirley Duvall has been baking for the Northwoods for fifteen years and is locally (perhaps regionally) known for her delicious banana pie. The fresh fruit and pecan pies are also worth trying.

There are two dining rooms, the original Cedar Room, a cozy and cheerful room seating about 40, and the much larger Fireside Room, facing the woods in back (ask for tables 11-14 by the windows). Both rooms are pleasantly woodsy with fireplaces and a rustic log and stone decor. A new and charming addition to the Northwoods is the flagstoned, terraced garden for outdoor dining in summer. The tables are nicely separated on varying levels, and the greens and yellows of the linens and directors' chairs blend well with the shrubbery and flowers. Dinner here is cooked in a barbeque pit: steaks, chops, trout, chicken, and ribs. And there's a band and dancing on the terrace on weekends. But in any kind of weather you might enjoy the intimate piano bar in the lounge off the Cedar Room.

Woodsy and well established.

THE NORTHWOODS SUPPER CLUB, Box 97, Marquette, MI 49855. Four miles west on U.S. 41, then ½ mile south on M-28. Telephone (906) 226-3531. Hours: noon-1 a.m., smorgasbord on Tuesday 5-9 p.m., Sunday brunch 11 a.m.-2 p.m. Full bar service. Children's plates. Background music; piano bar Thursday-Saturday; band on weekends starts at 8 p.m.; dancing nightly on terrace in summer. Baked goods and wines available for takeout. All major credit cards. Reservations recommended on weekends.

THE NORTHWOODS' POPPY SEED CAKE

Blend together 1½ cups sugar, ½ cup shortening, ¾ cup milk, ½ cup poppy seeds, 2 teaspoons baking powder, 2 cups flour, ½ teaspoon salt, and 4 whipped egg whites. Pour into a round springform pan (8 or 9 inch) that has been greased and then dusted with flour. Bake in a preheated 350-degree oven for 30-35 minutes or until the cake springs back when touched in the center. Remove cake from the pan, and allow to cool.

Mix the filling. Combine ¾ cup sugar, 2 cups milk, 1 teaspoon vanilla, 1 tablespoon butter, ½ cup chopped walnuts, 2 tablespoons cornstarch, and 4 lightly beaten egg yolks. Cook over medium low heat until thickened. Let cool, and spread this on top of the cake. Then top with whipped cream. Sprinkle with chopped walnuts.

96
MADELYNE'S PASTIES
Ishpeming

The Cornish pasty is, literally, a taste of Michigan history. Pasties (pronounced "pass-tees") were first prepared for miners in Cornwall, England, as portable meat pies for their lunch at work. As the miners emigrated to other parts of the world, the pasty went with them. Pasties vary tremendously in quality, flavor, and texture. The best we've found are those indigenous to the metal-mining areas of the Upper Peninsula: one in the iron-mining district west of Marquette, Madelyne's, and the other in the copper range at Laurium, north of Houghton (see Toni's Country Kitchen).

Any visitor to the Upper Peninsula should try an authentic Cornish pasty—a generally flavorful but simple blend of beef, potato, onion, and "bagies" (big yellow turnips called "Swedes" in Cornwall and rutabagas here), all encased in a pastry so that it can be easily eaten by hand or with a knife and fork. This sounds pretty uncomplicated, but in fact there are as many versions of pasties as there are cooks who put them together. In Cornwall they're likely to be filled with anything from eel to rabbit, herring to chicken, apples to jam. But the more familiar beef and potato variety is what you'll get in Michigan. It's a surprisingly tasty thing eaten in a Cornish pub, and can be as good for a carefree lunch at home or on a picnic.

Madelyne's mixes suet and parsley into the meat filling and uses a short lard pastry dough, slightly less tender than piecrust. Accompaniments vary to suit individual tastes. They can be eaten as is, but more often the customers add catsup. A few even top their pasties with mustard, hot sauce, or vinegar. We tend to think they're probably at their best with a well-seasoned beef gravy, but you won't get this at the restaurant. However, Madelyne's pasties are now being commercially manufactured, frozen, and widely distributed, so you can enjoy them at home—with gravy, if you wish. This is high-quality food at a bargain price and is ideal for lunch or a snack (but order one or two at a time and share, because they're quite substantial).

Madelyne started preparing pasties more than thirty years ago for the lunch pails of construction workers on the highway on which the restaurant is located. The place is easy to miss, so be alert when seeking it out. Look for the Green Acres Motel on the south side of the highway; Madelyne's is adjacent, a white cabin with green trim. You can eat here at one of three tables or at the counter, but most of the business is carryout. If you're driving through or camping at the large and popular Van Riper State Park a few miles west, you might consider stopping at Madelyne's to pick up a few pasties—they were created to travel well—and warm them up in camp, if you'd like. For a very reasonable price you can treat the family to a nutritious and filling meal—and, like the miners, you won't need to worry about who does the dishes.

For a hearty Cornish treat.

MADELYNE'S PASTIES, Route 1 (Greenwood Location), Ishpeming, MI. Four miles west of Ishpeming on U.S. 41. Telephone (906) 485-5531. Hours: 8 a.m.-8 p.m. daily in the summer; till about 7 p.m. from Labor Day to December. Closed Christmas, New Years Day, Thanksgiving, Easter. No alcoholic beverages. Free parking. Credit cards and reservations not accepted.

CORNISH PASTIES

Make pastry: Sift 1⅓ cups flour with a large pinch of salt. Blend in ¼ cup margarine till crumbly. Add 2 tablespoons cold water, and stir with a fork until the dough leaves the sides of the bowl. For a flakier crust, roll out the dough, dot the surface with small pieces of butter or margarine, fold both sides toward the center, and chill. After 20 minutes or so, roll out again. Cut out 6 rounds of dough.

Mix the filling: Toss together till moist ½ pound stewing meat or steak cut in ½-inch cubes, ¼ cup finely diced potato, ¼ cup finely diced rutabaga, ¼ cup finely diced onion, 1 teaspoon salt, ¼ teaspoon pepper, 2 tablespoons chopped parsley (optional), 1 dash thyme, 1 teaspoon Worcestershire sauce, 2 tablespoons water. Place the filling on the rounds of dough. Fold pastry in half over the filling and seal the edges with fingers, a fork, or a pastry crimper. Bake 45 minutes on an ungreased cookie sheet in a preheated 400-degree oven. Serve hot or cold. Makes 6 pasties.

If you like our recommendations, tell the proprietor. If you don't, tell us. Write Beech Tree Press, 2673 Rampart Path, Holt, Michigan 48842.

97
THE BLIND DUCK INN
Kingsford

A low, rustic building constructed of vertical dark logs and affording a pleasant view of a small lake, the Blind Duck Inn, though in business only three years, is one of the most popular dining places near Iron Mountain. The owners are duck hunters, hence the name; but the cuisine is, interestingly, Mexican-American. The inn houses a large, roomy bar and lounge with a handsome fireplace; a porch for outdoor dining in the summer; and an informal, comfortable dining room enhanced by four mirrors that reflect the view of woods and lake and contribute to a feeling of spaciousness. Sit by the window if you can. (Reserve tables 15, 16, and 20—for four persons—or 17, 18, 19 for larger groups.)

The fairly limited menu offers steaks, hamburgers, fish fillets, spaghetti, and ravioli; but we recommend the "famous wet burrito," the Mexican dinners, and the other dishes on the back page: Chimi Chunga (turkey-filled, deep-fried tortillas), enchiladas, and the Mexican combination plates. The mountainous servings are reasonably priced, and the budget-minded can eat here comfortably. At lunch you might even ask for smaller portions unless you're really hungry. We found two enchiladas instead of the three on the menu quite adequate. Favorite items on the menu are the wet burrito and the Pintail—a sandwich of ham, Swiss cheese, lettuce, and tomato with a special sauce and on a Grecian roll. Reduced prices on regular menu items are offered as specials on Monday (fish) and Wednesday (burrito and Chimi). And on Sunday a sensational all-you-can-eat Mexican combination dinner goes for a mere $3.

Patrons from Grand Rapids will recognize a certain familiarity in the Mexican dishes—the famous wet burrito is a winner in that city and has now, through the Blind Duck Inn, become a drawing card as far away as in the Upper Peninsula. If you like cocktails before dinner, you might consider the Blind Duck's Margarita, an enormous, frothy version blended with ice and large enough for two.

Fiesta in the firs.

THE BLIND DUCK INN, Cowboy Lake, Kingsford, MI 49801. Across from the Iron Mountain airport terminal. Telephone (906) 774-0037. Hours: 11 a.m.-10 p.m. Sunday-Thursday, 11 a.m.-11 p.m. Friday and Saturday. Closed Thanksgiving, Christmas, New Years Day, and Easter. Full bar service. Background music. Free parking. No credit cards.

THE BLIND DUCK'S MUD DUCK PIE

This is very simple and very good. It also has the advantage of advance preparation. Make a crust of 5 ounces Nabisco Chocolate Wafers (crushed) and 4 ounces melted butter or margarine. Press into a pie tin. Fill with coffee ice cream. Freeze. To serve, top with hot fudge sauce.

Hints from the Winters: Baskin and Robbins' is good, but if you buy the hot fudge sauce, why not try Michigan's own Sanders Hot Fudge? Or, if you're a purist, here's a recipe. Mix 2 cups sugar, ⅔ cup cocoa, ¼ cup flour, and ¼ teaspoon salt in a saucepan. Add 2 cups water and 2 tablespoons butter. Cook to the boiling point. Lower heat and cook about 8 minutes, stirring. Cool. Stir in 1 teaspoon vanilla extract.

98
ALICE'S
Iron River

The name might remind you of an old song by Arlo Guthrie or a newer television program. But there are no guitars or grits here—Alice is Italian. Don't let the location near a motel or the unimposing exterior fool you (it's not Alice's fault, because it's not Alice's building). You'll be delighted with the warm snugness of the interior—varying shades of red, including velvet chandeliers, and an especially pleasing, cozy atmosphere. All the tables are inviting, but smaller groups might prefer the alcove off the main dining room for a little more seclusion. The window air conditioner takes some getting used to, but we're certain that the food and the cheerfulness in decor and service will compensate for that minor fault.

The menu is limited but excellent, offering such Italian specialties in the finest Capeccian tradition as chicken Cacciatore, lasagne, ravioli (we love Alice's small, less doughy kind), noodles, spaghetti, mostaccioli, and the popular gnocchi. Accompanying the pasta dishes is a choice of meat balls, beef rollups, Italian sausage, or chicken. The Saturday special is a captivating chicken breast Valdostana. Everything is homemade, even the breadsticks, rolls, and absolutely delicious onion bread (which we feel fortunate to include in this book). Dinners include these as well as soup and salad. Non-Italian entrées (for the less experimental) are served with soup, spaghetti or potato, salad, and that wonderful bread. We strongly recommend that you try the soup with cappelleti ("little hats" filled with breast of chicken), a rare item on most Italian menus and well worth the little extra. As for quality and price, we urge you to order from the right side (Italian) of the menu. Or, if you must order meat, you might consider the pork chops. We're told they're very good.

Wine (American) is available by the carafe, but for a little more money, we suggest that you enjoy a bottle of one of the Italian wines with this fine, authentic Italian food. It's a small but acceptable wine list, offering four Italian whites and six Italian reds at very modest prices. In fact, there are some real bargains here, both in wine and food.

Iron mining is now inactive at Iron River, but the legacy of earlier days—and of the Italian immigrants who came here originally as miners—is this marvelous little restaurant. On our visit we weren't fortunate enough to meet Alice, but we enjoyed our talk with the friendly cooks—Mabel Tarsi, the day cook and Alice's sister-in-law, and Lynn Damp, the night cook. Their enthusiasm (not to mention their gnocchi and onion bread) was impressive. We hope to meet Alice soon. **Priceless, a little gem.**

ALICE'S TRAV-LURES SUPPER CLUB, West U.S. 2, Iron River, MI 49935. Next to the Trav-Lures Motel, 2 miles west of the city center on U.S. 2. Telephone (906) 265-4764. Hours: dinner only, 5-10 p.m. daily. Closed on major holidays. Full bar service. Background music. Free parking. No credit cards. Reservations recommended on weekends.

ALICE'S ABSOLUTELY DELICIOUS ONION BREAD

Combine 4¼ cups flour, 3 tablespoons shortening, and 1 teaspoon salt in a large bowl. Soften ¼ pound fresh yeast in 1½ cups lukewarm water with 3 tablespoons sugar. Add to the flour mixture, and mix thoroughly. If necessary, add more flour, and mix to a dough that won't stick to hands or bowl. Knead lightly on a floured surface. Place in a greased bowl, cover, and let rise until doubled in bulk. Punch down lightly, and let rise again till doubled in bulk.

Divide dough in 2 portions. Spread in 2 greased 15½ x 10½ x11-inch jelly roll pans. (Do not pull dough; spread gently with fingers.) Cover, and set in a warm place until doubled in bulk. Slice 2 large onions thinly. Place evenly over dough. Sprinkle lightly with salt and pepper. Pour ½ cup corn oil over the onions in each pan (1 cup oil in all). Bake in a moderate oven (350-375 degrees) for 20-30 minutes, until crisp and golden brown in color.

Hints from the Winters: This bread, considering the ease in preparation, is delectable. We found the baking time in our oven to run somewhat longer, about 35-40 minutes. Remove the bread when the onions begin to turn brown around the edges. The bread reheats nicely, too, covered with foil and set in a 350-degree oven for about 10 minutes. We haven't tried it yet but think that it might be good also with some grated Mozzarella cheese spread over the onions.

99
KONTEKA
White Pine

Konteka, named for a leader of the Chippewa, is certainly one of the best restaurants and meeting places in the far western Upper Peninsula. We could go so far as to label it a veritable oasis in an area so limited in facilities (other than for campers and sportsmen) that it is worthwhile to drive a little farther to get here. We haven't found anything open to the general public that matches Konteka in this part of the state. The comfortable dining room has a number of large windows that provide a pleasant view of the woods. At the entryway you can see a large piece of native copper; and all of the wine available, about twenty, are effectively displayed near the salad bar. An adjacent oval bar and lounge overlooks an automated eight-lane bowling alley and is well insulated for sound. There is also a small, utilitarian coffee shop that serves breakfast and delicious freshly baked cinnamon and pecan rolls and doughnuts.

The luncheon menu includes standard fare—sandwiches and salads, homemade soups and chili, bread and rolls. Sandwiches may also be ordered in the bar at any time. On the regular dinner menu the most interesting items are, aside from a notable assortment of steaks and seafood, especially well-prepared grilled lamb chops. If you order these, try to guess what's done to them to make them so meltingly tender. There are also scallops à la Mona (in a creamy sauce, served over broccoli) and Konteka's Trio, a fortuitous combination of barbequed ribs, pork chop, and lamb chop. Soups are well made at Konteka, with one or two available each day; favorites include the cream of cabbage, minestrone, chicken with dumplings, and corn chowder. The bread is baked fresh, and for dessert a peanut butter ice cream pie and several ice cream dessert drinks are offered. One item that impressed us was the Lithuanian dumplings available as an appetizer. These represent homestyle eastern European cooking at its best. Some customers are so enamored of them that they order only dumplings and salad for dinner. We think that's not a bad idea at all except that it's so hard to pass up the lamb chops or Trio. Ideally, if one skipped lunch, it would be a good idea to order both.

A variety of weekly specials are offered by Konteka: on Tuesday, prime rib; on Wednesday, lake trout; Thursday, small tenderloin; Friday, the especially popular seafood buffet; Saturday, beef Wellington—as well as other specials on Sunday and Monday evenings and a breakfast buffet on Sunday. The reasonably priced seafood buffet includes walleyed pike, clams, oysters, ocean perch, shrimp, all deep fried, and German potato salad, French fries, and a salad bar. The wine list is modest, and a carafe can be ordered.

The restaurant is within view of the White Pine mine's

smokestack that towers over 500 feet and is the tallest in Michigan. The last of the copper mines, it is still in operation. Though once it employed as many as 3,000 men, it now uses only 1,200 who work at two levels, 500 feet and 1,800 feet. A third of the men commute from Ironwood, Calumet, Houghton, and other mining towns. Konteka is also in close proximity to the Porcupine Mountains State Park, one of the most popular backpacking areas in the Great Lakes region and famous for the easily accessible view of Lake of the Clouds.

The best in the west.

KONTEKA, Mineral River Plaza, White Pine, MI 49971. Off M-64, 13 miles west of Ontonagon, then 6 miles south. Telephone (906) 885-5215. Hours: 6 a.m.-9 p.m. Closed Christmas. Full bar service. Children's luncheon menu. Background music. Free parking. Credit cards: MC, V. Reservations recommended for Friday evenings.

KONTEKA'S RAW VEGETABLE SALAD

This is without a doubt the most popular dish on Konteka's salad bar. Mix together in a large bowl 1 head of broccoli, cut in flowerets; 1 head cauliflower, cut in flowerets; 1 bunch green onions, sliced; 1 can water chestnuts, drained and cut in half; 1 can pitted ripe olives; 6 tomatoes, cut in wedges; 1 pound sliced fresh mushrooms; 1 package Good Seasons Cheese Garlic dressing mix, sprinkled on dry; 2 teaspoons garlic salt; and 2 teaspoons Italian seasoning. Marinate for several hours or overnight. It'll stay nice for several days. Serves 8-12.

100
THE SUMMER PLACE
Chassell

On a hot July or August day in the Copper Range, we can't think of a more refreshing spot, especially for luncheon, than the Summer Place in Chassell, just outside Houghton. The light, airy garden decor with trellises, plants, leaf green and white table settings, and a lovely hillside view of shady green lawns and Portage Lake all contribute to a most enjoyable hour or two. Once the private home of a local judge, the white frame building was converted to a restaurant in August 1975. In addition to the attractive Porch, where we much prefer to be seated, are a cocktail lounge in the former living room (cozy on cool days) and a separate, less interesting downstairs lounge.

The luncheon menu offers an imaginative "crepe of the day," a noteworthy quiche Lorraine, the Summer Place Salad (with turkey, white grapes, walnuts, and celery in a sour cream dressing), other salads and sandwiches, and several hot daily specials. The dinner menu provides standard steak and seafood entrees as well as a specially glazed roast duckling and barbequed back ribs. Steaks are marinated and broiled over an open hearth. A daily selection on the order of Cornish hen or stuffed baked trout is another possibility. On Saturday evening, prime rib is the feature. And the seafood buffet served on Friday nights is the best bargain: a mouth-watering array of shrimp, crab, stuffed trout, red snapper, and whiting on herbed rice. If either is on the menu, you might also like to try the cockaleekie or cold garden soup. Entrées are accompanied by a choice of potato or herbed rice (our preference), Carousel Salad, and homemade bread.

All the baking is done on the premises, and some savory desserts are on hand for the sweet-toothed: pies, tortes, and a sumptuous cheesecake flavored with chocolate and Amaretto. The wine list is modest, with most selections under $10. House wines may be ordered by the glass or liter. Prices for meals are about what one would expect at a better restaurant.

A northwoods lakeside retreat.

THE SUMMER PLACE, U.S. 41, Chassell, MI 49916. Two miles north of town; 3 miles south of Houghton. Telephone (906) 523-4915. Hours: luncheon 11:30 a.m.-2:30 p.m., dinner 5-11 p.m. seven days a week until January 1; then January 1-May 1 open Fridays, Saturdays, and Sundays only. Full bar service. Children's plates. Background music. Free parking. Credit cards MC, V. Reservations not taken on Friday and Saturday.

101
THE LIBRARY
Houghton

Anyone who can encourage so many young people to eat *escargots* and steak *tartare* surely has reached an epitome of restauranteurship. And that's exactly what Big Jon Davis appears to have done at the Library. The restaurant is housed in an old (certainly 100-year) building on what was once the main street of Houghton at the turn of the century. It was then called the Board of Trade and Palm Gardens Cafe and was an elegant dining place during the heady mining days, replete with potted palms and brass spittoons. Now, as the Library, with attractive old and new stained glass windows and carpeting on even walls and doors, it caters to Michigan Tech students and others of any age who are young at heart. (Wear your jeans.)

The Library has two dining areas on two levels, each with its own bar and the same menu. The atmosphere in both is relaxed though somewhat different from one another. We suggest that you visit the two rooms and then take your choice—but the house rule is that you can't take drinks from one room to the other. We prefer the upper level, known as the Homonym. The enormous bar stools are downright bizarre in appearance but surprisingly comfortable. We also find the light jazz background music in the restaurant very enjoyable.

The menu is extensive and fun to ponder over. Most items are priced less than $4, putting the Library in the bargain category; but the offerings are primarily pizza, sandwiches (including several bagel creations), salads, soups, and chili. Of the sandwiches the R.B.2 is the most popular—hot beef with cheese and mushrooms on pumpernickel or rye (and in two sizes)—as is the Epicurean, devised by the help (roast beef, bacon, cheese, lettuce, tomatoes, and mayonnaise on a choice of bread). The fish is refreshingly labeled "frozen," and there's a reasonably priced 10-ounce steak. Occasional luncheon specials are offered as well as a soup of the day—especially good are the crabmeat bisque and the cream of broccoli. A modest selection of wines and low-priced liters of house wines are available, though beer seems to be the favorite here. The Library hosts periodic wine tastings, featuring five or six wines, and dinners on various themes.

After eating, you might enjoy a brief walking tour, either out the main door to the left to look at the relic depot and the wharfs or to the right uphill to see the reconstructed Douglass House Hotel, named in honor of Douglass Houghton, the state's first geologist, who perished in a storm off the coast of the peninsula and after whom the town was named.

A library of fun and flavors, a bargain.

THE LIBRARY, 62 N. Isle Royale Street, Houghton, MI 49931. A half-block off north U.S. 41 in the city center. Telephone (906) 482-6211. Hours: 11:30 a.m.-1 a.m., Sundays 5 p.m.-1 a.m. Closed Christmas (check on other holidays). Full bar service. Background music. Parking difficult in the daytime; street parking or nearby city lot. No credit cards. Reservations recommended at lunch hour, especially for groups.

THE LIBRARY'S ORANGE-BRANDIED ROCK CORNISH HEN

This is a popular dish that was featured at one of the Library's recent wine tastings. For the sauce, combine in a saucepan one 6-ounce can frozen orange juice concentrate, 8 to 16 ounces brandy (to personal taste), and the juice from a 3-ounce jar of Maraschino cherries (reserve cherries). Heat to simmering. Add 3 tablespoons honey (or to taste) and 1 tablespoon freshly grated orange peel. Thicken with a mixture of 2 teaspoons cornstarch and 2 teaspoons water.

For the stuffing, combine 3 cups long-grain rice (or a mixture of long-grain and wild rice) that has been rinsed and cooked in chicken broth, 3 cups salted croutons (made from Jewish rye or dark pumpernickel), ½ to 1 cup slivered almonds and 1 large orange (peeled and cut in small pieces). Chop the reserved cherries and add. Add enough of the sauce to moisten the stuffing, saving about half of it for basting.

Stuff 6 Rock Cornish hens with this mixture. Garnish the breast of each bird with an orange slice and cherry. Bake at 275 degrees until brown and tender, basting about every 15 minutes with the remainder of the sauce. Salt and pepper should not be added during the cooking. Serve each bird on a base of chopped raw spinach and chopped almonds over a bed of Romaine lettuce. Serves 6.

102
TONI'S COUNTRY KITCHEN
Laurium

For the past twelve years or so, Toni's has become well known throughout the state among the more discriminating pasty fanciers for her excellent Cornish meat pies and other baked goods. Ninety percent of her business is takeout, but the small bakery-restaurant, decorated in early American style, seats 24 if you want to eat your pasties still steaming from the oven. The kitchen is spotless, the aromas tantalizing, and in the morning the glass showcase is laden with delicacies (and sadly depleted each afternoon). Unlike Madelyne's outside Ishpeming, the pasties here contain no suet or parsley and are encased in a flaky crust. The regular pasty weighs one pound, but three-quarter or half-pound pasties may be ordered. Whatever the size, this is basic homespun nourishment—food fit for a peasant, or a king. In all of Michigan, we favor Toni's, but decide for yourself.

Toni's pasties sell like—well—pasties, and she's likely to run out of them before the end of the day. Avid customers usually call ahead to be sure, and we advise you to do the same. You might also try some of Toni's other baked goods: saffron bread, date crumbles, tarts (fruit filled, like *kolackis*), Cousin Jacks—soft, biscuit-like raisin cookies—or her popular ginger cremes (see the recipe for them below).

Laurium, a company town like so many others in this part of the Upper Peninsula's copper range, is picturesquely and historically characterized by vertically elongated Cornish houses. It's worth a drive-through for a look at what mining life was once like in this area of Michigan. And it's well worth stopping at the Country Kitchen for a sample of a dish that conjures up the past, the typical miner's lunch—one of Toni's suberb pasties.

Tops for pasties and pastries.

TONI'S COUNTRY KITCHEN, 79 Third Street, Laurium, MI
49913. In village center; 11 miles northeast of Houghton.
Telephone (906) 337-0611. Hours: 7 a.m.-5 p.m. Closed Sundays and holidays. No alcoholic beverages. Free parking.
Credit cards and reservations not accepted.

TONI'S GINGER CREMES

Mix in order: 1 cup shortening, 1 cup brown sugar, 2 eggs,
⅔ cup molasses, 1 teaspoon baking soda, 1 teaspoon cinnamon, ½ teaspoon ginger, 4 cups flour, and ¾ cup sour milk.
Chill this mixture. For each cookie, place a spoonful of dough
on the cookie sheet, and flatten with a glass dipped in cold
water or flour. Bake 12 minutes in a preheated 375-degree
oven. When cool, frost with confectioners sugar icing.

103
THE KEWEENAW MOUNTAIN LODGE
Copper Harbor

A large part of the adventure of eating at the Keweenaw
Mountain Lodge is getting there and back. The winding drive
is punctuated by a number of scenic stops, including Silver
Falls and the city of Copper Harbor. But the highlight without
a doubt is Brockway Mountain Drive, a narrow blacktop road
that winds along the often windy crest of one of the highest
ridges forming the Keweenaw Peninsula. From here you can
see, on a clear day, the rugged terrain and rocky coast, and
you'll get a better idea of the magnitude of the largest of
the Great Lakes, the well-named Lake Superior. Both coming and going to the lodge are many glimpses of the relics
of abandoned copper mines and near ghost towns, characterized by picturesque Cornish miners' homes. The sprawling
lodge itself is located high on the side of one of the highest
and rockiest ridges in an attractive woodland setting near
the end of the peninsula.

Begun by the CWA and completed by the WPA in 1936, the

Keeweenaw Mountain Lodge has been literally carved out of the wilderness. Clearing the land provided work for several hundred men over a period of two and a half years, during which time an estimated 187,000 trees were felled. The logs and poles were used in building the lodge and cabins; and the limbs, tops, and stumps were made into firewood to supply families in the area. The land cleared of timber is now a nine-hole golf course. A charming aspect of the Keeweenaw Mountain Lodge is the cabins, each with a bedroom or two and a fireplace that makes for especially pleasant evenings in chilly summer weather.

The large, somewhat rustic dining room with open rafters, paneled walls, two huge fireplaces at either end, and a circular lounge bar on the west seems quite appropriate for this rugged northwoods setting. The ample menu primarily appeals to popular tastes: whitefish and trout, freshly caught from Lake Superior; a fine selection of praiseworthy steaks and chops; and a generous salad bar.

While here, you won't want to miss visiting Copper Harbor, a resort village on a scenic inlet off Lake Superior. From Copper Harbor you can take the Isle Royale Queen to Isle Royale National Park, a day-long excursion with a three-hour stop at the island. Campers will also enjoy popular Fort Wilkins State Park nearby. You can even see wild black bear from the protection of your car in especially prepared parking areas at the city dump (if you don't mind the surroundings).

A sentimental Copper Country favorite.

THE KEWEENAW MOUNTAIN LODGE, U.S. 41, Copper Harbor, MI 49918. One and a half miles south of Copper Harbor on U.S. 41. Telephone (906) 289-4403. Hours: breakfast 8-10:30 a.m., luncheon 11 a.m.-4 p.m., dinner 5-9 p.m. Snacks. Full bar service. Tennis, lawn games, golf, nearby swimming, boating, fishing. Free parking. Credit cards: MC, V. Reservations recommended.

OVERNIGHT SWEET PICKLES

We don't know where this originated. We discovered it in Port St. Lucie, Florida, and it seems appropriate to include it with a lodge located on another peninsula and noted for

238

its salad bar. These are the easiest—and, believe it or not, some of the best—pickles you'll ever make.

Slice 1 large unpeeled cucumber paper thin. Place in a bowl. In a saucepan heat to boiling ½ cup vinegar, ½ cup sugar, ¼ cup water, 1 teaspoon salt, and ½ teaspoon dill seed. Pour over the cucumber slices. Cover and chill over night. Makes about 1-1½ pints.

POPULAR PIZZERIAS

This listing is based almost completely on student recommendations, and they're pretty good judges of this sort of thing. The   list is in alphabetical order by location; then, within each location, in order of popularity.

Algonac
  Capri
Allen Park
  Mike and Sylvia's
Ann Arbor
  Bimbo's
  Pizza Bob's
  The Brown Jug
Bellaire
  Sylvester's
Berkley
  Dominico's
Coloma
  DiMaggio's
Dearborn
  Lona's
Detroit
  Buddy's Rendezvous
  Buscemi's
  Salt Mine
  Woodbridge Tavern
East Detroit
  Morano's

East Lansing
  Bell's
  Dooley's
Fenton
  Johnnie's
Flushing
  Roger's
Garden City
  Leather Bottle Inn
  Angelo's
Goodrich
  John's Steak House
Grand Blanc
  Little Joe's
Grand Haven
  Fricano's
Grand Rapids
Roaring 20s
  Village Inn
  Fred's
Harrison
  Bercilie's

Hazel Park
  Louie's
Holland
  Mario's
Holt
  Sammy's Paddock
Houghton
  The Library
  Ambassador
Indian River
  Vivio's
Ishpeming
  Congress Bar
Kalamazoo
  Godfather's
Kalkaska
  Old Parlor
Lansing
  Casa Nova
  Willow Bar
  Emil's
Lapeer
  Lapeer Family Inn
Livonia
  Fonte da Amore
  Corsi's
Ludington
  The Cellar
Madison Heights
  The Green Lantern
Marquette
  Villa Capri
Mason
  Westside Party Store

Mount Pleasant
  Blackstone
Northville
  Northville Charley's
Orchard Lake
  Mr. Tony's
Oscoda
  Big Dave's
Ovid
  Tri-Ami
Owosso
  Val's
Pontiac
  Mitch's
Romeo
  Town Pump
Sterling Heights
  Frank's
Tawas City
  Big Dave's
Traverse City
  The Cellar
Utica
  Buscemi's
  Valeria's
Wakefield
  Club 28
Warren
  Buscemi's
Webberville
  Nick's
Ypsilanti
  The Spaghetti Bender
  Pizza Bob's

THE BEST HOT DOG
IN MICHIGAN

We don't know where the hot dog originated. Probably in some eastern European kitchen where a thrifty and clever *hausfrau* mixed up a batch of leftovers, stuffed it in a cloth bag, and left it to smoke in the fireplace. But no matter its humble beginnings, the hot dog today is an American favorite. And there's absolutely no question among students at Michigan State University that the best hot dog in the state can be savored at Tiger Stadium in Detroit. Even when the Tigers are losing, the hot dogs are winners. Long before Fat Bob Taylor, the Singing Plumber, starts up with the first few bars of the National Anthem, the crowds are lining up at the concessions stands.

What makes the Tiger Stadium hot dog so special? We started asking, and came up with some interesting answers. The essential ingredients are Hygrade (brand) hot dogs that plump up as they cook; there are six to a pound, and each is four inches long. The five-inch buns come from the Mark Eagle Baking Company in Allen Park. And the mild mustard you'll get is a product of Detroit's Red Pelican Foods. According to Hub Johnson, a Ph.D. from Purdue with Hygrade Meat Products in Detroit, what you get at Tiger Stadium are Hygrade's Ball Park Meat Hot Dogs, made of beef, pork, and veal, a recipe that originated in 1957 and has remained unchanged. You've probably all seen Ball Park dogs in Michigan supermarkets, with the packages containing eight to the pound. They're bigger at the Stadium. And they're prepared in two ways, either boiled or grilled.

What you buy from the vendors while you're watching the game is the boiled version. But if you buy your hot dogs at the concession stands, they're cooked on ¼-inch-thick iron grills that have been in use for more than thirty years. Although both varieties are delicious, Robert Sherman, concessions manager at Tiger Stadium, prefers the grilled hot dogs and attributes their superior flavor to those old iron grills, which may now be irreplaceable. Hub Johnson, too, opts for the grilled version.

On the average, Tiger Stadium sells hot dogs equal in

number to about 80 percent of the attendance, and during double headers the figure rises to 100 percent. On cooler days, hot dogs become even more popular. The record for any one day of sales at the stadium was during a double header when the first game went extra innings and the second was delayed by rain—that day 60,000 hot dogs were sold.

Last year approximately 1,280,000 were sold, and if the little devils were placed end to end, they would extend, as the crow flies, from Tiger Stadium to the Capitol in Lansing. But even more impressive, in the last ten years Tiger Stadium has sold enough hot dogs to stretch from Detroit to New Orleans.

FORTY SPECIAL RESTAURANTS IN AND NEAR DETROIT

The selections here are based on our personal choices, the popularity of these places among Michigan State University students, and polls among knowledgable friends and acquaintances. It is not an all-inclusive list, but we're sure you'll find many restaurants that will please you and at all price ranges. Each offers full bar service unless otherwise indicated. The area code for all numbers is 313. Restaurants are listed alphabetically.

ALIETTE'S BAKERY, 3459 Porter, Detroit. At 24th Street, 2 blocks west of the Ambassador Bridge. Telephone 554-0907. Hours: luncheon 11:30 a.m.-2 p.m., dinner 5:30-10 p.m. Closed Sundays and Mondays. Wine list, no spirits. No credit cards. By reservation only; reserve 2-4 weeks ahead. Very French, very popular; a tiny bistro with blackboard menu (veal and duck are favorites). Prices moderate (and for the quality, surprisingly reasonable).

BENNO'S, 8027 Agnes, Detroit. Telephone 499-0040. Hours: 6 p.m.-midnight. Closed Sundays and Mondays. Wine, no cocktails. No credit cards. Reservations essential. Continental menu; very posh (not even a sign in front), tiny and elegant. Try the dessert omelette. Expensive.

BODEGA, 25245 Van Dyke, Centerline. Just north of Detroit. (Second location at 14433 Telegraph Road, Redford.) Telephone 755-5660. Hours: luncheon 11:30 a.m.-3 p.m., dinner 5-10 p.m. (till 11:30 p.m. Fridays and Saturdays), Sundays 2-9 p.m. Credit cards: MC, V. Casual dress. Crowded, popular, a student favorite. Reasonable prices; bargain steaks, seafood, roast beef (in $6 range).

THE BOTSFORD INN, 28000 Grand River Avenue, Farmington Hills. Just north of 8 Mile Road. Telephone 474-4800. Hours: 7 a.m.-10 p.m., Sundays 10 a.m.-8 p.m. Closed Mondays and holidays for food service. Credit cards: AE, MC, V. Restored 1836 inn, authentically furnished by Henry Ford in the 1920s. Specialties: chicken pie, Dover sole, calves liver, turkey and dressing, veal Parmigiana, rainbow trout.

CAFE CORTINA, 30715 Ten Mile Road, Farmington Hills. Telephone 474-3033. Hours: 11 a.m.-11 p.m. Mondays Fridays, 4-11 p.m. Saturdays, 1-10 p.m. Sundays. All major credit cards. Great northern Italian cooking in bistro atmosphere (delicate variations of veal). Moderate prices.

THE CAUCUS CLUB, 150 W. Congress, Detroit. In City National Bank Building. Telephone 965-4970. Hours: 11 a.m.-7 p.m. Mondays, 11 a.m.-midnight Tuesdays through Fridays, 5:30 p.m.-1 a.m. Saturdays. Closed Sundays. All major credit cards. Jackets required. Clubby atmosphere, expert service. Noted for London broil, Dover sole, steaks, spareribs, good sandwiches. Expensive.

CHARLEY'S CRAB, 5498 Crooks Road, Troy. Just west of I-75; in the Northfield Hilton. Telephone 879-2060. Hours: 4 p.m.-midnight Mondays through Thursdays, 4 p.m.-1 a.m. Fridays, 5 p.m.-1 a.m. Saturdays, 3-10 p.m. Sundays. Closed Christmas. All major credit cards. A Chuck Muer restaurant; seafood specialties (*bouillabaise*, stuffed lobster, daily catch, plus steaks). Moderately expensive.

THE DEARBORN INN, 20301 Oakwood Blvd., Dearborn. A few blocks south of Michigan. Telephone 271-2700. Hours: luncheon 11:30 a.m.-2:30 p.m., dinner 6-10 p.m. on weekdays (till 11 p.m. Fridays and Saturdays), 10:30 a.m.-2 p.m. Sunday brunch, 6-9 p.m. Sunday dinner. All major credit cards. Historic inn built by Henry Ford in 1931. Honest, hearty dinners, traditional desserts. Specialties: lamb chops, clambake, lobster, duckling, red snapper, rack of pork, steaks. Expensive.

DOUG'S BODY SHOP, 22061 Woodward, Ferndale. Between 8 and 9 Mile Roads. (Second location at 22175 Michigan, Dearborn, between Southfield and Outer Drive.) Telephone 339-1040, 562-9600. Hours: luncheon 11:30 a.m.-3 p.m., dinner 5-11 p.m. (till midnight Fridays and Saturdays). Closed Sundays and holidays. All major credit cards. Booths constructed from car bodies; food secondary to decor and music (contemporary jazz). Specialties: steak, shrimp Creole, seafood, tacos, duckling, chicken Divan. Large portions. Reasonable prices.

DUGLASS, 29269 Southfield Road, Southfield. Just north of 12 Mile Road. Telephone 424-9244. Hours: luncheon 11:30 a.m.-2:30 p.m. Mondays through Fridays, 5:30-11 p.m. Mondays through Saturdays. Closed Sundays. Credit cards: AE, MC, V. Flamboyant and glamorous. Chef Duglass Duglass Grech is one of Michigan's most creative chefs. Continental menu (great pastries). Very expensive.

ELIZABETH'S, 227 Hutton, Northville. Telephone 348-0575. Hours: luncheon 11:30 a.m.-2:30 p.m. Tuesdays through Fridays, dinner 6:30-9 p.m. Tuesdays through Saturdays. Closed Sundays and Mondays. No alcoholic beverages. No credit cards. Reservations necessary. In a tiny Victorian cottage, seating only 34. Continental menu, lovely soups, pâtés, blinis, beautiful desserts. Some specialties: cream of olive soup, veal and duck pâté, poached red snapper. Reasonable to expensive.

FISHERS 666, 666 Lothrop, Detroit. Telephone 875-2666. Hours: 11 a.m.-11 p.m. Closed Sundays. Credit cards: AE, MC,

V. Continental menu with interesting choices, including Indonesian *sate*, beef Wellington, roast loin of pork *glacé*, calves liver Florence. Expensive.

FRANCESCO'S, 22302 Michigan Avenue, Dearborn. Telephone 561-1655. Hours: 11 a.m.-2 a.m. Mondays through Saturdays, 4 p.m.-2 a.m. Sundays. Closed most holidays. All major credit cards. Reservations not accepted on weekends. Several Italian entrées plus steaks, seafood, veal.

THE GARDEN CAFE, 301 Fisher Building, Detroit. On W. Grand Blvd. at 2nd Street. In the Gallery of Contemporary Crafts. Telephone 873-7888. Hours: 11 a.m.-4 p.m., Mondays through Saturdays for luncheon and afternoon tea. Closed Sundays. No bar service, but you can bring your own wine. No credit cards. Cascading Boston ferns, genteel atmosphere. Blackboard menu, light lunches, topnotch desserts. Soups, salads, and sandwiches—beautiful and beautifully served. No meat.

THE HILLSIDE INN, 41661 Plymouth Road, Plymouth. Telephone 453-4300. Hours: 11:30 a.m.-11 p.m. Closed Sundays and most holidays. All major credit cards. A historic site, many authentic 19th century antiques, 1930s decor. Specialties: seafood and steak combinations, Swiss steak, roast sirloin of beef, beef Stroganoff, pan-fried chicken, breaded pork tenderloin. Wednesday night smorgasbord featuring prime rib.

JACQUES PETIT JARDIN, 30100 Telegraph Road, Bingham Farms. In Southfield-Birmingham area, just north of 12 Mile Road. Telephone 642-1373. Hours: luncheon 11:30 a.m.-2:30 p.m., dinner 6-11 p.m. Closed Sundays and Christmas. All major credit cards. A lovely place, plush and romantic; darkly sophisticated mirrored dining room, atrium garden. Continental and French menu; steak, lamb, and veal specialties; superb dessert omelette. Very expensive.

JIM'S GARAGE, 300 W. Larned, Detroit. Across from Cobo Hall. Telephone 961-5175. Hours: luncheon 11:30 a.m.-3 p.m., dinner 5:30-10 p.m. Closed Sundays and holidays. Credit cards: AE, MC, V. Reservations recommended. Early automobile memorabilia. American/Continental menu. Specialties: veal scallopine, sliced beef tenderloin, red snapper with Bernaise, Dover sole, scampi *en brochette*, Swiss onion soup, French-fried ice cream. Moderately expensive.

JOE MUER'S, 2000 Gratiot, Detroit. Near end of Fisher Freeway. Telephone 962-1088. Hours: 11 a.m.-9:30 p.m. Mondays through Thursdays, 9:30 a.m.-10 p.m. Fridays, 5-11 p.m. Saturdays. Closed Sundays and holidays. Credit cards: AE, MC, V. No reservations; sometimes a wait. Comfortable and warm, a grand old Detroit favorite. Seafood and fish specialties; changing daily menu (softshell crab, tiny frog legs, Maine lobster, scrod, baked deviled crabmeat, steaks). Expensive.

KYOTO, 18601 Hubbard Drive, Dearborn. North side of Fairlane Town Center. Telephone 593-3200. Hours: 5:30-11 p.m. Mondays through Saturdays, 5:30-midnight Fridays and Saturdays, 3-9 p.m. Sundays. All major credit cards. Japanese razzle-dazzle; watch your food being cooked. Specialties: Hibachi chicken and steak, lobster, scallops, Oriental side dishes. Reasonable.

LELLI'S, 7618 Woodward, Detroit. Just north of Grand Blvd. Telephone 871-1590. Hours: 11 a.m.-10 p.m. Tuesdays through Fridays, 11:30 a.m.-10:30 p.m. Saturdays. Closed Sundays, Mondays, and holidays. Credit cards: MC, V. No reservations. Terribly busy at lunch; more charming in evening. Excellent steaks, numerous pastas, beautiful veal; also *noisettes* of lamb, rabbit, veal kidney, much more. Reasonable to expensive.

THE LITTLE CAFE, 12601 Gratiot, Detroit. Between McNichols and Outer Drive. Telephone 521-0450. Hours: 11 a.m.-10 p.m. Tuesdays through Thursdays, 11 a.m.-11 p.m. Fridays, 4-11 p.m. Saturdays, noon-9 p.m. Sundays and holidays. Closed Mondays. Credit cards: AE, MC, CB. Reservations recommended. German/American menu. Specialties: beef *rouladen*, *hasenpfeffer*, chicken Paprikash, pig hocks, duck and turkey, sausages, steaks.

THE LONDON CHOP HOUSE, 153 W. Congress, Detroit. Between Griswold and Shelby. Telephone 962-0277. Hours: 11 a.m.-2 a.m. Closed Sundays and holidays. All major credit cards. Celebrated Detroit restaurant, award winner. Continental/American menu. Specialties: poached salmon steak, beef strip steak Madagascar, veal Zurich-style, whole Dover sole, roadhouse frog legs. Great wine list. Very expensive.

MAHARAJAH, 18433 W. 8 Mile Road, Detroit. Just west of Southfield Freeway. Telephone 534-7050. Hours: 4:30-10 p.m. Tuesdays through Thursdays, 4:30-11 p.m. Fridays and Saturdays, 3:30-9 p.m. Sundays. Closed Mondays. No alcoholic beverages. Credit cards: AE, CB, DC. East Indian cuisine. Small family restaurant. Several full dinners from various parts of India, special banquets for 4 persons, Biriani dishes, dry and yogurt curries.

MARIO'S, 4222 Second Avenue, Detroit. Telephone 833-9425. Hours: 11:30 a.m.-1 a.m. Tuesdays through Fridays, 2 p.m.-1 a.m. Saturdays. Closed Sundays and Mondays. All major credit cards. Enormous Italian menu, great veal dishes, also Spanish shrimp, chicken Mario, gnocchi, cannelloni. Always ask about the special; have the Capuccino for dessert. Expensive.

MATTIE'S BARBEQUE, 7504 W. McNichols Road, Detroit. Telephone 341-0832. Hours: 8 a.m.-9 p.m. daily. No alcoholic beverages. No credit cards. Simple, family style, with only 13 entrees. Barbeque isn't on the menu, but other Southern specialties include ham hocks, candied yams, baked ribs with cornbread dressing, meat loaf, cornmeal muffins. Inexpensive.

NEW HELLAS CAFE, 583 Monroe, Detroit. At St. Antoine. Telephone 961-5544. Hours: 11 a.m.-2 a.m. daily. Closed Christmas. Credit cards: DC, MC, V. No reservations on weekends. Very popular Greek restaurant. Specialties: ouzo, stuffed grape leaves, shish kebab, *pikilia* combination plate, octopus and squid in wine sauce, lamb dishes, meatballs, Greek salad. Reasonable.

NEW KING LIM'S, 3550 Auburn Road, Auburn Heights. Telephone 852-8280. Open for luncheon and dinner daily. A very pretty Chinese restaurant; excellent regional specialties (Cantonese, Mandarin, Szechwan). Try the Mongolian beef, crystal shrimp, or *hoisin* chicken. Moderate.

EL NIBBLE NOOK, 27725 W. 8 Mile Road, Livonia. At Grand River. (Second location at 26645 Hoover, Warren.) Telephone 474-0755. Hours: 11 a.m.-11 p.m. Mondays through Saturdays, 2-10 p.m. Sundays. Closed holidays. All major credit cards. No reservations; extremely popular—get there early or stand in line. Casual, unpretentious. Mexican/American menu (enchiladas, chimichangas, tostadas, combinations, steaks). Modest prices.

PONTCHARTRAIN WINE CELLARS, 234 W. Larned, Detroit. Near Washington Blvd. Telephone 963-1785. Hours: 11:30 a.m.-10 p.m. Mondays through Fridays, 5:30-11 p.m. Saturdays. Closed Sundays and holidays and in early July. All major credit cards. Small and French-accented, excellent service. In 1880s building. All major credit cards. Specialties: brochette of beef, *ratatouille*, veal Cordon Bleu, braised sweetbreads, *pots de creme*, *babas au rhum*. Moderate to expensive.

THE PUSHCART, 1488 Winder Street, Detroit. In the middle of Eastern Market. Telephone 393-1986. Hours: 11 a.m.-10 p.m. (till 2 a.m. Fridays and Saturdays). Closed Sundays and holidays. No credit cards. 1930s decor. Specialties: beef, Maine lobster, catch of the day, fresh vegetables, Italian sausage and Kosher corned beef sandwiches.

THE ROMA CAFE, 3401 Via Roma, Detroit. Near north end of the Eastern Market. Telephone 831-5940. Hours: 11 a.m.-10:15 p.m. (till midnight Saturdays). Closed Sundays and holidays. All major credit cards. Italian/American menu; great pastas (homemade spaghetti). Other specialties: nine veal dishes, chicken Cacciatore, baked lasagne, and cannelloni. Entertainment Mondays and Wednesdays. Reasonable.

THE ROYAL EAGLE, 1415 Parker, Detroit. Former dining room of Parkstone Apartments, on Detroit's east side. Telephone 331-8088. Hours: 5-9 p.m. (till 10 p.m. Fridays and Saturdays), Sundays noon-9 p.m. Closed Tuesdays and some holidays. No alcoholic beverages. No credit cards. Charming lace-curtained room, costumed servers. Polish cuisine. Good, solid entrées including roast duckling, fine soups. Moderate.

SADYE'S BEIRUT GARDENS, 15703 E. 10 Mile Road, East Detroit. Telephone 775-8740. Hours: 4-10 p.m. Tuesdays through Saturdays, 2-8:30 p.m. Sundays. Closed Mondays and some holidays. No alcoholic beverages. Credit cards: AE, V. Arabic food, Lebanese specialties.

THE SHIEK, 316 E. Lafayette, Detroit. Between Brush and Randolph Telephone 964-8441. Hours: 11 a.m.-10 p.m. Tuesdays through Fridays, 4-11 p.m. Saturdays, 3-10 p.m. Sundays. Closed Mondays and holidays. No credit cards. Lebanese menu much like Sadye's and as authentic, but cocktails available here. Dependable, good service. Specialties: stuffed grape leaves and cabbage, *taboulee* salad, shish kebab, *hommus, kibbee*. Reasonable to moderate.

THE SIAMESE TWINS, 1587 Opdyke, Bloomfield Township. At South Blvd., not far from Silverdome; in a little shopping plaza. Telephone 332-8080. Hours: 11 a.m.-10 p.m. Closed Mondays and holidays. No alcoholic beverages. Credit cards: MC, V. Michigan's only Thai spot, as far as we know. The national dish is *tod mun pla* (curried red snapper and shrimp) and especially spicy dishes are marked on the menu. You might also like the *neau pad nor mai* (fried beef with onion and chiles) and the coconut ice cream for dessert. Moderate.

THE SOUP KITCHEN SALOON, 1585 Franklin, Detroit. At Orleans Street. Telephone 259-1374. Hours: 11 a.m.-10 p.m. Mondays and Tuesdays, 11 a.m.-2 a.m. Wednesdays through Saturdays. Closed Sundays and holidays. Youthful and fun;

live entertainment. Sandwiches, salads, blackboard special soups. No credit cards or reservations. A bargain.

TWEENY'S, 280 N. Woodward, Birmingham. In the Great American Building, just north of Woodward. Telephone 644-0059. Hours: luncheon 11:30 a.m.-3:30 p.m., dinner 5:30-11 p.m. Closed Sundays and Mondays. No alcoholic beverages on last report. Credit cards: MC, V. Casual courtyard setting, authentically gourmet food—good fresh food well prepared. Menu changes daily; imaginative dishes might include crepes Bretagne, curried shrimp, fresh tuna Provençale. Fantastic desserts. Between 5:30 and 7 p.m. the Boulevard Supper at $12.50 is served—a bargain for Tweeny's. Very expensive.

XOCHIMILCO, 3409 Bagley Avenue, Detroit. Telephone 843-0179. Hours: 11 a.m.-4 a.m. No credit cards. Small place with tin ceiling, clean, orderly. Mexican menu; excellent tacos, *chiles rellenos*, and other specialties. Inexpensive.

ZOSIA RESTAURANT, 2990 Yemans, Hamtramck. Telephone 871-6492. Hours: noon-9 p.m. Closed Sundays. No credit cards or reservations accepted. (Past patrons might note the new address and phone number.) Venerable Polish restaurant, authentic and generous. Menu changes daily. Specialties: cheese and prune blintzes, great hearty soups (cabbage, barley, beet), veal schnitzels, sausage, roast pork. Inexpensive.

ABOUT SELECTING
AND SERVING WINE

An appreciation of wine adds a marvelous and adventurous dimension to well-prepared food. In fact, for some people the selection of an appropriate bottle from the wine list is more important—and more delightful—than choosing an appetizer or entree from the menu. But, for others, the very thought of wine is a problem best solved by avoidance, even if this means that the pleasure of dining is diminished. These notes are designed to aid those of you who are just starting to explore the world of wines by offering some guidelines and suggestions that will put you at greater ease and help increase your enjoyment.

But there are some things you ought to accept. First and foremost, a dinner wine should be considered as food, not as just another alcoholic beverage. When you prepare or order a meal, you give a lot of attention to the selection of dishes that are complementary to one another. Wine deserves the same consideration. Second, wines need to be consumed regularly and studied carefully to be fully appreciated. What you don't especially care for now, with familiarity and partnered with just the right dish, may turn out to be one of your favorites. Finally, for most of us, there's a good deal to be said for matching the cost of the wine with the quality of the experience. For a carefully planned evening at a very special place, a fine (and probably more expensive) selection will most likely enhance the dinner, possibly making it memorable for years. But, for the average night out, a modest selection from the list or even the house wine may be quite adequate. The important thing is that both types of experience—the exceptional and the everyday—can be enjoyable and informative.

SERVING THE WINE

Wine lists at most restaurants in Michigan tend to fall into two categories. The first, and by far the most common, offers anywhere from fifteen to forty wines, including a few sparkling varieties (such as Champagne) and rosés, with the rest split between reds and whites. At places with this sort of list, vintages (the years produced) are rarely listed, few wines if any are great, your waiter or waitress also serves as *sommelier* (wine steward) and most likely knows little about the offerings, orders are often taken by bin numbers (102, 103, 104, etc.) because no one is apt to know how to pronounce or spell the names correctly, wines will most likely be handled roughly with awkward corkage, and little finesse can be expected in serving. In such situations, it's best to take charge yourself by giving specific suggestions or even instructions for serving. These might include the following. (1) Specify that the bottle be handled gently, with the cork side up (to keep any sediment where it belongs, at the bottom of the bottle). (2) Have the wine, if it's other than a still red, brought to you in a bucket of half ice and half water. (3) Ask to remove the cork from the corkscrew yourself. When you do this, grasp only the dry end of the cork, and then examine it (it should be in good condition, not crumbly or decomposed) and sniff at it for the aroma of wine. If the server removes the cork, it will probably smell of liver and onions or whatever he or she last delivered to or from the kitchen. (4) Request that a small amount of wine be poured into your glass. Examine the color and appearance (the main concern here should be cloudiness, which may indicate spoilage), and then taste it. If the wine is acceptable under these terms, let it remain in the bottle to "breathe" until the course it is to be served with arrives. (Watch out here; the server will probably want to pour it immediately.)

Red wines often improve if you follow this procedure, and the whites and rosés will stay cold in the ice bucket. Two more reminders: all sparkling wines should be served ice cold and remain corked until ready to consume; and wine should never be served with the salad course—the flavors tend to be uncomplementary. Finally, unless you have confidence in your server, indicate that *you* will do the pouring of the wine during the meal; and, when you do, handle the bottle gently to keep the sediment at the bottom. In general, at least one bottle or liter of wine is necessary for four people, and the glasses (be sure they're good-sized) should be filled one-half to two-thirds full. Serve yourself last, pouring out all but the final cloudy liquid (if any), which should be discarded.

A few restaurants in the state, however, including the London Chop House, the Castle, the Thornapple Village Inn, the Rowe Inn, the Jordan Inn, and the Top of the Park, have much more impressive wine lists, in quality and quantity. Here you can expect (but still not always get) better wine service. There may be a *sommelier*, but, if not, a nod to the headwaiter can quickly bring you information and advice regarding suitable selections for your meal. Here you may also request decanting of your wine if you think it advisable— this is most often done for red wines, and it's highly desirable for older, high-quality red wines that have been stored properly. Decanting involves the careful transfer of wine from the original bottle to a decanter; the purpose is to draw off the wine without disturbing the sediment that may have settled and accumulated over the years. In places with a *sommelier* or where wine is decanted for you, a tip to the appropriate person is in order (usually 10 percent of the price of the bottle). Also, don't be surprised if the wine steward asks for permission to taste a small amount of your wine from his tasting cup—it's not an uncommon request, and you might learn something from his observations on your wine.

SELECTING THE WINE

Generally beginners in wine appreciation tend to prefer either sparkling or white varieties before they develop a taste for the still, dry reds. Even for experienced wine drinkers, the reds offer a challenge, varying considerably as they do from the light and fruity to very robust, full-bodied wines. Some restaurants have a *sommelier* who can assist you in ordering, and many others have lists that provide descriptions of the wines' characteristics. Some, however, have neither, and often your server won't be knowledgable in this area. In these situations the following hints from the Winters might be useful. We've divided the wines into four groups for purposes of simplicity.

Sparkling Wines

Sparkling wines are largely white, come in a variety of prices (some quite reasonable), tend to be rather versatile because they go nicely with many foods, and are festive and fun to open, serve, and drink. The finest are the true French Champagnes, the cheapest are certain California bulk-process wines, and the least sophisticated are the red and pink varieties. You'll see a lot of Great Westerns and Taylors from New York state, and they're not bad in terms of price and flavor if you're leaning towards this type of wine. Just watch the waiter when he opens the bottle because the corks can pop out at high velocity.

White Dinner Wines

These should in most instances be consumed while fairly young, generally within five to seven years after the vintage and often younger. They vary considerably in color, degree of dryness, and complexity of taste. A review of the wine lists from restaurants in this book shows that practically every one offers at least one of each of the following white wine types: (1)semisweet, light, and fruity; (2) steely, dry, and flinty; and (3) a softer but dry, full-bodied wine. If you're ordering a white, decide which of these appeals to you, and for the first type order one of the German wines; for the second look for anything described as a Chablis; and for the third try to find a white Burgundy labeled Pinot Chardonnay. One word of caution: some restaurants list sweet or semi-sweet white dessert wines along with the drier dinner wines. Often these go under the name "sauterne" (or, if French, "Sauternes"). Such a selection would rarely be appropriate with the main course of a dinner.

Rosé Wines

You'll probably find from one to three rosés on the wine list. In our opinion, the best thing about these wines is their color—they can be absolutely beautiful. But unfortunately none are really distinguished, and most are much less interesting than the still whites and reds. Their popularity appears to stem from the impression that they offer a reasonable compromise for that awkward situation where one person orders fish and prefers a white wine while the other has a steak *au poivre* and wants a red. Both may end up disappointed. We suggest that, if you find yourself in this dilemma, you choose two suitable half-bottles of red and white or even consider the house wine by the glass or half-liter, rather than expect the rosé to accomplish the impossible. There are, however, occasions where this is the wine to order. When chilled, as it should be, it can be very pleasant served with a light meal on a warm summer day. More importantly, you might find a rosé the best complement to ham, salmon, or any main course served with a sweet or semisweet sauce or glaze. But, aside from these situations, it's probably a better idea to look elsewhere on the list because most of the time, we think, rosés are ordered for the wrong reasons.

Red Dinner Wines

These are the best, and most of the best still come from France. It's also true that some superb red wines are produced elsewhere, such as in Italy and Spain, and there's a growing number of enthusiasts for the red wines of California. Fortunately many of the restaurants described in this book offer an adequate selection of both domestic and foreign red wines, and a few are even extraordinary. Prices and quality vary greatly—from low-cost, undistinguished jug wines sold by the liter to $100-plus bottles of fine French Bordeaux or Burgundy produced in such great years as 1961 or 1966. Here, as with the finer still white wines, you may need help because the offerings are so varied in terms of variety, source, vintage year, and price. An especially convenient and useful source of information is Hugh Johnson's *Pocket Encyclopedia of Wine*, a thin, wallet-sized book that fits nicely in purse or pocket. It can generally be purchased in good wine stores. And if you begin to become really enthusiastic, you should buy Alexis Lichine's latest encyclopedia on wine. We were fortunate enough to meet

Mr. Lichine at his chateau in Margaux during the summer of 1978—and it just increased our appreciation of his knowledge and that fine reference. But if these sources of information aren't handy, here are some suggestions.

For a reasonably priced, light, fruity wine, order a Beaujolais—but only if it's less than four years old. This wine should always be consumed young, in fact, the younger the better. For a wine with more character and finesse, look for a French Bordeaux that's been bottled at a chateau. 1959, 1961, 1964, and 1966 are fine years, and wine of these vintages, although generally scarce and expensive, are now ready to drink. The high-quality 1970s and 1971s, though on the wine lists, probably won't be at their best for several more years. Some spectacular masculine wines come from Burgundy in France, but like the Bordeaux their quality is directly reflected in the price (high). Good red Burgundies should be ten years old before you drink them, but avoid 1963s, 1965s, 1967s, and 1968s. If you want an exceptionally robust Italian wine, look for a Barolo that's been in the bottle for more than a decade. But on the Italian section of the list, look out for the Lambruscos unless you prefer something semisweet.

You might also consider ordering the often-seen Torres wines from Spain (such as Sangre de Toro), a decent selection at a reasonable cost. And from California two good varietals are the Cabernet Sauvignons and the Zinfandels; vintages here are not as important, but the wine shouldn't be consumed young. All in all, red wines offer the most difficult problems in selection. But if you begin to appreciate them, they also present the best opportunities for the enjoyment of wine. There's no question in our minds that learning about these wines can and should be an adventurous part of eating out in Michigan.

Johnson

Seafood, Steak

Cornwell's

KEY

M
S
U

Wallis

& Drink

The

TON SHANTY CREEK

Golden

nter

GATE

ornapple

ne, Ltd.

DAW

heep

ern

arian

A FINAL COMMENT

Several years ago, we heard and have never forgotten a remarkable observation by Sam Sebree Baskett, native of Missouri, veteran naval officer, Hemingway scholar, distinguished professor, and one of the most enthusiastic and delightful of dinner guests: "There is nothing in life I enjoy more than pleasure." At the time we were savoring some wonderful food and a miraculous bottle of Chateau Margaux 1966 in a restaurant high on a bluff outside of Istanbul. But our travels and dining in Michigan, resulting in this book, have shown us that we needn't be on the Bosporus for an exceptional eating experience. There's pleasure and a sense of adventure to be found right here in Michigan.

INDEX OF RECIPES